W9-BCK-604

The Novelistic Vision of Doris Lessing

The Novelistic Vision of
DORIS LESSING

Breaking the Forms of Consciousness

Roberta Rubenstein

UNIVERSITY OF ILLINOIS PRESS
Urbana   Chicago   London

Publication of this work was supported in part by a grant from the Andrew W. Mellon Foundation.

LIBRARY OF CONGRESS CATALOGING IN PUBLICATION DATA

Rubenstein, Roberta, 1944–
   The novelistic vision of Doris Lessing.

   Bibliography: p.
   Includes index.
   1. Lessing, Doris May, 1919–   —Criticism and interpretation.   2. Psychology in literature.
I. Title.
PR6023.E833Z87   823'.9'14   78-25916
ISBN 0-252-00706-9

For Chuck

Acknowledgments

I would like to express my appreciation to Doris Grumbach and Sydney Janet Kaplan for their careful reading and helpful comments; and to Jean Gentry for her impeccable typing and editorial skills in the preparation of this manuscript. I am especially indebted to my husband, without whose special support, both tangible and intangible, this book would not have come to fruition. And I thank Doris Lessing, not only for her willingness to answer my perhaps impertinent questions about her life and work, but for the inspiration of her fiction, which became the impetus for this study.

Roberta Rubenstein
Chevy Chase, Md.
1978

Contents

Opening   1

Breaking Down, Breaking Out

1   *The Grass Is Singing*   17
2   *Martha Quest* and *A Proper Marriage*   33
3   *Retreat to Innocence* and *A Ripple from the Storm*   49

Breaking Through

4   *The Golden Notebook*   71
5   *Landlocked*   113
6   *The Four-Gated City*   125

Returning to the Center

7   *Briefing for a Descent into Hell*   175
8   *The Summer before the Dark*   200
9   *The Memoirs of a Survivor*   220

Closing   243

Bibliography   259

Index   267

Opening

The reader of an author as provocative, prolific, impassioned, and demanding of engagement as Doris Lessing faces a number of conflicting possibilities: by which gate of the four- (or more) gated city should one enter? The rich choice of alternative entrances is even more challenging for the literary critic, for Lessing's wide-ranging expression of interlocking matters of social, political, psychological, and philosophical importance forbids a comprehensive topical reading of her works. Yet the broad range of issues that occupy the center of her canon demands that she be addressed critically as one of the significant writers of this century.

A formal approach poses entirely different, but equally intimidating, problems, since that ideological complexity cuts across each literary form in which Lessing has written: novel, short story, play, poetry, essay, memoir. Moreover, within any one of these genres the author's artistic method ranges from apparent indifference to decided attention to the structure itself. Even when she is concerned with aesthetic or formal problems, the language often exists in uneasy alliance with the provocative ideas that it bears. As Florence Howe has (representatively) observed,

> No one will read Doris Lessing in order to learn how to write a good novel or in order to admire a beautiful work of art. She disdains—is suspicious of—smoothness of most sorts. There is nothing subtle about her fiction; its bulk alone is formidable. She is careless even about sentences; she overwrites; her "symbolism" tends to be self-conscious; she preaches when she should be demonstrating; she tells us too much and too often. But frankly I don't care.[1]

Even limiting oneself to the literary form in which her major writing appears, the novel—as I have chosen to do here—does not resolve the overlapping difficulties of addressing Lessing's canon critically. In that genre alone Lessing has written eleven works that utilize both conventional and innovative structures and techniques, including *Bildungsroman*, speculative fiction, "psychological" fiction, romance, and other narrative forms. The five-volume *Bildungsroman*, *Children of Violence*, while tracing the life of a central protagonist, not only gathers other dimensions of Lessing's writing into itself both thematically and formally, but its internal chronology covers nearly a century in time while its chronology of publication spans two decades. During that period it was interrupted by the appearance of two other novels that are not part of the series but that signal or crystallize important shifts in the general direction of the author's work. Of the two full-length studies that have been published since the completion of *Children of Violence*, one groups the novels by discussing *The Grass Is Singing* and *The Golden Notebook* in separate chapters, *Children of Violence* in one extended chapter, and *Retreat to Innocence* and *Briefing for a Descent into Hell* together because they do not seem to fall into any other organization.[2] The second study more successfully addresses Lessing's longer fiction, along with a number of shorter works, through five major thematic groupings.[3] Admittedly the chronological approach I have taken here sacrifices the cumulative unity provided by *Children of Violence* in order to establish the larger continuity of Lessing's work as a whole, within which the series holds a central place.

To these preliminary problems I must add the even more perplexing one of how to interpret Doris Lessing's fiction without oversimplifying her works by synopsis or by topical, biographical, or other reductions. It would be folly for any critic to presume that she could do justice in one book to what it has taken Lessing eleven novels (aside from her other writing) to express. While any perspective has its limitations, certain approaches suggest themselves as likely ones. Biographical glossing might be tempting, since there are ample parallels between the author's own remarkable life and the lives and preoccupations of her characters. Born of English parents in Persia in 1919, Doris Lessing spent her childhood on a farm in Southern Rhodesia, leaving southern Africa in 1950 to take up residence in England (where she still lives). Twice married and divorced, she was for a time an active Leftist and member of the Communist party; more recently, she has become a serious and enthusiastic student of Sufi mysticism. Yet, despite the resemblances between life and work, Lessing's canon ultimately

4

must be judged not as disguised or transformed biography but as imaginative literature in its own right. As Lessing has equivocally remarked,

> As far as I am concerned, anything of value I have to say is in my books.
> ... If a writer has spent years and years—her whole life—working out how to live in such a way as to write, how to express the essentials of that life in what she writes, why then go back to the raw material? You'll say, this is the stuff of literary criticism, the literary approach. Well, that is so, but ought it to be?
> I maintain that anyone with a halfpence of sense, reading, let's say, *War and Peace*, can deduce the rest from that. *We all know* that life is raw, bleeding, painful, and without any shape discernible till much later. We know this. Reading the majestic distillations of *War and Peace*, or the tumult of *The Possessed*, do we have to be told these books were fed by the raging tornado that was Tolstoy, the seethe of Dostoievsky? Of course not: it is in our own lives, and it is there we will find the answer to anything that puzzles us in literature.[4]

Comparable limitations of focus would derive from considering Doris Lessing as an "African" or "Marxist" writer, since those aspects of her work, while central at some points in her canon, gradually diminish as her own development, chronologically and psychologically, distances her from those phases of her experience.

A feminist perspective suggests a more promising entrance into her work; as a woman writing, often, about women, Lessing has certainly articulated many of the issues that concern us. In fact, her major characters, particularly Martha Quest and Anna Wulf, are central figures in the roll of twentieth-century female literary protagonists. Their efforts to understand and ultimately transcend the biological and social expectations incumbent upon them as women occupy an important position in Lessing's fiction. Yet such a focus should in no way imply that either her subjects or her audience are delimited by gender. Lessing has remarked with some heat, "I'm impatient with people who emphasize sexual revolution. I say we should all go to bed, shut up about sexual liberation, and go on with the important matters."[5] Her impatience is an index to her own distance ahead of her readers, many of whose consciousnesses (male and female) she has helped to form by grappling with feminist issues long before we were aware of—or ready for—what she was saying.

Still, Lessing's fiction should not be read through political spectacles only. Ultimately, the deepest task of her characters is to achieve a personal wholeness that subsumes sexual identity or gender under a larger principle of growth. The challenge to the protagonist of a mythic work—as the major novels certainly are— is in the enlargement of the human spirit that is shared equally by both sexes. Without denying the importance of their progress or development of awareness as women, I view Lessing's protagonists as representative figures in the larger mythic sense, in their symbolic roles as "everyperson"—an identification that includes but goes beyond their sexual identities. The body may be enclosed by biology; the mind is not.

In the face of Lessing's dismissal of scholarly inquiry itself, expressed with insistence in the Preface to *The Golden Notebook*,[6] I can only offer an apologetic and humble justification for this study. Major artists—whether composers, painters, poets, or novelists—who cast their works on a vast scale, with a complexity of vision that is both exhilarating and bewildering, may be served by intermediators who ponder their works at some depth. Like concert-goers who hear a Mahler symphony for the first time, readers who enter the initial experience of *The Golden Notebook*, for example, may be so overwhelmed by the largeness of the whole that they cannot comprehend it in its entirety—and, having gotten lost in the parts, may not return to repeat the experience. Enthusiasts will return on their own. But for those who might be intimidated by the scope and size of the work, a few suggestions of what to listen for, what to look for, might enrich the experience of the whole by orienting the listener or reader. To stand back far enough to see the entirety of *The Golden Notebook* and *The Four-Gated City* as analogues of the experiences they encompass should enhance, rather than diminish, the appreciation of the works as wholes.

Furthermore, though Lessing has conceded that no one else can really know her conception of the work, a critic or many critics can increase its richness to the degree that they develop its diversity of meanings. Since no interpretation can be assumed to accord exactly with the author's intentions, my reading offers one of a number of possible angles of perception that might illumine for others the complexity and underlying continuity that I find in Lessing's extraordinary vision.

Given these provisions then, I have sought a perspective that provides a unifying thread among the numerous ones that might be pursued within the fiction of Doris Lessing. While the focus of a particular novel may appear to be political, social, psychological, feminist, or mythic (and I hesitate to label them so arbitrarily, since her work may be read through several of these screens simultaneously), the common denominator in Lessing's fictional world is the mind: the mind discovering, interpreting, and ultimately shaping its own reality. That function cuts across and brings together all of the other possible entrances into her work. As she has commented, "What interests me more than anything is how our minds are changing, how our ways of perceiving reality are changing."[7] That particular fascination is present from the very outset of her fiction, as her various protagonists "map" their realities, beginning with what is external to them in the social and political environments in which they find themselves, and moving progressively inward as they seek to comprehend the raw material of experience within their own psychological universes.

Since the development of consciousness is an unfolding process both for any individual or character in a novel, and in an author's canon, what emerges from a chronologically ordered reading of Doris Lessing's eleven novels is the coherence expressed through the path traced by that evolution of consciousness as it perceives, moves through, and reinterprets successive layers of experience. The author's dramatizations of this process—the ideas, characters, and forms through which they are expressed—cluster around a central core that simultaneously discloses the continuity of the fictional worlds Lessing has created and reveals the author's own artistic consciousness in various stages of evolution.

The idea of a center around which the novels' ideas cohere is a crucial one in several respects. Though the concept of development implicit in a chronological or horizontal approach to Lessing's novels suggests a linear direction, the equally compelling pattern informing the novels—both singly and collectively—is circular. In the formal narrative design and the thematic organization of her works, the "end is in the beginning." Besides the fact that reading itself is a linear progress through the text, the linear direction is suggested through the unfolding of idea, form, personality, or energy; the cyclic design emerges from the frequent implications of a return to the beginning, a doubling back to an initial point, an intensification of an earlier focus—again, both within characters and in the fictional structures themselves.

These patterns, however, grow organically out of the fiction rather than being self-consciously imposed upon it. Far from being arbitrary or artificial constructs, they are in fact paradigms deeply embedded in different ways of perceiving reality. The linear mode is a metaphorical abstraction for the kind of mental activity associated with rational thinking, analysis, logic, the uni-directional unfoldings of history and of life through time. By contrast, the circular mode reverberates throughout myth and the nonrational, the suprarational and synthesizing levels of mental activity: symbol, dream, hallucination, madness, extrasensory perception, mystical vision. The contrast between these modes of cognition and the attempt to reconcile their often contrary orientations toward experience and the nature of reality produce a central tension and energy in Lessing's fiction.

Lessing's readers acknowledge that her most accessible and consistent preoccupation is her critique of conventions that initially predetermine private experience: the political, social, economic, and psychological "givens" of a particular time and place. Generally, her protagonists are challenged with becoming aware of and then either acquiescing to or rejecting those conventions as they identify themselves within or against them. Thus the relationship between the private individual and the larger society is almost invariably an adversary one; her protagonists uncover and ultimately create their identities "over against" societal expectations, values, and structures, setting up the tensions of division into two, or several, categories. The impulse of her central characters is to overcome the separations that their own perceptions generate.

The tendency toward division functions not only between the individual and her milieu but within the consciousness itself. We can observe from experience that consciousness straddles two dimensions—functioning outwardly as a recorder responding to the stimuli of the phenomenal world that exists outside the self and for many observers, though particularized by the subjectivity of each observer; and inwardly as a synthesizer of mental events, interpretations, thoughts, and feelings produced by the mediating and creative (or destructive) potentialities of the psyche. These modalities are hardly exclusive, since consciousness is simultaneously process and content, and thus creates and participates in both. Fields as diverse as physics and psychology remind us that the object is inevitably altered by the subject; there is no value-neutral or entirely "objective" reality, even in the pure sciences.

The expression of the bivalent nature of consciousness is a prominent thematic and formal structure in Lessing's fiction, reflecting not only the primary separation between "self" and "other" but also the internal self-divisions inherent in the progress of consciousness as it accommodates the shifting relationships between internal and external modalities. Linearity is the mode in which such contradictions are expressed, and circularity is the mode in which they are overcome, reconciled, or transformed through some larger synthesis. The tension of these opposing modes, and the presence of antinomies seeking reconciliation, echo the classical Hegelian dialectical model. Lessing's work is, in fact, profoundly dialectical,[8] illustrating what N. O. Brown aptly describes in another context as the "dialectical imagination": manifested in such diverse forms as poetry, dreams, mysticism, and psychoanalysis, it is "an activity of consciousness struggling to circumvent the limitations imposed by the formal-logical law of contradiction."[9] That same dialectical paradigm is embedded in Marx's formulation of the direction of collective progress in reorganizing social and material experience, as well as in Jung's conception of the development of the individual psyche as it balances complementary psychic energies. Without presuming any consistent influence, we might view the three thinkers (Hegel, Marx, and Jung) as the philosophical, political, and psychological mentors of Lessing's fictional and intellectual universe.

Given an adversary relationship between protagonist and world through which Lessing frames inquiries about the validity of conventions and norms with (or against) which her characters struggle to define themselves, I have chosen the concept of "abnormal consciousness" as a way to approach the unfolding perspective of her fiction in this study. The term "abnormal" immediately implies a "normal" from which that consciousness might be said to diverge; in common usage "abnormal" also conveys a pathological deviation. It is difficult to find another term that embraces the mind's potentiality for diverging from an implicit norm in both positive and negative senses—a nuance particularly hard to pin down, since the value orientation given the implied norm will depend upon the source of the judgment. (That problem itself directly occupies Lessing in at least two of her novels.)

In his now classic work, *The Varieties of Religious Experience*, William James described the unconventional states of consciousness by observing that

> our normal waking consciousness, rational consciousness as we call it, is but one special type of consciousness, whilst all about it, parted from it by the filmiest of screens, there lie potential forms of consciousness entirely different. We may go through life without suspecting their existence; but apply the requisite stimulus, and at a touch they are there in all their completeness, definite types of mentality which probably somewhere have their field of application and adaptation. No account of the universe in its totality can be final which leaves these other forms of consciousness quite disregarded. How to regard them is the question—for they are so discontinuous with ordinary consciousness. Yet they may determine attitudes though they cannot furnish formulas, and open a region though they fail to give a map. At any rate, they forbid a premature closing of our accounts with reality.[10]

More recently, Charles T. Tart has used the term "altered states of consciousness" to designate particularly those mental states which diverge in a pleasurable or positive direction from the state of ordinary waking consciousness—the latter defined as that which "for any given individual . . . is the one in which he spends the major part of his waking hours."[11] The altered state is, by contrast, "one in which he clearly feels a *qualitative* shift in his pattern of mental functioning, that is, he feels not just a quantitative shift (more or less alert, more or less visual imagery, sharper or duller, etc.), but also that some quality or qualities of his mental processes are different. Mental functions operate that do not operate at all ordinarily, perceptual qualities appear that have no normal counterparts, and so forth."[12]

Because Doris Lessing frequently dramatizes her characters' mental experiences and states as altered in either a positive or negative way—increasingly so in her later fiction, but present from the beginning—I use the term "abnormal consciousness" in what I hope will be taken, until further elaboration, to be a value-neutral term embracing the mental experiences and states encountered by her protagonists as they interpret, respond to, and create relationships with their milieux.

Such an approach implies a subjectivity of perception that imbues both the characters and their worlds with a particularly psychological cast. In fact, the subjectivity of perception and the psychology of consciousness are concerns that Lessing confronts directly in the course of her fiction. An admirer of the psychological realism of the great nineteenth-century novelists, Lessing's own initial artistic orientation could be described by that same term. As she has commented, "For me the highest point of literature was the novel of the nineteenth century, the work of Tolstoy, Stendhal, Dostoevsky, Balzac, Turgenev, Chekhov; the work of the great realists. I define realism as art which springs so vigorously and naturally from a strongly-held, though not necessarily intellectually-defined, view of life that it absorbs symbolism." [13] As her fiction evolves and increases in complexity, however, the emphasis shifts from what is an essentially realistic narrative method, in which detailed descriptions of experiences are filtered either through an omniscient narrator or a central protagonist's point of view, to one heightened by a substructure that connects interior to exterior phenomena and states of mind or being in an increasingly symbolic way.

The search for a different method for communicating the complex nature of consciousness itself led Lessing to change the form of her fiction in order to conceptualize that subject. Midway through her career, with the publication of *The Golden Notebook* in 1962, the author described that novel as her attempt to "break a form; to break certain forms of consciousness and go beyond them." [14] In that statement Lessing refers not only to the tradition of the narrative form which she had recognized—after writing five conventional novels—as inadequate to express her particular vision but also to the assumptions about the relationship of mind to reality. Adumbrations of those shifts appear in the earlier fiction, in her examination of the relationship between perception and experience; with *The Golden Notebook* and the novels that follow it, the author continues to break through forms of consciousness, and to express her discoveries in narrative structures that occasionally become analogues for the unconventional experiences they describe.

Starting with these principles of organization—the chronology of publication and the gradual unfolding of consciousness through a series of protagonists who struggle to define or discover themselves within (and against) the norms of their milieux—I have grouped Lessing's eleven novels into three sections. This arrangement reflects what I see as different formal and conceptual stages in the author's depiction of the mind as it interacts with the reality that it creates and that creates it.

"Breaking Down, Breaking Out" encompasses the first five novels that Lessing wrote: *The Grass Is Singing* (1950), *Martha Quest* (1952), *A Proper Marriage* (1954), *Retreat to Innocence* (1956), and *A Ripple from the Storm* (1958). Each of these works is a novel of initiation, taking as its starting point a young woman who has not yet discovered her own values within the matrix of her geographical, social, political, and psychological universes, or who is unable to act in a way that is consistent with her own ideals. "Breaking out" describes the interplay of forces within as well as outside the personality that produces certain kinds of relationships and self-discoveries. "Breaking down" is the extreme form of that struggle, resulting from the enclosure of the self by constraints that, whether external or internal, are perceived as barriers to it. The chronological arrangement presented here enables us to see the evolution of those themes and patterns in both the initial volumes of *Children of Violence* and the two novels that precede or digress from the sequence.

While the novels discussed in the first section are primarily concerned with the protagonists' efforts to achieve self-awareness and autonomy, the novels grouped under the second heading, "Breaking Through," concern more self-conscious protagonists confronting the same, and additional, constraints to their freedom. This section includes the most significant novels of Lessing's canon—*The Golden Notebook* (1962) and *The Four-Gated City* (1969)—and the novel that comes between them chronologically and provides the transition, *Landlocked* (1965). The latter two are the concluding volumes of the *Children of Violence* series. Both of the major novels are qualitatively and quantitatively vast, encompassing and transforming the themes and patterns explored in the earlier novels and extending the parameters of form and idea in increasingly symbolic ways.

"Returning to the Center," the final grouping, delineates another stage in Lessing's fiction: a distillation of language that reduces the sheer verbal density—and ideological diversity—of the preceding works, while pursuing further some of the same concerns. Shifting away from the large canvas of the collective with the completion of *Children of Violence*, Lessing focuses on more private experiences in the three novels she has written since that series. In *Briefing for a Descent into Hell* (1971), *The Summer before the Dark* (1973), and *The Memoirs of a Survivor* (1975), the evolution of consciousness moves toward further heights (or depths) and resolutions. In these later works Lessing continues to press innovatively against formal conventions as well, incorporating in her narratives characteristics of the nonrealistic genre of romance.

Each of Doris Lessing's novels is both a movement forward and a return to the concerns of the earlier fiction at deeper levels of meaning and complexity. As Anna Wulf's psychoanalyst in *The Golden Notebook* says, "'All self-knowledge is knowing, on deeper and deeper levels, what one knew before'" (p. 205). Or, to paraphrase Kierkegaard, we live forward, we understand backward. The organization and interpretations offered here are thus only preliminary maps of the multiple forms of reality that Lessing has explored for herself and for her readers.

NOTES

1. Florence Howe, "Doris Lessing's Free Women," *Nation* 200 (11 Jan. 1965), 37.

2. Paul Schlueter, *The Novels of Doris Lessing* (Carbondale: Southern Illinois University Press, 1973). The one earlier study of Doris Lessing discusses all of her work to that date, grouping the fiction by genre (short stories, novels) with a separate chapter on *The Golden Notebook*. See Dorothy Brewster, *Doris Lessing* (New York: Twayne Publishers, 1965).

3. Mary Ann Singleton, *The City and the Veld: The Fiction of Doris Lessing* (Lewisburg, Pa.: Bucknell University Press, 1977). Singleton's study appeared as this book was in preparation for press. I note, however, the compatibility of our independent interest in Lessing's psychological concerns and in her use of Jungian and esoteric imagery.

4. Letter from Doris Lessing to Roberta Rubenstein dated 28 Mar. 1977.

5. "Doris Lessing at Stony Brook: An Interview by Jonah Raskin" (1969), in *A Small Personal Voice*, ed. Paul Schlueter (New York: Alfred A. Knopf, 1974), p. 71.

6. *The Golden Notebook* (1962; rpt. London: Michael Joseph, 1972), p. xx. Unless otherwise noted, all subsequent page references to the novel are to this edition.

7. "Doris Lessing at Stony Brook," p. 66.

8. For Lessing's own comments on the relationship between Leftist ideology and the presence of dialectical patterns in her writing, see p. 66 below, n.1.

9. Brown, *Life against Death* (Middletown, Conn.: Wesleyan University Press, 1959), pp. 318–19.

10. James, *The Varieties of Religious Experience* (1902; rpt. New York and London: Longmans, Green, 1929), p. 338.

11. Tart, ed., *Altered States of Consciousness*, 2nd ed. (New York: Doubleday, 1972), p. 1.

12. Ibid., p. 2, emphasis in original.

13. "The Small Personal Voice" (1957), in *A Small Personal Voice*, p. 4.

14. From the dust jacket of the original British edition (London: Michael Joseph, 1962).

Breaking Down, Breaking Out

1

The Grass Is Singing

In retrospect, it is remarkable to discover the seeds for so many of Doris Lessing's later preoccupations in her first novel, *The Grass Is Singing*. Among her concerns with social, economic, and political structures, with being female in a conventional man's world and white in black Africa, one also finds the central cluster of her ideas concerning the abnormal consciousness: fragmentation, self-division, breakdown, the subjective distortions of perception, and implicit questions about the relationship between internal and external perspectives or events. In fact, fragmentation itself is a process embodying both dimensions of that experience. Outwardly, it is an index of inadequate or coercive social and political structures—such as the oppression of blacks or women. Inwardly, it is the manifestation of one particular response to those life-denying or intolerable social edifices. The mental breakdown of Mary Turner anticipates a variety of acute and disorienting mental experiences in the characters of Lessing's later novels: Anna Wulf (*The Golden Notebook*), Thomas Stern (*Landlocked*), Martha Quest and Lynda Coldridge (*The Four-Gated City*), Charles Watkins (*Briefing for a Descent into Hell*), Kate Brown (*The Summer before the Dark*), the narrator of *The Memoirs of a Survivor*.

Viewed developmentally in both individual psychopathology and in the course of Lessing's fiction, chaos is first confronted as a construct of the external world and then (though not always) recognized as a construct of internal reality: outer hell is the counterpart or even the projection of inner hell. In each case violence, fragmentation, and self-division are indicative of a breakdown within the self, in personal relationships, and in the relationship between people and their ongoing institutions. Moreover, the dialectical focus suggested by this correspondence evolves in Doris Lessing's fiction to reflect different aspects of the relationship between mind and world.

The Grass Is Singing is the point of origin not only for Lessing's fictional formulation of the processes of breakdown but also for what become the characteristic patterns of linearity, circularity, and duality that inform her artistic and psychological universe. In many ways a "traditional" novel in the shaping of plot through a male/female relationship and its consequences, *The Grass Is Singing* traces the story of Mary Turner, a conventional white South African woman, as her personal vulnerabilities intersect with the repressive social and psychological pressures of her environment. The narrative begins not with the unfolding account of her life, however, but with the factual newspaper account of her death at the hands of her black servant, Moses. Thus the cyclic pattern of the narrative is initiated with the end at the beginning.[1] The remainder of the novel uncoils like a slow spring as the extended linear flashback develops the events culminating in that murder. On the narrative level, tension is created partly through the sense of inevitability established by the opening, as the reader later comes to understand the psychological significance of that impersonal report, and partly from the gap between the "facts" and the truth—the objective and the subjective reality—of Mary's life and death.

Mary Turner's character slowly emerges as a result of the dialectic between her personal situation and the larger societal forces that create her personality. Shaped from childhood by the values promulgated by the conservative English settlers in South Africa, she is the daughter of a boozing shopkeeper and a mother made bitter by the struggle for sheer economic survival. By the time Mary achieves financial independence at the age of twenty as a typist in a small town she has already become an emotional cripple, repelled by intimacy, preferring the "impersonality" of a solitary existence. Little happens to her between the ages of twenty and thirty besides the deaths of both parents, which hardly move her—an intimation of her incipient psychic stagnation.

To be thirty and single in a white colonialist society is almost a form of heresy. Since Mary is far from being a feminist, her personal status becomes a cause for anxiety, reinforced by her awareness that others discuss her peculiarities openly. She develops a slight tendency toward paranoid perceptions, suspecting "double meanings where none were intended, [expecting] to find maliciousness in the glance of a person who felt nothing but affection for her."[2] Unconsciously she looks for a husband as a way out of her anxious state, not realizing that her genuine "aversion towards the personal things like love and passion" (p. 42) will foredoom the success of any intimate relationship. Because her earlier confidence is gradually eroded by other people's expectations for and judgments of her, she marries in desperation the first man to offer an acceptable possibility—Dick Turner.

Dick's motivations are equally ill-considered. Lacking self-knowledge, he yearns for marriage in its romantically idealized form, as a way of fulfilling a set of socially created expectations for himself. He is as subject to the cultural role expectations, and as out of touch with his true feelings, as Mary is; he chooses to fall in love with her "because it was essential for him to love somebody" (p. 49). Though identical in their emotional flatness, Dick and Mary Turner are matched only through their needs, not their affections. Dick is a farmer who thrives on isolation and the physical labor and hardship of his chosen vocation, while Mary needs the stimulation of town life and the responsibility of a job. Their sexual relationship is a disaster from the beginning, given their mutual inability to share any intimacy. While Dick unintentionally makes her a sexual object by idealizing her, Mary can only accept him when he approaches her submissively. Then, yielding to him in a martyr-like way, "expecting outrage and imposition, she was relieved to find she felt nothing. She was able maternally to bestow the gift of herself on this humble stranger, and remain untouched" (p. 57).

Lessing describes their frigid relationship as typical of so many in which "two people, both twisted and wrong in their depths, are well matched, making each other miserable in the way they need . . ." (p. 58). This negative and symbiotic connection reappears throughout her fiction as the paradigm of unhappy male/female relationships. For Lessing, emotional frigidity is the symptom of a problem with multiple causes, originating in the cultural roles and attitudes toward men and women, sexuality, and intimacy as well as in the individual's own thwarted psychic resources.

It is important to see that the seeds for Mary Turner's eventual psychic breakdown are sown years earlier, in her progressive alienation from herself. Thus the part of the story concerning her inability to handle the black servants—a male/female relationship overlaid with the tensions of black/white roles—is merely the culminating crisis in a process already well underway. Even it begins imperceptibly. Having quickly exhausted the few household tasks available for her to do (sewing, putting the bare house right), Mary finds herself lonely and bored. The clearly inadequate sexual relationship between her and Dick is a symptom of the deeper schism separating them; she can only feel affection toward him when she is in a position of moral superiority. She alters the prior understanding between Dick and his houseboy by canceling the few unspoken kitchen liberties that had guaranteed the latter's loyalty and efficiency. Her emotional hardness finds a ready outlet apart from Dick, for "she could not understand any white person feeling anything personal about a native" (p. 69).

A series of houseboys who leave because of Mary's abuse develops her distaste for Africans into open hatred. Ironically, her emotional antipathy is based on misunderstandings of both a personal and cultural nature—such as a servant's aversion of her glance, a sign of politeness that Mary interprets as dishonesty. Her own emptiness and impersonality are projected onto the African servants; she is enraged by each one's objectlike presence, "as if he were not really there, only a black body ready to do her bidding" (p. 73).

One element after another in Mary's empty life becomes the catalyst for her increasing anxiety and alienation: the heat, the primitive bathing facilities, the neighbors, Dick's successive failures as a farmer. She once tries ineffectually to walk out on these entrapments, but Dick follows her to town and reclaims her, and she weakly capitulates, since she sees no real alternatives. Only Dick's bout with malaria, which temporarily restores Mary's feeling of being needed and her superiority of position, staves off the inevitable breakdown. However, the recognition that Dick is in fact an incompetent farmer who has created their economic misery by mismanagement cancels her tenuous sympathy for him. Paradoxically, having played a major role in reducing him to that state through her sexual and psychic frigidity, she still unconsciously craves submission to "a man stronger than herself" (p. 145). Hating him for his weakness, she hates herself.

At this stage in Mary's unacknowledged self-contempt, the black servant Moses enters her life. Two years earlier, in another context, she had whipped him across the face; her fear that he might in some way retaliate contributes a further tension to the sexual and racial ones that ensue. As a man, Moses exudes a sexual power that Mary unconsciously seeks; but as a black, he must be controlled, subordinated to her will. Moses is impersonal, indifferent to her chastisements and her efforts to cow him. Yet his very impersonality, so much a reflection of her own, enrages her: Moses becomes the personification of her self-hatred. The more she feels herself losing power over him, the more she asserts whatever power she still has through her culturally defined superiority by making unreasonable demands on him.

Split between Dick's ultimatum not to lose Moses, the best houseboy they have had, and the highly charged emotional ambivalence Mary feels toward him, her psychic energy is progressively consumed. Lessing details the deterioration of a personality under acute stress, as Mary begins to lapse into apathetic silences in the middle of sentences, weep at the smallest provocation, and neglect household details. Only her relationship with Moses retains a negative vitality. Recognizing his mistress's distraught state, the servant one day steers her to bed to rest. His very solicitousness and assumption of control further distress her, since she consciously denies the "personal" dimension and, beneath it, the attraction she feels toward him. Yet the more she denies it, the more she feels herself in his power. Her dreams haunt her with images of her submission to Moses's control and kindness.

The relationship between Mary and Moses depicts in microcosm several forms of power relationships. On the political level it duplicates the imbalance between the oppressive white minority and the black majority in South Africa. More suggestively, on the physical level it reflects the shifting tensions of sexual dominance and submission between male and female. On the psychological level it dramatizes the splits within the fragmenting personality. This correspondence between the microcosms of private relationship and the elements of individual personality on the one hand and the macrocosm within which they develop on the other later becomes one of Lessing's most consistent fictional techniques. Moreover, the division into opposing polarities—whether typified as conscious/unconscious, white/black, male/female, dominant/submissive—corresponds to the paradigm of the psyche elaborated by Carl Jung. Since that model of consciousness is a central one in understanding Lessing's use of the abnormal perspective, it bears elaboration here.

Both Freud and Jung conceived of the psyche as divided into areas with different functions corresponding to degree of accessibility. Freud characterized those as conscious, subconscious, and unconscious, while Jung identified them simply as conscious and unconscious. In the Freudian model the unconscious aspect of psychic function contains material repressed from conscious awareness, primarily of a sexual nature, derived from past experiences and fantasies. Jung's model proposes that the unconscious contains not only these but also contents of a nonsexual nature, as well as psychic materials that may never have been conscious but that are capable of entering awareness through the symbolic language of dreams. In essence, Jung describes a compensatory psychic system in which elements of the personality not functioning at the conscious level are contained as a kind of potentiality or "shadow" opposite of the conscious self. As he describes it,

> the activity of the unconscious [is] a balancing of the one-sidedness of the general attitude produced by the function of consciousness. ... The more one-sided the conscious attitude, the more antagonistic are the contents arising [in dreams] from the unconscious, so that we may speak of a real opposition between the two. ... As a rule, the unconscious compensation does not run counter to consciousness, but is rather a balancing or supplementing of the conscious orientation.[3]

Various aspects of this compensatory and self-regulating system function at different levels of psychic energy and accessibility, and are manifested in dreams as well as in projections onto external objects and persons in different forms. The most rudimentary one is the "shadow" itself—the hidden and alien opposite component of the conscious or acknowledged personality. The shadow corresponds to the generally same-sex mirror opposite of the acknowledged self; at a deeper layer of the psyche the complementary qualities are personified in the form of a figure of the opposite sex—the anima (for the male) and the animus (for the female). These entities are, according to Jung, products of an aspect of the mind's activity shared by all human beings, and thus may correspond with psychic contents related not only to a person's actual life situation but also to the larger collective experiences of the human race.

Jung uses the term "archetype" to designate those symbolic configurations, often personified, of dynamic mechanisms and experiences within the unconscious. The deepest and most difficult to actualize of these potentialities is the "Self," a hypothetical construct representing the totality of the personality in all of its realized and unrealized aspects. Thus, though the center of the field of *consciousness* is the ego, it is contained within the larger entity of the Self—an encompassing and regulating psychic center that stands for the potential whole of the personality.[4] The process by which that entirety is gradually realized is called "individuation" —the "conscious coming-to-terms with one's own inner center (psychic nucleus)."[5]

The importance of these symbols of various aspects and processes to the development of consciousness in Lessing's characters will be discussed in more detail in due course. At this point, several essential connections deserve emphasis. First, the Jungian model —in its proposition that the psyche is inherently divided but with an inner dynamic pressing toward wholeness—is compatible with Lessing's own orientation. As she has commented, "There are difficulties about the Freudian landscape. The Freudians describe the conscious as a small lit area, all white, and the unconscious as a great dark marsh full of monsters. In their view, the monsters reach up, grab you by the ankles, and try to drag you down. But the unconscious can be what you make of it, good or bad, helpful or unhelpful. Our culture has made an enemy of the unconscious."[6]

The Jungian model of psychic growth through the accommodation of opposing qualities is analogous to the dialectical paradigm of thesis/antithesis/synthesis. In this sense duality can be understood as both a psychological configuration within the self and a philosophical function defining the relationship between mind and world. Without having to assume that Lessing was consciously adapting the Jungian model of the psyche, one can still identify her essential artistic and psychological compatibility with it; the Jungian orientation becomes increasingly visible in her fiction, both in the design of the works and in the conceptualization of her characters' psychic realities.[7]

In *The Grass Is Singing* the pattern of duality is already present: Mary Turner's consciousness is split into conscious and unconscious aspects, the latter of which is psychologically and narratively realized through her relationship to and perception of Moses. Functioning on the symbolic level of the narrative as a kind of alter ego or complementary double, Moses becomes a screen upon which Mary projects her own denied negative self. As Jung has stated in describing the "shadow" mechanism in the psyche, "The psychological rule says that when an inner situation is not made conscious, it happens outside, as fate. That is to say, when the individual remains undivided and does not become conscious of his inner opposite, the world must perforce act out the conflict and be torn into opposing halves."[8] Lessing dramatizes this process as it takes place in Mary Turner, exploring her experience as measured against the other characters' perceptions of her behavior.

As Mary's unwilling involvement with Moses progresses, her mind wanders and she loses her sense of time. Dick becomes ill again. Interestingly, his stress results in physical breakdown while his wife's takes the form of mental breakdown; as incomplete as he may be, he is not forced to confront his inner conflicts the way Mary is. One night while Mary is overwhelmed by terrifying sexual dreams about her father, Moses assumes responsibility for Dick's care.

At this point Lessing shifts from the objective narration of the earlier part of the novel into a subjective point of view, describing events as if perceived by a consciousness highly distorted by emotional anguish. Looking in on Dick, for example, Mary sees one of

Moses's legs, "an enormous, more than life-size leg, the limb of a giant" (p. 191)—suggestive, also, of her denied sexual feelings. Nightmare and reality become indistinguishable as she dreams that Dick is dead and ambivalently feels both relief and guilt. Moses merges into the image of her father, who approaches her lasciviously, smelling foul. "He came near and put his hand on her arm. It was the voice of the African she heard. He was confronting her because of Dick's death . . . but at the same time it was her father menacing and horrible, who touched her in desire" (p. 192). Lessing condenses the several important male figures in Mary's life into one—an image revealing through her protagonist's feelings toward her father the sources of Mary's frigidity, her need/dread of domination, and her repressed sexuality. This technique of splitting and condensation recurs in more complex ways in Lessing's subsequent novels, paralleling the primary process mechanisms of dreaming described in depth psychology.[9]

The obsessive and distorted quality of Mary's perceptions increases as Dick becomes not just dreamlike but unreal; the sole reality is the ubiquitous presence of Moses. Knowing that he senses her fear of him, which gives him power over her, Mary fears him even more. "They were like two antagonists, silently sparring. Only he was powerful and sure of himself, and she was undermined with fear, by her terrible dream-filled nights, her obsession" (p. 196). Like the double in Dostoevsky's story of the same name, Moses absorbs more and more of the positive attributes of Mary's own disintegrating personality.

The last two chapters of *The Grass Is Singing* juxtapose two very different perspectives: the external, conventional reality and values of South Africa, represented by the Turners' opportunistic neighbor, Charlie Slatter; and Mary's disintegrating inner reality. On a rare visit to the Turners Charlie notices the altered power relationship between mistress and servant, and is shocked by the undercurrent of coyness on Mary's part and the impersonal contempt on Moses's. Charlie's motive for urging the Turners to leave their failing farm conforms to the "first law of white South Africa, which is: 'Thou shalt not let your fellow whites sink lower than a certain point; because if you do, the nigger will see he is as good as you are'" (p. 210).

A second external perspective is supplied by Tony Marston, a more compassionate young man whom Charlie calculatingly sends to the Turners to learn how to manage the farm that he will buy from them. Marston observes that Mary's behavior and speech are often disconnected, that she giggles, inserts *non sequiturs* into dinner conversations, or lapses into staring silences. He confidently labels her condition to himself as "complete nervous breakdown" (p. 217). Later he accidentally witnesses Mary being dressed by Moses. Her behavior is emotionless, revealing the radical division between the conscious and unconscious dimensions of her experience. The reader sees the degree to which the self-alienated woman also categorizes and objectifies others, depersonalizing Moses so completely in her conscious mind that he is only a machine who caters to her wishes. At the same time she is unconsciously acting out the sexual intimacy that she cannot consciously acknowledge.

Marston can only comprehend such bizarre behavior in terms of a story he has heard about a Russian empress "who thought so little of her slaves, as human beings, that she used to undress naked in front of them" (p. 220). He would like to think that Mary is "mad as a hatter" (p. 221)—but at the same time he admits to himself that "she can't be mad. She doesn't behave as if she were. She behaves simply as if she lives in a world of her own, where other people's standards don't count. . . . But then, what is madness, but a refuge, a retreating from the world?" (p. 221). Through Tony's own uncertainties, Lessing suggests the indistinct boundary between sanity and madness, and condemns the facile compartmentalization of mental illness that becomes both a judgment and a way of depersonalizing the sufferer. That position, already radical at the time of the publication of *The Grass Is Singing*, becomes even more central and explicit in her subsequent fiction.

The final chapter of the novel is told almost entirely from the perspective of the abnormal consciousness. It begins with Mary's mind in a rare relaxed moment (p. 224), mulling over an image that later appears in Anna Wulf's consciousness (*The Golden Notebook*, p. 469) as well: the imagined reconstruction of her physical surroundings, beginning with the immediate details of the room and expanding outward to the house and beyond. In both cases this mental exercise—which Anna Wulf calls "the game"—

involves a progressive movement outward from the core of the subjective self to greater and greater objectivity, distance, and psychic release from tension. For Mary it is not so much a therapeutic exercise as a powerful representation of her self-alienation, analogous to that of characters in Robbe-Grillet's *Jalousie* or *Le Voyeur* who concentrate obsessively on the outer object world in order to suppress the uncontrollable emotional turmoil within.

Mary's detachment from her husband is total, for, as she recognized, "it had been a choice, if one could call such an inevitable thing a choice, between Dick and the other, and Dick was destroyed long ago" (p. 226). Significantly, the "other" is not named, for in psychological terms that other is both Moses and what Moses has become for Mary: her shadow, her own denied self, embodying the intimacy, submission, and sexuality excluded from her conscious awareness.

The description of Mary Turner's last day dramatizes the extreme point of her breakdown, amplifying the dissonant forces within her psyche. The day dawns, unlike the preceding ones, clear and fresh. She feels a rare sense of euphoria—a temporary neutralization of her isolation from her surroundings and an anticipation, perhaps, that release (which is also her death) awaits her. Her black-and-white world is momentarily suffused with intense sounds and "a miracle of color, and all for her, all for her! She could have wept with release and lighthearted joy" (p. 227). That sensation of heightened connection with the phenomenal world recurs later in Doris Lessing's fiction as the more positive form of the dissolution of boundaries between inner and outer modalities of being.

But for Mary Turner it is short-lived. The intensity of the sun and the shrill din of the cicadas cancel out her ecstasy, as the narrator describes the external object world perceived through the protagonist's abnormal consciousness: ". . . that insistent low screaming seemed to her to be the noise of the sun, whirling on its hot core, the sound of the harsh brazen light, the sound of the gathering heat. . . . The sky shut down over her, with thick yellowish walls of smoke growing up to meet it. The world was small, shut in a room of heat and haze and light" (p. 228). Mary's emotional claustrophobia is symbolized by the room closing in upon her like a prison—the reverse of the outward movement recounted earlier (p. 224) and a metaphor for the correspondence between mental state and outer surroundings that appears frequently in Lessing's fiction. Mary's consciousness is dominated by an awareness of "he" (Moses) outside somewhere, waiting for her until nightfall.

Further distortions of "external" reality occur: time becomes space, so that in attempting to review her life, Mary feels herself "balanced in mid-air" (p. 230). Her vision of what will happen to her surroundings once she is gone takes shape in a moment of psychotic insight: the successive encroachments of rats, beetles, rain, grass, bushes, creepers, branches, trees, toads, and worms suggest the terrifying impingement of an unbearable reality upon her own fragmenting self. The impersonal world she has constructed to protect her from her unacceptable feelings finally comes to mirror the depersonalization that has reduced her to a shell with "nothing left" (p. 230).

The particular form of Mary's psychic state at this point resembles what the British psychiatrist R. D. Laing calls "engulfment" or "implosion." In *The Divided Self*, Laing pursues the Sartrean observation that reducing others to objects ("depersonalizing" them) is to some degree a function of most human relationships. However, the "ontologically insecure" individual may be incapable of keeping that process under control, and may thus come to experience himself as constantly threatened by other people and by the external world.[10] This existential state of "implosion" is characterized by

> the full terror of the experience of the world as liable at any moment to crash in and obliterate all identity as a gas will rush in and obliterate a vacuum. The individual feels that, like the vacuum, he is empty. But this emptiness is him. Although in other ways he longs for the emptiness to be filled, he dreads the possibility of this happening because he has come to feel that all he can be is the awful nothingness of just this very vacuum. Any "contact" with reality is then itself experienced as a dreadful threat. . . . Reality . . . is the persecutor.[11]

As with the Jungian parallels noted above, these correspondences between the mental state of Lessing's character and Laing's observations on the existential and phenomenological aspects of the schizoid consciousness are instructive in view of Lessing's later fiction, in which such resonances become more explicit. It is important to note that Lessing's portrayal of Mary's psychological state in *The Grass Is Singing* pre-dates Laing's publication of *The Divided Self* by nearly a decade.

In one of Mary Turner's few remaining acts of will, she submits herself to the dreaded "other," walking out into the bush to confront her destruction. With astonishment, she realizes that this is the first time she has ever *experienced* the bush, has ever strayed from the familiar paths. Symbolically, she is, for the first and last time, experiencing part of the tangled undergrowth of her own personality, that part of the potential consciousness that must be slowly admitted into awareness if the personality is to achieve integration. In the altered perception induced by her mental breakdown, she momentarily overcomes the split between acknowledged and denied self.

Her mind gropes for order again and seizes on the image of young Tony, who might be able to save her from the terror (herself), just as, years earlier, she had chosen Dick, to be "saved from herself by marrying him" (p. 237). Confronting Tony, however, she sees that there is no escape, that neither he nor anyone else can save her now. To his sympathetic observation that she is ill, she replies, "'I have been ill for years. . . . Inside, somewhere. Inside. Not *ill*, you understand. Everything wrong, somewhere'" (p. 238). Concerned but helpless, Dick and Tony cannot see the presence that Mary knows is waiting for her in the darkness, since he exists primarily in her own inner darkness. Lessing dramatizes with accelerating intensity the distortions of Mary's subjective reality as her terror increases: "Now it seemed as if the night were closing in on her, and the little house was bending over like a candle, melting in the heat. She heard the crack, crack; the restless moving of the iron [roof] above, and it seemed to her that a vast black body, like a human spider, was crawling over the roof, trying to get inside. . . . She was shut in a small black box, the walls closing in on her, the roof pressing down" (p. 241). Lessing's portrayal of her protagonist's mental state dramatizes the degree to which Mary inhabits a psychic universe of her own creation. As she expects and wills, Moses comes to meet her, cutting off her scream, and her life, in the midst of her one final thought—that the bush had avenged itself upon her. "The trees advanced in a rush, like beasts, and the thunder was the noise of their coming" (p. 243).

Returning to the perspective of limited omniscience after describing Mary's final day, the narrator leaves the reader to reflect on the inscrutability of Mary's antagonist. The novel ends with Moses retreating into the bush and then abruptly turning back to await his own certain fate—"though what thoughts of regret, of pity, or perhaps even wounded human affection were compounded with the satisfaction of his completed revenge, it is impossible to say" (p. 245). For the central reality of Mary's psychic breakdown is based finally not on Moses but on what her own disturbed consciousness has made of him. As the "other" for her, he is the only route left for her desired escape from herself. The tension between acknowledged and unconscious feeling is so extreme that the one possible release is her total annihilation. Moreover, only Moses, the embodiment of her self-hatred and need for punishment of her illicit desires, can bestow that upon her. The physical death of Mary Turner is the form of her psychic death made tangible.

The Grass Is Singing thus anticipates many of Doris Lessing's subsequent explorations of the abnormal consciousness, particularly as manifested in mental breakdown and madness. Mary Turner's slow disintegration is meticulously and realistically developed, so that her helpless descent into chaos makes sense in terms not only of her own personality but of the external world. The fragmentation to which she succumbs is a product of both private emptiness and political realities (understood through sexual power relationships: male/female and black/white). One might say that Mary's submission to Moses is the inevitable end for a personality shaped by the interlocking dialectics of both sexuality and power —the conflicting needs to assert power over and to be overpowered by a male "other." That pattern recurs repeatedly in Lessing's subsequent fiction.

What Lessing has made so vivid in this first novel is the evolution of psychic realities as they transform the outer world into projections of the character's own denied self. As Jung has observed, "Projections change the world into the replica of one's own unknown face."[12] In addition, Lessing makes clear that other perspectives contain their own distortions as well; there is no value-neutral reality. Though Dick Turner's pathetic illusions never become delusions, they do prevent him from responding to Mary's profound alienation. And Charlie Slatter's conventional values make it easy for him to judge but not understand Mary's situation, only part of which is self-created.

In addition to these thematic concerns, one finds in *The Grass Is Singing* the structural patterns that continue throughout Lessing's fiction; the psychic determinism suggested in Mary's situation is mirrored in and reinforced by the organization of the narrative. Each development grows inevitably out of the dialectic of the plot: the formation of Mary's character in response to the alternatives available to her, which in turn shape her subsequent choices; and the inner dialectic of her mind, split between allowed and prohibited feelings, dominance and submission, hostility and desire. Both dialectics unfold toward a single end, achieving a negative resolution in the murder already announced at the beginning of the novel. Thus the return to the beginning is the formal expression of Mary's life. The novel describes a circle that encloses and shapes the reality from which she cannot escape—the empty imprisonment of her own fragmented being.

While Mary Turner's breakdown is an essentially private one, the novel as a whole provides the corresponding societal context within which it takes place, through its dramatization of the dehumanization imposed on both races by the color bar. The political reality of South Africa is an institutionalized form of fragmentation and madness in the macrocosm: depersonalization practiced as a culturally accepted norm. *The Grass Is Singing* economically conceptualizes Lessing's early identification of the correspondences between private and societal fragmentation, a theme to which she repeatedly returns.[13] It also anticipates the inference of several of the later novels that in an insane situation, madness may not only "make sense" but may be the only option available to the individual. In those later novels the characters themselves provide the insight into the connection between personal and societal fragmentation, breakdown, and madness—as well as the potential for synthesis into unity, vision, and wholeness.

NOTES

1. Though the title of the novel comes from Part V of T. S. Eliot's *The Waste-land* ("In this decayed hole among the mountains/In the faint moonlight, the grass is singing/Over the tumbled graves . . ."), the novel's circular structure suggests the variations of "the end is in the beginning" in Eliot's *Four Quartets*.

2. *The Grass Is Singing* (1950; rpt. New York: Crowell, n.d. [1975]), p. 41. All subsequent page references are indicated in the text.

3. Jung, *Psychological Types*, trans. R. F. C. Hull, vol. 6 of *The Collected Works*, Bollingen Series XX (New York: Pantheon Books, 1959), p. 419.

4. Jung, *Aion*, trans. R. F. C. Hull, vol. 9 of *The Collected Works*, Bollingen Series XX (New York: Pantheon Books, 1959), p. 3.

5. Marie-Louise von Franz, "The Process of Individuation," in Carl G. Jung et al., *Man and His Symbols* (1964; rpt. New York: Dell, 1970), p. 169.

6. "Doris Lessing at Stony Brook: An Interview by Jonah Raskin" (1969), in *A Small Personal Voice*, ed. Paul Schlueter (New York: Alfred A. Knopf, 1974), p. 67.

7. Lessing was in direct contact with the ideas of Jung's psychology through a Jungian analysis. For her observations on that model of therapy, and for her most recent judgment of Jung, see pp. 110–11, n. 14, and 231 below.

8. Jung, *Aion*, p. 71.

9. See Charles Brenner, *An Elementary Textbook of Psychoanalysis*, rev. ed. (New York: International Universities Press, 1973), pp. 52–57.

10. Laing, *The Divided Self* (1960; rpt. Middlesex, England: Penguin Books, 1965), p. 39.

11. Ibid., pp. 45–46.

12. Jung, *Aion*, p. 9.

13. Michele Wender Zak focuses on the Marxian dimension of the novel, examining the ways in which material and economic causes facilitate Mary's breakdown. Her analysis also makes use of R. D. Laing's view of schizophrenic withdrawal from an impoverished reality. See "*The Grass Is Singing*: A Little Novel about the Emotions," in *Doris Lessing: Critical Essays*, ed. Annis Pratt and L. S. Dembo (Madison: University of Wisconsin Press, 1974), pp. 64–73.

2

Martha Quest and
A Proper Marriage

Martha Quest, the protagonist of the five-volume series *Children of Violence*, is, briefly, Mary Turner's successor. Reared in almost the same claustrophobic family circumstances in fictional Zambesia[1] (corresponding to southern Africa), and exposed to the same conventional colonial attitudes about sex, race, and female roles, Martha also chooses the limited route initially available to her: leaving her family to take a job as a small-town secretary and, much earlier than Mary, an utterly wrong-headed marriage. What ultimately saves Martha from Mary Turner's fate is her altogether different consciousness, aided by a strong will and a ruthless self-critical honesty. It is almost as if Lessing posed for herself the challenge of starting with the same setting and values, and then worked them out through a quite different female protagonist.

Despite these initial similarities of character and geography, *The Grass Is Singing* and *Martha Quest* are substantially different in conception and structure. The former novel is more economically written, and its shape emphasizes the tension of the whole. *Martha Quest*, as the first novel of a slowly unfolding series published over two decades, is necessarily more formless and indeterminate in both thematic and narrative design. In following the traditional *Bildungsroman* form (an intention Lessing makes explicit in her "Author's Note" at the conclusion of the series), it traces in chronological fashion the developing consciousness of a young protagonist.

Readers who discover Lessing first through her later fiction or short stories are often disappointed when they encounter the decidedly flat, prosaic, and two-dimensional qualities of the early volumes of the *Children of Violence* series. In proportionate weight of narrative expression to idea, these novels are prolix, cumbersome—more easily summarized because, unlike the later fiction, they are less saturated with symbolic significance. If Lessing had not completed the series but had written only the first two or three volumes, her early work might well have been lost in the large company of conventional fictional narratives of adolescence and young adulthood. While psychologically accurate, they are nonetheless rather pedestrian in style and conception. As Mary Ellman has bluntly observed, ". . . the probable truths of this feminine history [*Children of Violence*] might almost as well be probable untruths, the effect of tedium is so often predominant. . . . It is not, of course, Doris Lessing's fault that a flock has fabricated what she attempted genuinely. . . . But still, its whole intention seems to have driven the writer towards the dulling of her own talent."[2]

If unremarkable by themselves, these early volumes of the series achieve significance in the context both of Martha Quest's later life and of Doris Lessing's evolution as a writer. Their shape and content, like the shape and content of Martha Quest's consciousness, only slowly assume the depth of vision and the increasing artistic control of it that inform Lessing's later fiction. One can observe the overlap of linear and circular dynamics at work: while Martha Quest's history unfolds chronologically, Lessing circles back to re-examine and deepen certain themes, images, and motifs. Thus a number of events and images easily missed in their initial context reappear later, assuming greater prominence each time they recur. In tracing the progress of the unfolding consciousness, it is useful to identify these recurring motifs—not to exaggerate their importance in the context of any particular volume, but to indicate their contribution to the unity of vision that permeates Lessing's novels from the beginning.

While in *The Grass Is Singing* each of Mary Turner's acts further reduces her freedom, in *Martha Quest* the protagonist slowly enlarges her consciousness through her greater capacity for introspection and self-reflection. She watches "the movements of her own mind as if she were observing a machine."[3] However, for much of her adolescent and young adult life Martha struggles with some of the same ambivalent psychic tendencies that finally destroy Mary Turner: passive compliance accompanied by repressed hostility. Later her hesitant and then increasingly open rebellion against the confining social structures of her world enables her to direct herself away from a psychic determinism and toward free choice and emotional stability.

In *Martha Quest* and *A Proper Marriage*, Lessing takes her protagonist through the rites of passage of adolescence and young adulthood: social, intellectual, and sexual initiations; marriage, first child, and dissolution of her marriage.[4] The landmarks of Martha's early experiences and gradual development of consciousness are deliberately representative, even archetypical, ones, such as her awareness of herself playing the "young girl" role (p. 12) for her elders; or her recognition, as she departs for a first date, that, "moving inescapably through an ancient role, she must leave her parents who destroyed her" (p. 80). Martha's mother, May Quest —the epitome of all the conventional attitudes toward politics, social behavior, sexuality, and experience from which Martha must extricate herself—appears through her daughter's eyes as "the eternal mother, holding sleep and death in her twin hands like a sweet and poisonous cloud of forgetfulness—that was how Martha saw her, like a baneful figure in the nightmare in which she herself was caught" (p. 34). Some time after leaving home Martha observes that a letter from her friend Joss Cohen steering her toward a more fruitful intellectual milieu had "released her from her imprisonment like the kiss of the prince in the fairy tales..." (p. 207).

From these ritualistic stages Martha moves through further specific experiences that shape her character and personality: her introduction to the social life of the town through the Sport Club and sundowner parties; her exposure to socialist thought through her friends Joss and Solly Cohen and the Left Book Club; her courtship with a latent homosexual named Donovan; and her sexual initiation with an earnest young man named Adolph whom she does not love. In each circumstance she observes not only the new people and events as they enter her experience but also her own reactions to them. Making Martha a more introspective character than Mary Turner, Lessing presents the development of her awareness in considerably more detail, and primarily through the girl's own reflections.

Martha's actual experiences are supplemented by what she calls "that other journey of discovery" (p. 209), reading. "She read like a bird collecting twigs for a nest. She picked up each new book, using the author's name as a sanction, as if the book were something separate and self-contained, a world in itself. And as she read, she asked herself, What has this got to do with me?" (p. 210). The world disclosed to her through books provides a crucial source of values against which she can measure those of her immediate milieu. What she reads also generates in her susceptible imagination ideals and philosophies that must inevitably be tested through her own experience and often shattered. In the course of her reading Martha discovers Schopenhauer, Nietzsche, Freud, and others whose deterministic views of human development puzzle her. The atmosphere of necessity hangs heavily over these early volumes of *Children of Violence*, in Lessing's portrayal of her protagonist's struggle to discover the nature of the forces that continue to shape and limit her.

Despite her desire to gain rational control over the direction of her life, Martha's actions are rarely deliberate and consistent. More often, they emerge out of her own self-division and her effort to discover her truest self in the welter of competing feelings and needs. Subject to the emotional vicissitudes typical of adolescence (and later), she often feels as if "half a dozen entirely different people inhabited her body, and they violently disliked each other, bound together by only one thing, a strong pulse of longing; anonymous, impersonal, formless, like water" (p. 153).

Such self-division is incipient from Martha Quest's very birth. Conceived (like the author herself) during World War I—the manifestation of cultural breakdown in its most massive dimension—by parents "'both having severe nervous breakdowns, due to the Great Unmentionable'" (Martha's father's euphemism for the war), Martha has known from childhood that "she was unwanted in the first place, and that she had a double nervous breakdown for godparents" (p. 249). Already alert to the ubiquitous divisions of her world by the age of fifteen, when the first novel of the series opens, she acknowledges that "the effort of imagination needed to destroy the words *black*, *white*, *nation*, *race*, exhausted her . . ." (p. 57).

Later that sense of categorization is understood as a construct not exclusively of the external world or of Martha's perception of it but of consciousness itself. Unlike Mary Turner's pathological self-division, however, Martha's is more nearly a critical regulator through which she gradually reduces the disparity between what others expect of her and what she really feels. Frequently her choices and decisions are negative ones, acquiescences arising out of a desire *not* to do something else. Her marriage at nineteen to Douglas Knowell is typical of the way in which her rebellion against one set of values forces her to re-define herself in the context of another, often equally mistaken, set—a judgment which she is only later able to make.

Lessing establishes the two poles of her protagonist's universe early in the first volume of the series. The literal center of Martha's emotional and geographical world is represented by her family's mud hut on the veld, located

> in the center of a vast basin, which was bounded by mountains. In front, there were seven miles to the Dumfries Hills; west, seven miles of rising ground to the Oxford range; seven miles east, a long swelling mountain which was named Jacob's Burg. Behind, there was no defining chain of kopjes, but the land traveled endlessly, without limit, and faded into a bluish haze, like the hinterland to the imagination we cannot do without—the great declivity was open to the north. (P. 13)

The symmetry of the location suggests a metaphorical as well as a literal place; Martha's environment forms the external and real pole of her universe, the internal and ideal pole of which is the symmetrical four-gated city of her imagination:

> a noble city, set foursquare and colonnaded along its falling, flower-bordered terraces. There were splashing fountains, and the sound of flutes; and its citizens moved, grave and beautiful, black and white and brown together; and these groups of elders paused, and smiled with pleasure at the sight of the children—the blue-eyed, fair-skinned children of the North playing hand in hand with the bronze-skinned, dark-eyed children of the South. Yes, they smiled and approved of these many-fathered children, running and playing

among the flowers and the terraces, through the white pillars and tall trees of this fabulous and ancient city. . . . (P. 21)

The latter image becomes the central emblem for the goal of unity and wholeness that Martha seeks within herself, as well as the shaping symbol of the later volumes of *Children of Violence*, culminating in the final work, *The Four-Gated City*.

Between these two poles of the real and the ideal, Martha Quest's consciousness slowly develops, breaking out of a succession of enclosures as (in the later volumes) she approaches the fantasied four-gated city that represents an overcoming of division. Her first real break from her family home propels her to the nearest town, where she lives in a small impersonal room and pursues a secretarial course at the local polytechnic; her employer at a law office sends her there because he recognizes her intelligence but does not know how to utilize it, since she is female. Seeing no clear future for herself in the town as a single woman in a job which does not challenge her or fulfill her imagined possibilities for herself, she passively accepts the role of wife—having first slept with Adolph and then Douglas Knowell in defiance of her parents' Victorian sexual attitudes. Ironically she is most her mother's daughter when she rebels against her, for her rejection of the values of her parents' generation merely traps her in a repetition of the very kind of marriage from which she had hoped to escape. As Martha's marriage to Douglas approaches, Lessing metaphorically suggests the exchange of one enclosure for another: "It was odd that Martha, who thought of the wedding ceremony as an unimportant formula that must be gone through for the sake of society, was also thinking of it as the door which would enclose Douglas and herself safely within romantic love. . . . She thought of the marriage as a door closing firmly against her life in town, which she was already regarding with puzzled loathing" (pp. 237–38).

Lessing frames the process of psychic growth in an image that characterizes her protagonist's divided universe, in which freedom is conceived as a limited space between fixed alternatives. Describing Martha's trip with Douglas from the town to the veld to announce their marriage to her parents, the narrator observes that "the town was a long way behind, the farm was not yet reached;

and in between these two lodestones, this free and reckless passage through warmed blue air. How terrible that it must always be the town or the farm; how terrible this decision, always one thing or the other, and the exquisite flight between them so short, so fatally limited . . ." (p. 240). Though Martha has never felt lonely in the veld before, when she reaches it this time, her anxiety extends outward into the physical world, transforming it into the correlative of her inner state: "She was now feeling lost and afraid. She was vividly conscious of the night outside, the vast teeming night, which was so strong, and seemed to be beating down into the room, through the low shelter of the thatch, through the frail mud walls. It was as if the house itself, formed of the stuff and substance of the veld, had turned enemy . . ." (p. 245). In that moment Martha is most like her fictional predecessor, Mary Turner, whose anxieties transform her house and the bush into the external forms of her own inner enemy. However, while Mary's abnormal consciousness becomes radically fragmented and ultimately psychotic, Martha's self-division gradually moves toward unity and even into visionary capacities.

There are only a few adumbrations of the latter aspect in the first two novels of *Children of Violence*. The earliest suggestion of visionary perception is her fantasy of the four-gated city, imagined when she is still a young girl on the veld. Her experience of "intense, joyful melancholy" (pp. 60–61) is undeveloped, fleeting, a product more of daydreaming than of psychic insight or control. Yet even in its early manifestations, one recognizes Martha's hunger for the ideal of wholeness that transcends the divisions of what is initially understood as her external world and ultimately recognized as her psychological universe as well.

A subsequent vision anticipates the sensitivity that will, later in Martha's life, enable her to enter other people's consciousnesses empathetically and even telepathically. These experiences are, the narrator comments, typical of the simultaneously painful and ecstatic experiences of Martha's "religious" phase:

> Suddenly the feeling in Martha deepened, and as it did so she knew she had forgotten, as always, that what she had been waiting for like a revelation was a pain, not a happiness; what she remembered, always, was the exultation and the achievement, what she

forgot was this difficult birth into a state of mind which words like *ecstasy, illumination,* and so on could not describe, because they suggest joy. . . .

There was certainly a definite point at which the thing began. It was not; then it was suddenly inescapable, and nothing could have frightened it away. There was a slow integration, during which she, and the little animals, and the moving grasses, and the sun-warmed trees, and the slopes of shivering silvery mealies, and the great dome of blue light overhead, and the stones of earth under her feet, became one, shuddering together in a dissolution of dancing atoms. She felt the rivers under the ground forcing themselves painfully along her veins, swelling them out in an unbearable pressure; her flesh was the earth, and suffered growth like a ferment; and her eyes stared, fixed like the eye of the sun. Not for one second longer (if the terms for time apply) could she have borne it; but then, with a sudden movement forwards and out, the whole process stopped; and *that* was "the moment" which it was impossible to remember afterwards. (Emphasis in original, p. 62)

The experience that Martha describes resembles the state of consciousness variously described by the terms "cosmic emotion," "peak-experience," "oceanic feeling," "cosmic consciousness," *satori, samadhi,* and others.[5] Regardless of the terminology used, they share the quality of what Evelyn Underhill describes as the "expression of the innate tendency of the human spirit towards complete harmony with the transcendental order; whatever be the theological formula under which that order is understood."[6] Martha Quest is not a mystic so much as a young woman with a decided psychic sensitivity that occasionally expresses itself through the classic experience of transcendent unity. She comes to recognize that "sense of movement, of separate things interacting and finally becoming one, but greater" (p. 210) as her "lodestone," even her conscience, and eventually the manifestation of the most authentic dimension of her reality.

The dissolution of the subject/object dichotomy between self and world, inner and outer, becomes the deepest expression of the unconventional consciousness in Lessing's fiction. The integrating mystical vision that Martha Quest experiences in brief glimpses, and the disintegrating, psychotic vision that overwhelms Mary Turner, represent its complementary manifestations, each of which ramifies further in Lessing's subsequent novels.

One further form of the dissolution of the boundaries of the self is the temporary merging with an other that occurs in ecstatic sexual union—an event that Lessing's female protagonists rarely experience; the moment of union is more often a psychological than a physical event for her characters. Martha Quest's first sexual experience with Adolph, for example, is disappointing both physically and emotionally. Her ideal of sexual communion is a fantasy that, like the image of the four-gated city, is projected into a potentiality for the future: "For if the act fell short of her demand, that idea, the thing-in-itself, that mirage, remained untouched, quivering exquisitely in front of her . . . her mind had swallowed the moment of disappointment whole, like a python, so that he, the man, and the mirage were able once again to fuse together, in the future" (p. 194).

Despite Martha's occasional illuminations, the general progress of her emotional, sexual, and social education in the early volumes of *Children of Violence* is more often along the path of self-division. Her anxiety and ambivalence over her imminent marriage to Douglas Knowell near the end of *Martha Quest*, for example, typify her inability to distinguish clearly which of her many selves is her true center. "She need not marry him; at the same time, she knew quite well she would marry him; she could not help it. . . . She also heard a voice remarking calmly within her that she would not stay married to him . . ." (p. 253).

The same sense of inevitability, the same circular imprisonment that Mary Turner enters, hovers symbolically over young Martha Quest's emotional universe. In the beginning and again in the concluding sections of the first volume of *Children of Violence*, Lessing describes the figure of a hawk circling overhead, tracing an invisible pattern that suggests both the harmonious natural order and the restrictive emotional geography that awaits Martha as she leaves it. Her marriage to Douglas places her emphatically outside the circle of wholeness described by the hawk's flight and simultaneously inside a circle of emotional constriction; she spends the rest of her life trying to move from one back to the other. The linear movement of Martha Quest's development is thus framed by a cyclic one: at the end of the first volume Martha has broken out of the circle of her family only to enter another form of enclosure through her marriage.

The symbol of enclosure modulates to another circle in the second volume of *Children of Violence*. In *A Proper Marriage*, Lessing traces Martha's experiences as a young wife, taking her through the ambivalent feelings and accompanying physical experiences of early marriage, maternity, and childbirth. Outside the Knowells' small characterless flat revolves a great glittering Ferris wheel whose lights "mingled with the lamps of Orion and the Cross."[7] Initially Martha finds serenity in its steady rotation; later it reflects her acute sense of repetition and entrapment. The anxiety underlying her marriage "seemed to be of the same quality as that suggested by the great dragging circle of lights, which continued to flicker through her sleep like a warning" (pp. 289–90). The Ferris wheel *is*, in fact, a warning: an objectification of the inner biological rhythm whose movement she ignores at her peril. While she resists the truth of her negative feelings about Douglas and her new role as his wife, she learns that she has already conceived a child, and is indeed dragged into a biologically inevitable cycle concluding with the birth of her daughter, Caroline. Lessing describes that process in detail, grounding Martha's developing consciousness in her physical being.

While many of Martha's choices and acquiescences come from her sexual and psychological naiveté, her rebellions are frequently motivated by her efforts to reject the negative determinism of her sex in its biological as well as its sociological context. Much of her early character develops through attempts to reconcile that sexual identity—understood through the constraints and expectations placed upon her as a female in a world shaped by conventional male values—with her desire to be a complete person, due all the rights of her male counterparts. She is distressed to discover the disparity between the idyllic life she has been led to expect from the fiction she reads, and the disillusionments of her own experience, created partly by her own unrecognized compliance. The inner contradictions of Martha's roles as wife, lover, mother, and what she describes "vaguely but to her own satisfaction as 'a person'" (p. 466) are the most crucial challenges of her growth toward freedom and self-definition in both her social universe and the universe of her mind.[8] Behind her effort to reconcile her romantic expectations with her real circumstances and goals is Doris Lessing's own artistic determination to create a believable, unidealized female protagonist by including the aspects of female experiences excluded by other (mainly male) practitioners of the novel form.

Martha's journey to awareness is charted not only through her discovery of her physical identity as a woman but also through the larger circles that intersect with and shape her personal history. Lessing details her protagonist's involvement in the social and cultural institutions of her time and place: the "swinging circle of intoxicated dancers" at sundowner parties (p. 329); the discussion circle of the Left Book Club, to which she has been introduced by Joss Cohen's letter; the "circle of women" friends meeting in a "circle of grass chairs" (p. 510) as they exchange information on babies, husbands, money, and household affairs; and, most invisible and distressing, the "cycles of guilt and defiance [that] ruled her living . . ." (p. 461).

These concentric circles of Martha's experience are inevitably disrupted by her ambivalent, self-critical consciousness. Even during the minutely documented experiences of her pregnancy and childbirth, she feels herself "essentially divided."

> One part of herself was sunk in the development of the creature, appallingly slow, frighteningly inevitable, a process which she could not alter or hasten, and which dragged her back into the impersonal blind urges of creation; with the other part she watched it; her mind was like a lighthouse, anxious and watchful that she, the free spirit, should not be implicated; and engaged in daydreams of the exciting activities that could begin when she was liberated. (P. 387)

During her effort to remain in control of the course of labor and delivery, she observes from "the small lit place in her brain" (p. 404) the parallel divisions within her own physical experience itself. Following a particularly intense pain,

> She went limp, into a state of perfect painlessness, an exquisite exhaustion in which the mere idea of pain seemed impossible—it was impossible that it could recur again. And as soon as the slow flush of sensation began, the condition of painlessness seemed as impossible as the pain had seemed only a few moments before. They were two states of being, utterly disconnected, without a bridge, and Martha found herself in a condition of anxious but exasperated anger that she could *not* remember the agony fifteen seconds after it had ended. (P. 404)

Martha's daughter Caroline is born on the eve of World War II, recalling that Martha herself had been born during the first war. Thus her personal odyssey is set against the recurring cycles of collective violence. Her husband's year-long absence from her as a drafted soldier emphasizes the schisms at work in both the larger political universe and Martha's private one. While she is temporarily husbandless but very much involved in the demands of child-rearing, she reflects on the series of events that have resulted in an existence in which she is utterly miserable. In spite of her intentions and beliefs, she finds herself having done the exact opposite of what she intended to do. "If she had remained in the colony when she had wanted to leave it, got married when she wanted to be free and adventurous, always did the contrary to what she wanted most, it followed that there was no reason why at fifty she should not be just such another woman as Mrs. Quest, narrow, conventional, intolerant, insensitive" (p. 294). Yet the only way she can find out who she is is by making choices and learning from them what she is not.[9] The sheer sense of fatality and determinism in Martha's experience (perhaps unintentionally reinforced by the density of the prose style itself) underscores Lessing's portrayal of the struggle of consciousness to overcome both the external prescriptions for social behavior and the unknown forces within the personality.

Resuming her political education through the Left Book Club, Martha gains further insight into the culturally conditioned choices she has made. She becomes aware of how many members of her milieu have reinforced the masquerade of marriage, including Dr. Stern, who, having presided over her unintended pregnancy, recommends a second one as a cure for her restlessness. The doctor's collusion in her destiny is an early adumbration of Lessing's indictment of the medical establishment as the carrier of conventional and often personally destructive values. Dr. Stern and May Quest—though not Martha's father—repeatedly undermine Martha's legitimate negative feelings by assuring her that they are unreliable, predictable, and temporary. Too often lulled away from those inner voices by such explanations, Martha finally acknowledges that *they* represent her true self, and that the cajoling voices of her elders and contemporaries are the ones that must be resisted.

By the time her husband returns (discharged from the army for health reasons), the rift between them has widened to expose the falsity of their relationship, the emotional and intellectual chasms that separate them. In the final section of *A Proper Marriage*—ironically prefaced by an epigraph from Jung on marriage—Lessing details Martha's painful and hesitant efforts at extricating herself from the confinements of that social institution. As a further irony, Martha and Douglas move into a house whose location is almost a parody of the visionary four-gated city that Martha's deeper consciousness seeks—a house "in the older part of the city, at the corner of a block. From its gate one could see a mile in four directions along tree-bordered avenues. . . . Everything was straight, orderly, unproblematical" (p. 506).

Such details reinforce a prominent, though not always consistent, element of Lessing's early fiction: the importance of irony to her narrative method. Read "straight," these first volumes of *Children of Violence* are indeed rather plodding in pace and commonplace in incident; their narrative success may ultimately depend upon the reader's awareness of the deliberately dry tone, which gains in subtlety and control as Lessing makes Martha herself the ironic observer in later volumes of the series. In *Martha Quest* and *A Proper Marriage* the tone occasionally oscillates between earnestness and irony, resulting in the reader's vacillation between identification with and distance from Martha Quest.

Martha's involvement in the Left Book Club, at first a temporary distraction from her private doubts, later gives her the moral strength to make the final break. The duality of her inner world is transferred from the personal to the political, a form of escape that she only later understands as a repetition of the same pattern of self-division. As Martha focuses her attention on the "socialist sixth of the world," "she had two clear and distinct pictures . . . one noble, creative and generous, the other ugly, savage and sordid. There was no sort of connection between the two pictures. As she looked at one, she wanted to fling herself into the struggle, to become one of the millions of people who were creating a new world; as she looked at the other, she felt staleness, futility" (p. 545).

These ambivalent images—reflections, in a political context, of the same antitheses that structure Martha's private life—do not

45

move toward a synthesis. Instead she chooses to believe whole-heartedly in the first and reject the second, again endorsing the same romantic idealism that persistently clouds her perception. "For the first time in her life she had been offered an ideal to live for" (p. 546). The fact that she has been reborn, metaphorically, is underscored by her "new" parents. As Mr. Maynard observes, "'I suppose with the French Revolution for a father and the Russian Revolution for a mother, you can very well dispense with a family'" (p. 605).

The final pages of *A Proper Marriage* juxtapose the two imme-diate dimensions of Martha's growth at this stage in her life—personal and political. Whereas the circle of family life has en-closed and shaped her development up to this point, her decision to leave Douglas and to set her young daughter free from "the "tyranny of the family" (p. 343) is her extraordinary act of inde-pendence, embodying the extreme degree of both her political zeal and her personal confusion. As part of her new radical perspective, she believes that "a child without any parents at all clearly had a greater chance of survival as a whole personality" (pp. 371–72), an attitude rooted in Martha's perception of her own negative childhood and her need to repudiate her destructive mother. Bru-tal as that choice may be in personal terms, it does temporarily liberate Martha from the "tyranny" of family life that had, as she perceives it, restricted her growth as a person. What she does not see at the time is that escape is not so easy. She must bear the guilt and pain of her choice for many years—an emotional tyranny that is at least as oppressive as the one she thought she had terminated.

While *Martha Quest* and *A Proper Marriage* together frame the same setting as *The Grass Is Singing*—of growing up female in southern Africa, with the attendant cultural, sexual, and social implications of that geography—the psychic geography develops in a completely different direction. Mary Turner tries to escape from anxiety and inner chaos by running first into the arms of Dick Turner and then of Moses; Martha Quest runs in the oppo-site direction—away from the arms of husband and daughter, determined to face her own inner self and answer to it. In that extraordinary choice she does break out of the cycle of family life by severing the connections among the three generations of females otherwise doomed to the inevitable repetitions of family history and misery. The second volume of *Children of Violence* thus ends with a sense not of enclosure but of release. Disburdened of her idealistic expectations of marriage and motherhood, Martha Quest has yet to be disillusioned by the impossible idealism of the Leftist political movement, or by the limits of reason and will as shapers of her destiny.

NOTES

1. Though the name has been used by Africans to refer to the same geographical area, Lessing notes that she has used Zambesia in a fictional sense to represent "a composite of various white-dominated parts of Africa . . ." rather than a specific country like Zambia or Rhodesia. See Author's Note, *The Four-Gated City* (New York: Alfred A. Knopf, 1969), p. 615.

2. Ellman, *Thinking about Women* (New York: Harcourt Brace Jovanovich, 1968), p. 198.

3. *Martha Quest* [*Children of Violence*, vol. 1] (1952; rpt. New York: Simon and Schuster, 1964), p. 61. All subsequent page references will be indicated in the text.

4. F. R. Karl suggests that the early volumes of *Children of Violence* seem to be almost a working out of the stages of female development—minus the existential ideology—in Simone de Beauvoir's *The Second Sex*. See "Doris Lessing in the Sixties: The New Anatomy of Melancholy," *Contemporary Literature* 13 (Winter 1972), 25. De Beauvoir's landmark study was published in an English translation in 1953—a year after *Martha Quest*—suggesting affinity rather than influence.

5. William James, *The Varieties of Religious Experience* (1902; rpt. New York and London: Longmans, Green, 1929), p. 79; Abraham H. Maslow, *Toward a Psychology of Being*, 2nd ed. (New York: Van Nostrand Reinhold, 1968), pp. 74–114; Sigmund Freud, *Civilization and Its Discontents*, vol. 21 (1927–31) of *The Complete Psychological Works of Sigmund Freud*, trans. and ed. James Strachey (London: Hogarth Press and the Institute of Psychoanalysis, 1961), pp. 64–65; Richard M. Bucke, *Cosmic Consciousness* (1901; rpt. New York: E. P. Dutton, 1969). *Satori* is the term used in Zen Buddhism; *samadhi* is the name for that state in Yogi tradition.

6. Underhill, *Mysticism* (1910; rpt. New York: E. P. Dutton, 1930), p. xiv.

7. *A Proper Marriage* [*Children of Violence*, vol. 2] (1954; rpt. New York: Simon and Schuster, 1964), p. 284. All subsequent page references will be indicated in the text.

8. In her study, *Feminine Consciousness in the Modern British Novel* (Urbana: University of Illinois Press, 1975), Sydney Janet Kaplan devotes a perceptive chapter to the fiction of Doris Lessing. Analyzing the cycles of "rebellion, acquiescence," and the elements of biological and cultural conditioning of women, Kaplan focuses on the specifically female aspects of Martha Quest's (and Anna Wulf's) development—the "'feminine consciousness,' made up of pas-

sivity, submissiveness, resentment against men, and disassociation between body and mind" (p. 171). She interprets Martha's extrasensory perceptions in the final volume of the series as an extrapolation of her essential "passivity," linking those intuitive, visionary powers to the "feminine consciousness" that only much later transcends sexual identity and is understood as part of a "universal" consciousness.

9. In that regard Lessing's protagonist follows the Hegelian path toward self-consciousness through the dialectic of affirmation and negation.

3

Retreat to Innocence and A Ripple from the Storm

Lessing's next two novels address themselves more directly to the political dimension of her fictional universe hinted at in the closing pages of *A Proper Marriage*. However, her fourth novel is not the next volume of *Children of Violence* but an independent work, *Retreat to Innocence*. As a digression from her chief work in progress that explores certain ideas within a more limited fictional framework, it reveals the concerns of the author that were pressing for immediate expression, as well as some of the same themes that are later incorporated into Martha Quest's perspective. While *A Proper Marriage* is primarily about Martha Quest's personal life, with her political education hovering on the periphery of her consciousness, the volume that follows it in the series (*A Ripple from the Storm*) reverses that emphasis. *Retreat to Innocence*, published between the two volumes, provides the fictional and intellectual bridge between them, in its exploration of political and philosophical polarities depicted in the context of a male/female relationship.

Retreat to Innocence clearly sprang from the author's politically bifurcated experience during the mid-1950s. After more than a decade as a communist, and several years as a committed party member in Great Britain, Lessing—along with other intellectuals who foresaw the increasingly dogmatic direction of Stalin's leadership, which was to culminate in the Hungarian Revolt of 1956—left the party. The influence of socialist thought is present in both the conception and design of the novel; the central characters form a distinctly dialectical pair, expressing antithetical issues in both political and psychological contexts.[1] Julia Barr, a sentimental and politically naive young English girl recently fledged from a wealthy liberal family, meets Jan Brod, a Leftist German Jew from Czechoslovakia who is old enough to be her father. Again the female protagonist's sexual, psychological, and political coming of age is the shaping theme of the novel, this time set in England rather than southern Africa. The measure of the gap between values and generations, between ideal and actual politics in the mid-1950s, emerges as Lessing traces her protagonist's discovery of her own feelings and sympathies.

While Julia "loathes" politics, preferring "happiness" to "misery and heroics,"[2] Jan Brod is a political animal by nature. Julia is unable to understand Jan's complex personality and the irregularities, as she sees them, of his personal life, both of which are consistent with his political values and have been shaped by conditions quite different from Julia's. An alien to England both literally and figuratively, Jan had been forced to leave Eastern Europe because of the war, but he feels ideologically out of place in England. He longs for a home compatible not only with his politics but with his need for personal and intellectual freedom.

Jan's livelihood in England is as a clerk, though he was a lawyer in Prague; but his real passion is his work on a manuscript detailing World War II from a radical perspective. Eager to be involved in Jan's life though indifferent to his real center of energy, Julia volunteers as his research assistant and secretary, typing her way through his manuscript without ever reading the words. That blindness is emblematic of her brief involvement with him. During their two-month-long relationship, Julia wants to simplify Jan, to turn off his vital political dimension and isolate the aspects of his personality that concern her. Her typical attitude toward his references to peasant revolts in Kenya or British Guiana is, "'I don't want to hear it. I know it's all horrible, but I wasn't asked. It's not my fault'" (p. 227).

As in the preceding novels, Lessing signals the shape of consciousness in her characters through the analogy of rooms. Significantly, Julia Barr's room is tidy, frilled, and romantic—a "parody of a bedroom 'suitable for a young girl'" (p. 19). In fact, it is not a parody so much as a statement of who Julia actually is. She admits to herself, "'This room . . . *is* me; it wasn't a joke at all when I made it like this, even though I pretended it was a joke so that my mother wouldn't laugh at me'" (p. 19). When Julia first meets Jan at his room in his friend Friedl's house, she wants to break through its locked door: "The walls of her self had collapsed, and left nothing but desperate need to enter the room beyond it" (p. 82). Yet her first reaction to Jan's cluttered room is an urge to "tidy" it (p. 83)—metaphorically, to reduce the chaotic disorder that her simpler consciousness cannot accommodate. That impulse characterizes her approach to their entire relationship. While denying the dimensions of his personality that do not interest her, she impinges on his life in unintentionally destructive ways by trying to "help" him. Using her little-girl role with her father (a minor titled lord), she tries to generate money and influence to improve Jan's employment, find a publisher for his manuscript, pay off an old debt, and exert pressure on his request for citizenship. In each case her intervention in his private affairs not only is based upon a profound misunderstanding of Jan's character but actively worsens his situation, eventually resulting in his forced departure from England.

Even after her sexual encounter with Jan, she feels as if she is "standing outside a door firmly locked against her. . . . Before she could go, however, he must come and set her free. She was still shut within the walls of his breast, stifled" (p. 84). Julia needs Jan to "set her free" from what she is—a conventional, sentimental young woman. But because she fears her own emotions and is incapable of understanding what being "free" means, she is unable to grow in that direction. Instead she reduces her lover's freedom through her manipulations of his private life for either naive or selfish motives. One of the novel's ironic reversals is the symbolic destruction of "experience" by "innocence."

Julia's actual physical loss of innocence (inferred rather than described) is underscored by the corresponding, and disorienting, changes that take place in her consciousness. Alone in her own flat again following that first sexual encounter, Julia experiences a sensation like falling. At the same time, "the rooms of the flat lost solidity, the walls of the building dissolved; Julia was suspended on nothing but her own consciousness above the roofs and

51

tree-tops of summer London" (p. 103). This free-floating sensation is a feature of abnormal consciousness shared by several of
Lessing's characters when they enter the chaotic uncharted area
within their own psyches.

Lessing frames her protagonist's anxiety over her indistinct
identity through the analogue of rooms, and also through the
juxtaposition in Julia's mind of the two father figures who per-
sonify her self-division:

> "If I were really the daughter of Sir Andrew Barr, I wouldn't be
> here at all." It was like a discovery. "And I wouldn't be with Jan
> Brod." She saw her father, saw Jan Brod, and the incongruity of
> the two images left her divided and nil. Nothing. She was nothing.
> "They can't be my parents. Who am I, then? Supposing I left my
> flat, supposing I left Betty [her flatmate], supposing I never went
> back home—if I walked out of my life, out of myself, and found
> a room in a part of London I'd never been in, *who would I be
> then?*" (Emphasis in original, p. 126)

Her late-night perambulation spent in search of her true self discloses the splits in her self-image (and incidentally adumbrates
Martha Quest's more extended pilgrimage through London and
her interior geography at the beginning of *The Four-Gated City*).

Later during the same walk Julia imagines a kind of warning
message contained in a neon-lit advertisement for *Madame's
Models*, and recognizes a bizarre distortion in her perceptions:
"The word Madame was written in a flowing looped script; it
seemed to have a secret and intimate significance; as if it had been
set there for Julia, as a warning. 'That light is what I am,' thought
Julia, feeling herself dissolve again: she could feel herself flowing
out, away from a disintegrating centre. For a moment, she did not
exist; it was a moment of unconsciousness" (pp. 132–33). Julia's
self-alienation is manifested on a number of other occasions, such
as her sense that her emotions are blocked, her anxiety that her
irrational passion for Jan is a kind of madness, her feelings of
nothingness, and her discovery that she is doing things that surprise her.

From the beginning of the relationship Jan, who understands
so much more about human relationships through his own experience than Julia does as a student of "social psychology," warns
her that she will probably feel hate as well as love toward him.

Jan has learned to accommodate such emotional contradictions. His view of life, expressed through his political commitment to the Communist party as well as his personal affairs, is that the beginning of man's freedom (both historically and individually) comes in believing that "'we accept the responsibility for what we do, we accept all the good and all the evil of the past, we reject nothing'" (pp. 228–29). Julia cannot accommodate or synthesize such dichotomies, in either emotional or intellectual terms.

Ironically, while Jan paternally counsels her to accept ambiguity, her own father points out her unresolved self-division as sexual ambivalence. Sir Andrew observes that his daughter's intention "'to be taken a virgin to the altar in white lace has been proclaimed with positively embarrassing insistence. . . .' Until he had put it before her, Julia had not seen herself as divided. Now she saw, very painfully, Julia in white lace before an altar; Julia lying on the bed waiting for Jan Brod to finish his work and come and make love to her" (p. 194). Later Lessing describes the corresponding psychic geography of Julia's emerging self-awareness: "Inside her were two landscapes, one a quiet and leafy park, walled against intrusion; the other a shabby cracked plain, full of rickety villages, policed by young men in heavy black thighboots, whips in their hands. When she slept, she moved between them, a small ghost, invisible to everyone" (p. 202). Julia's attitude toward Jan also becomes more obviously bifurcated, "half-provocative, half-contemptuous" (p. 229).

If Julia is a conventional "bourgeois" romantic, Jan is equally a romantic, though in a less limited sense. Though he identifies himself as a Jew first and a communist second, it is clear that his party identification grows from an almost religious belief and commitment. His allegorical story of the messiah—described not for Julia but to his friend Franz in her presence—suggests both Christ and Stalin: "'He's coming, he's coming soon. . . . When he is born, he is not of the rich, but of the poor, in the hut of a shoemaker. The rich men hate him. . . . The wise men know him at once, and shout to the whole world that here he is'" (p. 316). When Franz points out the obvious religious overtones in this parable, Jan insists that his description is an allegory not of an individual but of a nation, class, or people, and adds that all of the myths of the birth of a great man were "'forecast[s] of the birth of Communism'" (p. 317). The strength of his ideological commitment rests on his faith in Stalin—the "new man" who, through a self-discipline that occasionally erred in the direction of ruthlessness, preserved the future for his successors.

The long eulogy to Stalin in the context of the whole novel suggests a radical ambivalence between commitment and complacency, between artistic and political freedom. The self-sacrifice of a generation idealistically committed to improving life for the masses had degenerated not only into the excesses of Stalin himself but into young people like Julia Barr who think that "'it's much more sensible just to take things for granted'" (p. 327). Though Julia achieves a very dim recognition of the meaning of pain through her relationship with Jan, she shortly thereafter separates from him, the damage to his life already done.

In contrast to Martha Quest's need to rebel against the reactionary values of her parents, Julia's rebellion is ironically staged against reasonably enlightened liberal parents. That process of self-definition ultimately results in her rejection of both her "fathers"—both aspects of her self-division—in favor of the utterly conventional ones reflected in her marriage to a barely characterized young man named Roger. (Julia's future husband is introduced at the beginning of the novel and then too conveniently dismissed for a long holiday in Europe.) Having sampled the no longer forbidden fruits of sexual freedom and of radical political commitment, she chooses the more comfortable simplifications of bourgeois life. Despite the warning issued to her from her own unconscious during her midnight walk, Julia in effect becomes one of "Madame's Models" in a wedding ceremony replete with all the trappings.

The pattern of rebellion repeated from one generation to the next traces in cyclic fashion a return to the beginning—the static circular repetition on the collective level that Lessing mourns repeatedly in her work. The novel itself embraces that pattern and comes almost, but not quite, full circle. Despite Julia's conscious rejection of ambiguity, political complexity, and emotional depth, the division of consciousness initiated by her involvement with what Jan Brod stands for seals off her retreat to innocence. The Fall has taken place, both literally and figuratively; virginity can be lost only once. The small advance in consciousness is her regretful recognition that her involvement with Jan has changed her permanently. "'I must have been mad. Why did I do it? I'll never be simple and ordinary again as long as I live. I'll never be able to do anything with an undivided mind—I'll always be seeing myself as Jan Brod would.' . . . She realized that the tears which filled her eyes were of passionate regret, and not because of the triumph she wanted to feel" (pp. 332–34).

If there is any synthesis of opposites within Julia Barr or within the novel as a whole, it is in a negative direction—in retreat. Jan returns to his home in Eastern Europe, where he is doomed to a life entangled in bureaucratic red tape; Julia resumes her sentimental view of marriage and family life, though haunted by the lingering shadow of self-doubt beneath her shallow image of happiness. The dichotomies run right down the middle of the novel: East/West, youth/age, innocence/experience, bourgeois/radical, capitalism/communism, WASP/Jew. The novel's polarizations unfortunately oversimplify its characters and issues. Lessing herself has dismissed *Retreat to Innocence* as a minor work (it is the only one of her novels out of print), feeling that it reflects two characters "wasted, because their possibilities were not fully developed," "a good theme spoiled by lack of thought," and "a good many very serious questions . . . far too easily, lightly, treated. I'd like the book to get lost altogether." [3]

Yet despite its admitted intellectual and formal weaknesses, *Retreat to Innocence* contributes to an understanding of Lessing's fictional universe and her charting of the paths to wider and more integrated consciousness. Julia Barr's unconscious effort to keep politics and emotion in separate compartments anticipates Martha Quest's similar self-division in the next two volumes of *Children of Violence*, as well as Anna Wulf's more complex partitioning of experience in *The Golden Notebook*. Her brief episodes of abnormal consciousness link her both to Mary Turner and to Lessing's later protagonists.

The impassioned portrayal of the idealistic aspects of communism in Jan's allegory of the messiah embodies Lessing's growing use of symbolic allegory, as well as the teleological dimension of Leftist politics that continues to permeate her fiction long after her formal break from active participation in the party. The predisposition to believe in human perfectibility in the face of present disillusionment remains a constant in Lessing's fiction, modulating from political to psychological expression through her characters' increasingly inner-directed quests for wholeness and unity.

The evolution from the teleology of communism to that of mystical illumination is not as discontinuous as at first might appear. Jan Brod's allegory of the hero is a variant of the mythic pattern of renewal and rebirth, a connection that Lessing articulates again in Anna Wulf's reflection (in *The Golden Notebook*, p. 143) on the day of Stalin's death: "I thought how odd it was we all have this need for the great man, and create him over and over again in the face of all the evidence." Mircea Eliade has observed that the reformulation of archaic patterns of regeneration and renewal in modern terms "betrays at least the desire to find a meaning and a transhistorical justification for historical events."[4] Furthermore, "At the end of the Marxist philosophy of history, lies the age of gold of the archaic eschatologies. In this sense it is correct to say not only that Marx 'brought Hegel's philosophy back to earth' but also that he reconfirmed, upon an exclusively human level, the value of the primitive myth of the age of gold, with the difference that he puts the age of gold only at the end of history, instead of putting it at the beginning too."[5]

The intersection of these two paradigms of human experience—linear and cyclical, or historical and mythic—asserts itself throughout Lessing's fiction, connecting the political and metaphysical dimensions of her work. Her own symbol of the "golden age," the image of the four-gated city, is understood eventually as a potentiality with private and collective, internal and external, significations. The tension between an ideology of the individual and an ideology of the collective initially framed in this novel is explored at greater length in the remaining volumes of *Children of Violence*.

If Freud and Jung are the intellectual overseers of the first two volumes of the *Children of Violence* series, Hegel and Marx are the reigning spirits of the next two, with *Retreat to Innocence* forming the intellectual link between them. Lessing's description of the series as "a study of the individual conscience in its relations with the collective"[6] finds its most explicit political matrix in the third—and middle—volume, *A Ripple from the Storm*. The action of the novel develops out of the isolated ripples of socialist revolution generated years earlier in Europe and Russia, and its narrative content embraces what seems like one endless Communist party meeting, as Martha tries to find her own self somewhere within the parameters of her moral and psychological universe.

As in *Retreat to Innocence*, the dialectical paradigm of Hegelian/Marxist thought structures the psychological as well as the political dimensions of the novel. Like Julia Barr, and Mary Turner before her, Martha Quest is (still) self-divided. But unlike Julia, who refuses political involvement, Martha embraces the Leftist ideal enthusiastically. The polarities suggested by the oppositions between Julia and Jan Brod in the preceding novel are incorporated into the character of Martha Quest, so that her own inner division between emotion and intellect straddles both the private and political aspects of her experience. Though the correspondences between them would thus seem to be more complex than the antinomies worked out in *Retreat to Innocence*, this novel that follows it chronologically in Lessing's canon is flat and undynamic; the stasis developing within Martha herself is corroborated by the somewhat tedious chronicling of the political activity that frames her emotional life. (Even the title, *A Ripple from the Storm*, is a rather mixed metaphor.)

In an attempt to flee her private confusions following the separation from Douglas Knowell and their child, Martha immerses herself in the idealistic talk and practical busywork of a group of dedicated left-wing activists. Her prior disillusionment with personal relationships leads her into a temporary identification with the group's ideological commitment to a collective future. Through the countless meetings and discussions Martha attends on policies, strategies, and procedures, Lessing details the development of her protagonist's political consciousness. Concurrently she exposes the factional processes in groups that work counter to their solidarity: the inconsistencies between principle and action that influence both public and private affairs.

Martha's political zeal is largely the result of her effort to conceal from herself her guilt over her abandonment of her daughter, Caroline, and the failures of her emotional life. The communist philosophy enables her to perceive division as a political rather than a personal problem, for "'capitalism creates divisions between human beings which will vanish on the advent of socialism.'" [7] The future orientation of the group seems to offer an intellectual escape from present difficulties, though, as Martha eventually learns through her own experience, politics cannot remedy her inner schisms. Nonetheless, her willing exchange of present reality for future possibility is consistent with the romantic idealism that has characterized her since adolescence, and that becomes even more pronounced when she has a cause larger than herself to embrace.

Periodically, Martha's real feelings about her own child and even the failure of her first marriage surface from the unconscious and repressed part of her self. They assume acute form in the breakdown of her physical health—one of Lessing's ways of equating psychic upheaval with its physical manifestations. Following some months of fervent political activity interlarded with business-like personal relationships, Martha submits almost gratefully to a fever, acknowledging that "it would be pleasant to be ill for a day or two, to have time to think, and even—this last thought gave her a severe spasm of guilt—to be alone for a little, not always to be surrounded by people" (p. 93). One symptom of her political zeal is her guilty feeling that the illness itself is an act of irresponsibility and disloyalty—as if even her body must submit, like her mind, to the rational framework of ideology.

In her fevered state her anxieties move to the foreground of her consciousness. She enters "'that country'; a phrase she used to describe a particular region of sleep which she often visited, or which visited her—and always when she was overtired or sick. 'That country' was pale, misted, flat; gulls cried like children around violet-coloured shores" (p. 94). As in the bifurcated dream landscape that Julia Barr identifies (*Retreat to Innocence*, p. 202), Martha's dream produces another image antithetical to her idealized country: an immense antediluvian lizard that emerges alive from a deep chasm in the earth. The appearance of a counterpart to the idyllic landscape of her fantasy characterizes the psychic tendency described by Jung for a particularly strong emotional content to generate its own opposite, or to be divided into pairs of opposing images in an enantiodromian process. [8] Martha ponders the incongruity of the two geographies; "the cold salt-sprayed shores and the deep sullen pit seemed to have nothing in common, not to be connected, and their lack of connection was a danger" (p. 95). That unexamined psychic schism is indeed a dangerous one, eventually leading to a second mistaken marriage.

Both of the images that appear in Martha's dreams suggest archetypal motifs from her deeper unconscious. The "shallow shores of nostalgia, where no responsibility existed" (p. 97), is a variant of the longing for escape or innocence that assumes different forms throughout Lessing's fiction. Its antithesis, the "dust-filmed half-closed eye of the great petrified saurian" (p. 97), is the monster of negative feelings in her unconscious self that Martha traces back, much later (in *The Four-Gated City*), to her mother. As Erich Neumann notes, following Jung, "anything deep—abyss, valley, ground, also the sea and the bottom of the sea" and other images of the underworld or of dragon figures, suggest the archetypal figure of the mother—the positive form of which is the source of life and wholeness, the negative form of which is a destructive monster.[9] In *A Ripple from the Storm* Martha's landlady, Mrs. Carson, is a stand-in for that figure. "A variety of psychological dinosaur" (p. 30), as Martha describes her, she embodies the conventional prejudices of Martha's mother pushed to their extreme form in the paranoiac fear of being attacked by natives.

As her fever worsens, Martha becomes delirious; Lessing describes her protagonist's altered state of consciousness through Martha's perceptions of her distorted body image.

Her body had taken over from her mind. She lay feeling every pulse of pain, every sensation of heat and cold. Her body lay stretched out among the sheets that felt gritty and sharp, as if she were lying on sand, or on moving ants. But her hands were not hers. [They] . . . were enormous, and she could not control their size. At the end of her arms she could feel them, giant's hands, as if she compressed the world inside them. . . . The world lay safe inside her hands. Tenderness filled her. She thought: Because of us, everyone will be saved. She thought: I am holding the world safe, and no one will be hurt and unhappy ever again.

. . . She kept her hands away from [Anton Hesse, the visiting group leader]; she had to keep them away because of their immense power: he might get hurt if he touched them. (P. 107)

R. D. Laing has observed, in his discussion of the divided self, that even "normal" individuals under certain circumstances may experience dissociation in the form of temporary estrangement of the self from the body.[10] The schizoid individual, more seriously alienated from his self and thus constantly feeling anxious and threatened by others, believes in his own destructive omnipotence because he feels that "to be loved threatens his self; but his love is equally dangerous to anyone else."[11] The temporary dissociation of Martha's perceptions described here approaches the schizoid condition, as Lessing symbolically condenses a number of implications about her protagonist's present psychic state: guilt about her child, anxiety about her conflicting emotional needs and ideological commitment, and the alarming perception of body distortion generated by her alienation. Her abnormal state of consciousness emphasizes the widening inner schism between intellect and emotion, mind and body.

The clearest measure of the growing rift between Martha's political activity within the group and the emotional undercurrents of her private life is her ambivalent attraction to the group's leader, Anton Hesse. Anton, like Jan Brod in *Retreat to Innocence*, is an alien Jew dedicated to the communist ideal. However, he is unlike Jan in virtually every other way. His inner contradictions are never acknowledged and accommodated, as are Jan's, but rather are expressed in a fanatical devotion to efficiency, duty, and discipline. These qualities initially conceal his underlying insecurity—the contradiction between expressed socialist values and unrecognized personal ones that surfaces only after he and Martha marry. While Martha admires his dedication to Leftist principles, at the same time she is disturbed by his rigid rationality. Observing his disapproving reaction to a member of their group who has crossed the color line in a romantic involvement, Martha feels Anton "to be logically right; she felt him to be inhuman and wrong. There was no way for her to make these two feelings fit together" (p. 109).

During Martha's illness Anton's concern and attentiveness disclose a more human aspect of his personality. In gratitude for his attention Martha intellectualizes her blocked emotions into a determination to feel affection for him. Her anxieties multiply further when Andrew, one of the RAF members of the group, marries Martha's friend, an uncomplicated, childlike young woman named Maisie Gale, in order to give a name to her unborn baby. Maisie's pregnancy reminds Martha of her own rejected motherhood and further confuses her feelings. Unable to decipher her emotions, she translates her communist principles into action as Andrew has done, by selflessly marrying Anton—thereby rescuing him from suspicion by Zambesian authorities because of his "enemy alien" status as a German.

Again Lessing reveals the dissonance between her protagonist's conscious actions and her deeper, unconscious feelings. Martha's "selflessness" in marrying Anton is actually a further denial of her negative feelings. Since her decision is a calculated one, motivated by guilt and logic rather than genuine affection—and one that conflicts directly with her emotional warning signals—the relationship is doomed to sterility from its beginning. What she and Anton have in common is not affection but their neurotic needs, and their efforts to rule the heart by the head. Martha views the marriage to Anton as a kind of compulsive necessity: "Already she was feeling, under the pressure of the snapping jaws of impatience, the need to move forward, as if the marriage with Anton and what she might become as a result of it were already done and accomplished. It was as if her whole being had concentrated itself into a movement of taking in and absorbing, as if she were swallowing something whole and hurrying on" (p. 185). Lessing's metaphor is particularly apt; until Martha can digest the experiences she swallows whole, she inevitably repeats previous mistakes and remains anxious and alienated from her deeper self. Psychologically, "assimilation" is the process of making conscious by digesting and thus integrating unconscious psychic material.[12] In this context, Martha suffers from indigestion for a large part of her young adult life.

Her ambivalence toward Anton, and her own guilt, are not assuaged but exacerbated by the marriage itself; the very "reasonableness" of their relationship is its most destructive quality. Underneath its logic is Martha's unconscious dependency on a man to create her identity, a need that overrides for the second time her conscious desire to be free, independent, and emotionally self-reliant. As Lessing has described that tendency in Martha earlier in the novel,

> There is a type of woman who can never be, as they are likely to put it, "themselves" with anyone but the man to whom they have permanently or not given their hearts. If the man goes away there is left an empty space filled with shadows. She mourns for the temporarily extinct person she can only be with the man she loves; she mourns him who brought her "self" to life. She lives with the empty space at her side, peopled with the images of her own potentialities until the next man walks into the space, absorbs the shadows into himself, creating her, allowing her to be her "self"—but a new self, since it is his conception which forms her. (P. 48)

(This "type" of woman is in fact the prototype of nearly all of Lessing's female protagonists.) In *A Ripple from the Storm* Lessing traces Martha Quest's failure to find a man who awakens that truest part of herself. Though she reminds herself that she must "try to keep [her]self free and open, and try to think more, try not to drift into things" (p. 182), her need for emotional sustenance is the stronger force. While she waits for the next man to "walk into the empty space" (p. 49) in herself, her need compels her to Anton.[13]

The fact that Anton is an "enemy alien" is also significant in a symbolic sense, for in exaggerated form he embodies both her inner enemy and her psychic alienation. In effect, she "swallows whole" without assimilating her male counterpart, requiring a man who will "[absorb] the shadows into himself" (p. 48). The process is reciprocal; Anton similarly projects his fantasies onto Martha. While he sees "something in her that she did not recognize as being any part of herself" (p. 240), within the first months of their marriage Martha struggles against the "final collapse of her conception of him": "She knew that the moment she put her arms about him to coax him out of his silence that creature in herself she despised would be born again: she would be capricious, charming, filial: to this compliant little girl Anton would be kind —and patronizing. . . . But this would be a mask for his being dependent on her; she would not be his child, but he hers. She found herself saying: Why, he's not a man at all—in anything!" (p. 265). Beneath Anton's rationality and calculated efficiency Martha discovers a dependent child who wants her maternal protection. But since she unconsciously sought in her marriage to Anton an escape from herself—including the maternal role she has already vacated

—their relationship see-saws between their ambivalent emotional dependencies. Its repetitive negative dynamic recalls the liaison between Mary and Dick Turner, in which neurotic needs generate a dynamic process of mutual destruction of the self that each wants to be and needs the other to confer.

Simone de Beauvoir has cogently described the psychic battle of the sexes that this pattern exemplifies, observing that "in those combats where they think they confront one another, it is really against the self that each one struggles, projecting into the partner that part of the self which is repudiated; instead of living out the ambiguities of their situation, each tries to make the other bear the abjection and tries to reserve the honor for the self." [14] The inner split dramatized by Lessing in the younger Martha Quest becomes more complex in *A Ripple from the Storm*. More than Julia Barr and Jan Brod, who together form an antithetical pair, Martha and Anton embody psychic antinomies not only together as a couple but separately within themselves.

The marriage between them inevitably disintegrates into a loveless stalemate; all of their passion is diverted into political activity, and the sexual incompatibility between them that Martha had sensed earlier but denied becomes the tangible form of their psychological incompatibility. Because she cannot become the person Anton wants to make of her, Martha's only means of maintaining wholeness is through her now characteristic defense of denying negative feelings or substituting for them fantasies projected into a future where they might still be attained. "She was on the point of indulging in fantasies of the faceless man who waited in the wings of the future, waiting to free the Martha who was in cold storage—but she suppressed them. . . . She restored her own wholeness by resting in imagination on the man who would enter her life and make her be what she knew she could be" (p. 240). However, it takes Martha the rest of *A Ripple from the Storm* and most of *Landlocked* to extricate herself from her second liaison to the wrong man—symbolically, to reconcile her confusing ambivalence and assimilate the "enemy alien" within her into consciousness. Significantly, the psychological dynamics of that process are worked out first not in Martha Quest but through Lessing's next protagonist, Anna Wulf.

Though the future may hold some promise of fulfillment of

Martha's fantasies of the man who will create her deepest self, the present dissolves in shambles as *A Ripple from the Storm* ends with a series of breakups and schisms. Fracture lines develop within the larger socialist movement because of differences of opinion on how to absorb the African branch of the party—resulting in several symbolic confrontations and finally in a division into a pro-African Socialist Democratic party and a white Labour party. Thus split, the political influence of the radical Left on existing government policies or upcoming elections is effectively dissolved and reduced to nil. The small political group whose activities have sustained Martha disperses because of these as well as more personal divisions: the defections of several members to pursue their private affairs; the departure of the RAF members for the war front; group hostility toward Anton Hesse's leadership.

The private relationships reflect the schisms of the group. Maisie and Andrew, unable to absorb the visit from Binkie Maynard, the real father of Maisie's unborn child, begin divorce proceedings; Martha senses that the deadness of her own relationship with Anton is irreversible. The novel ends with Martha enclosed, once again, in the concentric layers of a fragmenting universe, "cut off from everything that had fed her imagination" (p. 269) for two years. Each of the larger circles that intersects with Martha's personal history is revealed to be splintered rather than whole. The dichotomy in each dimension of her microcosm is between "two very clear convictions that existed simultaneously in her mind. One, it was inevitable that everything should have happened in exactly the way it had happened: no one could have behaved differently. Two, that everything that had happened was unreal, grotesque, and irrelevant. . . . But it's not possible that both can be true, Martha thought" (pp. 271–72).

In *A Ripple from the Storm*, as in *Retreat to Innocence*, the psychological dialectic underlying the Marxian one does not generate synthesis on any level—between individual and collective, principle and belief, feeling and intellect. Instead, the fissures deepen in every dimension of the universe that Martha inhabits, as Lessing places her protagonist in an existential trap in which the only means of defining and establishing the self is through a series of negations that eventually result in a chronic and nihilistic self-division. The atmosphere of alienation, failure, and sterility reinforces the sense of psychological determinism that has dogged Martha Quest since her youth. In her escape from the marriage to Douglas Knowell in order to be "free," Martha has merely backed herself into a second lifeless entrapment that repeats the circular pattern of need and disillusionment she has already traversed, revealing again the profound and troubling lack of control she exercises over her own destiny. Despite her efforts to achieve emotional honesty and autonomy, defiance and compliance are the antithetical responses that still shape her life. The political group provides only an illusory escape from those inner divisions, for it eventually duplicates the schisms in Martha's private life.

Though Lessing has dramatized the antithetical potentialities inherent in both the emotional (individual conscience) and political (collective) dimensions of experience in a more complex form in this novel than in *Retreat to Innocence*, the resulting narrative is as stultifying as Martha Quest's own psychological paralysis. Reconciling these impasses both narratively, in the form of the novel, and psychologically, in the bifurcations of consciousness portrayed within it, was obviously the challenge Lessing faced at the conclusion of the third volume of *Children of Violence*. It is as if she had taken Martha Quest as far as she could at that point and needed to conceive another character and another kind of novel in order to find a more vital way of expressing the complexity of experience.

The novel that follows *A Ripple from the Storm* is the author's second diversion from the *Children of Violence* series. Far more than *Retreat to Innocence*, the appearance of *The Golden Notebook* between volumes of the series marks a crucial shift in Lessing's fictional portrayal of the development of consciousness. In *The Golden Notebook*, Lessing accomplishes a qualitative transformation of the elements of her fictional universe. For the first time the themes and patterns contained in the five novels that precede it—the chronological narration and the antithetical tensions of the protagonists' mental lives—are brought together in a new way that achieves a true synthesis both aesthetically and psychologically. Martha Quest is left at the point where there is no way to break out of the self-created, closed circle of consciousness; Anna Wulf penetrates it by going further *in*.

NOTES

1. Lessing dates her involvement with Leftist politics from 1942. In reply to my query concerning the influence of the political thinkers she read during that period upon her own dialectical imagination, she wrote, "I read all the books in the Marxist canon of that period. . . . Some were: *The Socialist Sixth of the World*, various books by Stalin, the one most read at that time being *Stalin on the National Question*, Engels, some Marx—the *Manifesto* for one, collations of Marxist texts of different periods, *The Short History* . . . etc. and so forth. No, I don't think this influenced me much . . . I think I have already said that people have more influence than books—always and at all times. . . . As regards my writing being 'dialectical': the dialectical aspects of Marxism, as they reached me in Southern Rhodesia, 1942 (in other words, this is not how they would have reached let's say a peasant in Castro's Cuba)—seemed to me to sum up various ways of thinking I had already acquired. But the idea of 'dialectics,' that fashion of thinking was . . . part of philosophical thinking before Marx and Marxism. He took it over from other people and made it 'marxist.' There was nothing new in it." Letter from Doris Lessing to Roberta Rubenstein dated 28 Mar. 1977.

2. *Retreat to Innocence* (1956; rpt. New York: Prometheus, 1959), p. 46 (this edition is identical to the 1956 edition published in England by Michael Joseph). All subsequent page references will be indicated in the text.

3. Correspondences to Dorothy Brewster, Paul Schlueter, and Alfred A. Carey, quoted in Schlueter, *The Novels of Doris Lessing* (Carbondale: Southern Illinois University Press, 1973), p. 137.

4. Eliade, *The Myth of the Eternal Return, or, Cosmos and History*, trans. Willard R. Trask, Bollingen Series XLVI (1954; rpt. Princeton, N.J.: Princeton University Press, 1971), p. 147.

5. Ibid., p. 149.

6. "The Small Personal Voice" (1957), in *A Small Personal Voice*, ed. Paul Schlueter (New York: Alfred A. Knopf, 1974), p. 14.

7. *A Ripple from the Storm* [*Children of Violence*, vol. 3] (1958; rpt. New York: Simon and Schuster, 1966), p. 59. All subsequent page references will be indicated in the text.

8. Jung, *Two Essays on Analytical Psychology*, trans. R. F. C. Hull, vol. 7 of *The Collected Works*, Bollingen Series XX (New York: Pantheon Books, 1953), pp. 71–72.

9. Neumann, *The Origins and History of Consciousness*, trans. R. F. C. Hull, Bollingen Series XLII (1954; rpt. Princeton, N.J.: Princeton University Press, 1969), p. 14.

10. Laing, *The Divided Self* (1960; rpt. Middlesex, England: Penguin Books, 1965), pp. 78–79.

11. Ibid., p. 93.

12. Neumann, *Origins of Consciousness*, p. 30.

13. The "empty space" metaphor brings to mind Erik Erikson's controversial interpretation of the female inner space, with psychological implications deriving from anatomical configuration. In his article on "Womanhood and the Inner Space" (in *Identity: Youth and Crisis* [New York: W. W. Norton, 1968]), Erikson observes that "in female experience an 'inner space' is at the center of despair

even as it is the very center of potential fulfillment. Emptiness is the female form of perdition . . ." (p. 278). Extrapolating from the truism of psychoanalysis that patients of Freudian analysts tend to be Freudianized, and of Jungian analysts to be Jungianized, I shall not pursue the Eriksonian implications of Lessing's image here, though its metaphoric level may invite other interpretations.

14. De Beauvoir, *The Second Sex*, trans. and ed. H. M. Parshley (New York: Alfred A. Knopf, 1953), p. 728.

Breaking Through

4

The Golden Notebook

The seminal position of *The Golden Notebook* in Lessing's canon is without argument. In addition to its qualitative leap forward in the adaptation of form to content, and its sweeping inclusion of issues of social, political, and sexual import, it also advances with increasing complexity and extensiveness Lessing's exploration of breakdown, fragmentation of personality, and the abnormal consciousness.[1] Like *Retreat to Innocence*, a digression from *Children of Violence* during which Lessing explores a number of ideas (some of which are subsequently assimilated into Martha Quest's experience), *The Golden Notebook* interrupts the chronology of *Children of Violence* at a crucial point in the evolution of the central consciousness of her protagonist.

Each of the central female figures in Lessing's earlier novels struggles within the constructs of her social, political, and physical reality, as well as within her own psychological geography. The character of Martha Quest includes and extends the conflicts of Mary Turner and Julia Barr as she struggles for an ideal of freedom that is both external (her political activism) and internal (her rebellion against sexual roles and the constraining expectations and values of her family and society). While Martha is one of the children born of violence, Anna Wulf takes that violence into herself, as Lessing makes her protagonist's consciousness a microcosm of cultural upheaval and instability. Anna Wulf thus further extends the characteristics of Martha Quest's personality, including her radical alienation, her self-division, and her desire to live as a "free woman" by overcoming the entrapments imposed both from without and within.

Moreover, each of the five preceding novels concerns a protagonist who has no real vocation—though Martha Quest possesses a strong analytical and introspective intelligence. In her sixth novel Lessing provides her protagonist, Anna Wulf, with a vocation as a writer, thus enabling the author to increase the degree of self-consciousness concerning both the experiences of her central character and their narrative expression. Instead of Lessing narrating and commenting upon her protagonist's experiences, the writer Anna Wulf—the invention of the writer Doris Lessing—narrates and examines her experiences directly. Even the apparently omniscient narrator of the *Free Women* section is ultimately revealed to be Anna Wulf. In one sense *The Golden Notebook* is a metafiction—a novel about writing a novel—in which both the process and the form are examined.[2]

The concerns of character, theme, and narrative structure left unresolved at the conclusion of *A Ripple from the Storm* compelled Lessing to find a more malleable and three-dimensional form through which to communicate her multivalent vision. Chronologically *The Golden Notebook* marks the point at which the author recasts the metaphoric levels of her fictional world not only by abandoning convention but by reflecting meaning more directly through the narrative structure itself. The formal limitation of the earlier *Children of Violence* novels is apparent in the increasing disparity between the protagonist's perceptions and the conventional shape of the novel—omniscient chronological narration—through which they are presented. That the formal innovations of *The Golden Notebook* were virtually ignored at the time of its publication—because the novel touched so many other areas of interest on the level of ideas—is an indication of its extraordinary richness in both respects. The multiple layerings of the narrative are not simply a statement of Lessing's "sense of despair about writing a conventional novel"[3] but the result of a deepening of the author's artistic vision in both psychological and formal senses: in the changing nature of the evolving consciousness in its relation to reality, and in the more complex novel form required to express it. Lessing has described the breakthroughs, both willed and accidental, that took place in her own consciousness during the writing of the novel:

> ... this question of I, who am I, what different levels there are inside of us, is very relevant to writing, to the process of creative writing about which we know nothing whatsoever. Every writer *feels* when he, she, hits a different level. A certain kind of writing or emotion comes from it. But you don't know who it is who lives there. ...
>
> When I wrote *The Golden Notebook* I deliberately evoked the different levels to write different parts of it. To write the part where two characters are a bit mad, I couldn't do it, I couldn't get to that level. Then I didn't eat for some time by accident (I forgot) and found that there I was, I'd got there. And other parts of *The Golden Notebook* needed to be written by "I's" from other levels.[4]

The Golden Notebook begins conventionally enough, with two women alone in a London flat—an echo of the pairs of females introduced at the beginning of *Martha Quest* and *A Proper Marriage*. But despite this opening similarity, a shift in direction from the earlier approach is announced almost immediately, as Anna Wulf observes, "'the point is, that as far as I can see, everything's cracking up.'"[5] In fact, "cracking up"—which does characterize everything that Anna sees—is, paradoxically, the major unifying thread of the novel. It manifests itself at every layer of Anna's reality and of the novel's many layers, as divisions, splits, schisms: in marriages (Anna and her friend Molly are both divorced); between generations (Molly's son Tommy, whose loyalties are divided between his polarized parents, rejects most of the values for which Molly has fought, while Anna's daughter Janet is on the brink of similar rejection); friendship (Anna's own inner confusion alienates her from Molly); male/female relationships and sexual roles (the most frequently confronted set of schisms in the novel); politics (the Communist party to which Anna and Molly initially belong and later leave is itself torn by inner division of purpose); statesmanship (international news is dominated by McCarthyism, advances in H-bomb testing, and ubiquitous wars and violence on a world-wide scale).

This cross-section of themes demonstrates the greater complexity in *The Golden Notebook* of both the exterior and the interior worlds established in Lessing's previous novels. Anna Wulf, an intelligent and sensitive writer temporarily suffering from a "writer's block" but driven to write compulsively, reflects within her own consciousness the fragmentation and destruction of the external world. Symbolically the arts and the artist embody the schism that characterizes the times. As Anna notes, "The novel has become a function of the fragmented society, the fragmented consciousness. Human beings are so divided, are becoming more and more divided, *and more subdivided in themselves* . . ." (emphasis in original, p. 59).

The shape of *The Golden Notebook* dramatically bodies forth that correspondence, for Anna attempts to split off and fragment her experience by writing about it in four different notebooks which provide the structural organization of Lessing's novel: "a black notebook, which is to do with Anna Wulf the writer[;] a red notebook, concerned with politics; a yellow notebook, in which I make stories out of my experience; and a blue notebook which tries to be a diary" (p. 406). The fifth repeating segment of the novel is the envelope to the notebooks, the "conventional novel" entitled *Free Women*, written (one learns late in *The Golden Notebook*) by Anna herself after resolving her writer's block. In relinquishing the authorial omniscience of the earlier novels, Lessing assumes a more subjective narrative stance, for the only perspective available is the events and experiences filtered through Anna Wulf's own consciousness. Meaning and structure reinforce each other as Lessing illustrates through the narrative arrangement of *The Golden Notebook* that objectivity is an aesthetic and epistemological convention; there is only the subjective point of view, since all experience must be interpreted by some consciousness.

Anna's notebooks are written during a seven-year period beginning in 1950 (though parts of the Black notebook *describe* a much earlier time period, as Anna reconsiders her past life in southern Africa in the 1940s). However, the chronology of the notebooks is deliberately scrambled through Lessing's technique of presenting segments of each of the four notebooks—in sequence but not necessarily covering simultaneous time periods—preceded by a segment of Anna's novel, *Free Women*, which is written in 1957 and covers only the events of that year. This structure imposes on the reader the challenge of reconstructing Anna Wulf's experiences as one moves through the narrative, in a way that duplicates Anna's own reconstruction of her experiences. While progress through any narrative is necessarily linear from the reader's point of view, the novel's organization challenges that movement by emphasizing the cyclic repetitions, layerings, and recombinations of the same essential emotional events from a variety of perspectives.

The arrangement of the segments of *Free Women* followed by the notebooks is constant, though the proportion of space devoted to each varies: following each *Free Women* installment, the order of the four segments from the notebooks is always Black, Red, Yellow, and Blue. The complete sequence occurs four times in the novel, abstractly defining a circle in that it repeats the same pattern each time, with the exception of the unique Golden notebook and a fifth *Free Women* segment at the conclusion of the novel. At first the sequence itself may appear to be arbitrary; upon closer consideration, one realizes that the order is crucial to the development of the novel's themes. Each larger unit of five segments forms a continuum, moving from exteriorized and shaped reportage of experiences (*Free Women*) to the remoteness of recollected past experiences or business transactions (Black notebook); to the public but contemporary political experiences (Red notebook); to the private, fictionalized projections of Anna's immediate past emotional life (Yellow notebook); to the current, totally introspective, and unshaped material of the diary (Blue notebook). The progression of both time and emotional distance in each complete sequence modulates from detachment or "objectivity" toward the increasing immediacy and "subjectivity" of the Blue notebook/ diary.

The order of these five angles of perception is analogous to the effect created by focusing a camera at infinity and then gradually rotating the lens adjustment until only what is very close is in focus. In fact, the analogy of the camera lens can be applied in numerous ways to the form-breaking techniques as well as the themes of the novel. "Vision" is a primary motif, referring not only to Anna Wulf's extended effort to "see" herself as a unified person but also to Lessing's dramatization of many of Anna's psychic realizations through visual images and, ultimately, through the kinds of fusions, overlaps, flashbacks, and superimpositions of time that are more suggestive of film techniques than of the written medium.

Lessing divides the narrative voice itself into five different perspectives, a further adaptation of the technique of splitting and division that shapes the simpler antinomies of character in the preceding novels. Division functions in *The Golden Notebook* not only as a psychological phenomenon but as a formal one, as the structure of the novel becomes an objective correlative of the central character's consciousness.

Since so much of the material in *The Golden Notebook* concerns consciousness itself, it is important to see the way in which certain dynamics of the personality are implicit in the events formulated in this novel. The Jungian paradigm described earlier is a useful model through which to understand the dynamic processes of the conscious and unconscious aspects of the psyche, proposing as it does a compensatory system in which the unconscious or "dark" side of the personality is experienced in dreams and in waking life as a shadow or "other" which represents the denied aspect of the self.[6] Until the complementary (generally negative) elements at various levels of the psyche are acknowledged and accepted as part of the total personality rather than denied and perceived as aspects of other people, the self cannot achieve wholeness. The mechanism by which these elements are perceived in others—as outside rather than within the self—is known as projection. In literature that tendency is often symbolized by the figure of the double or alter ego.[7]

At deeper levels of the psyche the processes of image-making and projection are even more symbolic. In dreams or when rational consciousness is otherwise suspended, "primary process" (also called primitive or paleological) thinking takes over. In that process several ideas or figures or images may be superimposed upon one person or symbolic figure (a process identified in depth psychology as condensation). Its opposite, splitting (or division), involves the distribution of emotions among several figures or objects.[8] Since the unconscious mind works by analogy, association, and image-making rather than by rational logic, clearly the symbolic value of such processes can be dramatized in fiction, where many of the same overlappings of meaning and image function. In *The Golden Notebook* divisions, splits, and projections, as well as the verbal and visual metaphors of dream imagery, are played out in theme and character as well as in recombinations of the same basic concerns throughout the novel.

Ignoring for the moment the *Free Women* segments, the entries in the four notebooks disclose the rifts and splits that permeate Anna Wulf's psychic reality and grow wider during the course of the novel's unfolding. The first notebook in each sequence, the Black one, is itself further subdivided into two aspects of Anna's life as a writer: into "Money," a record of the financial and business history of her first and only novel, *The Frontiers of War*; and "Source," her attempt to recall and reconstruct the real experiences which she had fictionalized in that novel. The perspective in the "Source" entries is one of distance in time. Anna struggles to avoid what she sees as a false nostalgia, balancing factual events with the subjective interpretation of her past in order to come to terms with experiences filtered through the distorting lens of memory. That exercise, too, dramatizes her self-division, for it is "like wrestling with an obstinate other-self who insists on its own kind of privacy" (p. 122); the "other-self" of one's past, like the past itself, proves to be a fiction from the perspective of the present.

Other schisms in Anna's psyche are revealed in the Black notebook as well. As a younger woman her sexual ambivalence had split her along several fracture lines: she compares her frigid marriage to a German Jew, Max Wulf, with the fictionalized Willi Rodde of her novel; her ambivalent attraction to men like George Hounslow and Paul Blackenhurst recalls for her the inner conflict between the needs for submission and control in male/female relationships (examples of the way that Anna's past also embraces in condensed form aspects of the "pasts" of Lessing's earlier protagonists). She reconsiders the incestuous love of her friend Maryrose for her dead brother (which anticipates the more ambivalent brother/lover relationship between Anna and Saul Green developed later in the novel). Even on the level of explicit physical events the symbolism of division is ubiquitous: Paul, one of the men Anna admired most in the group of friends at Mashopi, dies by walking into an invisibly spinning propeller which cuts him in half.

In the second segment of the Black notebook dated 1954–55, the emphasis shifts from "Source" to "Money." Anna records her

77

repeated frustrating meetings with agents and editors of film or TV shows, in which she finds herself becoming more hysterical as she fights against total misunderstanding of her work. Ironically, one TV producer is from "Amalgamated Vision" (p. 243), but what he sees Anna doesn't, and vice versa. A second long excursus on memories from her African years focuses obsessively on violence and death in the natural world. Her writing in the Black notebook parallels the progressive deteriorations of her sanity described from different perspectives in the other notebooks as the inner splits widen; the Black notebook collapses into self-parody and then gives way in 1955–57 to collected newspaper clippings that describe war and violence in Africa. The clippings are the external form of what Anna feels happening within herself, and their presence in her notebooks is evidence of her growing inability to articulate it in her own words.

From the perspective of hindsight, Anna recalls early in the Black notebook that her private politics and the politics of the idealistic communist group in southern Africa were equally characterized by schism. Within herself she recognizes that "there were always two personalities . . . the 'communist' and Anna . . ." (p. 66); at the collective level, "inherent in the structure of a communist party or group is a self-dividing principle" (p. 64). These political divisions (recalling Martha Quest's impasses at the end of *A Ripple from the Storm*) are brought up to date in the first segment of the Red notebook, in which Anna reports her own and Molly's "two personalities" as Communist party members in Britain—the "dry, wise, ironical political woman, or the Party fanatic who sounds, literally, quite maniacal" (p. 141). That particular ideological division eventually results in their disaffection from the Communist party and their separate decisions to leave it. The later segments of the Red notebook trace that disillusionment, including Anna's admission that Stalin, once her hero, was "mad and a murderer" (p. 259).

Also in the Red notebook, in another variation of a major theme of the novel, Anna reflects on the problem of language itself, particularly as it is distorted by political didacticism. In that context it expresses for her "the fragmentation of everything, the painful disintegration of something that is linked with what I feel to be true about language, the thinning of language against the density of our experience" (p. 259). The Red notebook finally dead-ends in 1956–57 with a series of newspaper clippings recording the same pattern of war, violence, and chaos collected in the final segment of the Black notebook, but based on events taking place in Europe, Asia, and the United States rather than Africa.

The most profound dimension of Anna Wulf's psychic split is generated, however, not at the political but at the emotional level, by the dissolution of a five-year relationship with her lover, Michael, the dynamics of which form the central subject of the Yellow notebook. There, in the several installments of a fictionalized account entitled "The Shadow of the Third," written between 1950 and 1955, Anna examines the multiple facets of the relationship, hoping to understand the reasons for its failure and also to exorcise the pain that is partly responsible for her present psychic paralysis. She creates an alter ego for herself in the character of Ella and transposes Michael into a fictional double named Paul Tanner, her friend Molly into Julia, and her daugher Janet into a son, Michael (the name of her actual lover). To further accentuate the levels of the fragmented personality, Lessing has Anna conceive of her fictional persona, Ella, as a writer also, who is currently working on a novel whose theme is suicide.

Ella's preoccupation with psychic schism and negation is twice removed from Anna Wulf through the fiction-within-a-fiction principle that structures all of *The Golden Notebook*. In her novel in progress the male protagonist

> had not known he was going to commit suicide until the moment of death, when he understood that he had in fact been preparing for it, and in great detail, for months. . . . It would be understood, at the moment of death, that the link between the dark need for death, and death itself, had been the wild crazy fantasies of a beautiful life; and that the commonsense and the order had been (not as it had seemed earlier in the story) symptoms of sanity, but intimations of madness. (Pp. 151–52)

In this fiction the unconscious self moves counter to rational consciousness, disclosing the gap between surface sanity and underlying madness that Anna Wulf eventually confronts in herself without the cushion of aesthetic distance. Because so much of *The Golden Notebook* depends upon a complex pattern of repetitions and variations of equivalent ideas, events, and images, it is not surprising to find a variation of the suicide theme in the intercalated novel Anna herself later writes (*Free Women*). In that version Molly's son Tommy attempts suicide as a way of reconciling self-division and succeeds only in blinding himself—a reversal of Anna's own experience, in which self-division finally leads to vision.

Observations about schism, mental illness, and breakdown permeate the first long segment of the Yellow notebook, anticipating the more direct report of Anna's own crackup in her diary (the Blue notebook). Paul Tanner, Ella's lover, has two jobs which divide his loyalties and his abilities: as a psychiatrist at one hospital and as an administrator at another. The son of working-class parents who has made it into the professional establishment, he is a mirror, Ella observes, of the class split of England itself. He recognizes that psychiatrists like himself are anomalies, for "'what sort of a doctor is it who sees his patients as symptoms of world sickness?'" (p. 183).

While in *The Grass Is Singing* Mary Turner's breakdown is a particular woman's response to the enclosures of her private physical and mental worlds, in *The Golden Notebook* personal breakdown is the analogue of collective insanity. Thus madness and self-division are (as Anna's fictitious Paul Tanner implies) metaphors for a chaotic, fragmented reality, and to be adjusted to it is to acquiesce in madness of an even more insidious variety. Anna Wulf and each of Lessing's subsequent radically self-divided characters must be understood in this dual context, in which inner schism also serves as a metaphor for disunity in the collective reality. As the author has observed, "I think the people in the world are getting more and more mad. While I do not think the history of this world at least in historical times shows much evidence of sanity, what we are living in now is horror and awfulness. I think the Second World War accelerated a corruption the First World War started, and we are very corrupt and damaged people. Not everyone in the world of course." [9]

One of the most completely detailed fictional renderings of these many layers of personal schism functions at the most unconscious level of the relationship between Ella and Paul (the fictional projection of Anna and Michael), paralleling the Jungian shadow and its opposite-sex configurations of the anima and animus. Ella comes to experience Paul's personality in two emotional valences, his "positive" and "negative" selves. Because of her own emotional needs, she initially disregards the cynical, cruel side of Paul as "not his" personality, deluding herself into believing that she can isolate the qualities that open up her own loving potentialities without acknowledging the aspect that petrifies her emotions. The shadow dimension of Paul is a "self-hating rake, free, casual, heartless" (p. 180). Several times, when that side of him wounds or shocks her, Ella calls him a madman (pp. 177, 182, 184, 185), and Paul admits, "'I get madder and madder. Sometimes I wonder why they don't lock me up instead of my patients'" (p. 185).[10] As the relationship develops, Paul's inner division dovetails with Ella's and exacerbates it, for in creating the "naive Ella, [he] destroyed in her the knowing, doubting, sophisticated Ella and again and again he put her intelligence to sleep, and with her willing connivance ..." (p. 183). At the same time that he brings to life her vulnerable positive self, Ella activates Paul's destructive self. In dramatizing the sexually inflected emotional forces within the fictional characters created out of her own experience, Anna Wulf sees how certain attractions may operate on one level of emotional involvement while their antithetical qualities function at a deeper level, sabotaging the relationship.

The shadow, Anna's own term for that ambivalent underside of the male/female relationship, evolves during the course of the fictionalized love affair between Ella and Paul recorded in several installments of the Yellow notebook. First it is Paul's wife, a subtle presence in his relationship with Ella. Then it becomes an idealized version of Paul's wife who is, Ella recognizes, a fantasy of her own best self brought to life by Paul; then a memory of Paul himself after the relationship has ended; and finally, the other half of Ella —the assimilation of her animus—born out of her ambivalence toward Paul. The self-division that Ella projects onto him thus determines the destructive tension of the relationship. It recalls the characteristic emotional pattern in Lessing's women: their need for men who "complete" them—that is, on whom they can lean—and the resulting anxiety when their men upset that emotional contract by depending upon them for the same support.

As Jung has written, "The recognition of anima or animus gives rise, in a man, to a triad, one third of which is transcendent: the masculine subject, the opposing feminine subject, and the transcendent anima. With a woman the situation is reversed." [11] The dialectical triad implicit in Anna/Ella's relationship with Michael/ Paul becomes explicit as Anna identifies the synthesizing "third" element that enters the unstable balance between the other two constellations of emotion. She writes in the Yellow notebook, "As Ella cracks and disintegrates, she holds fast to the idea of Ella whole, healthy, and happy. The link between the various 'thirds' must be made very clear: the link is normality, but more than that —conventionality, attitudes or emotions proper to the 'respectable' life" (p. 385).

The contradiction between normal and abnormal, conscious and unconscious, emotional currents also manifests itself in Ella's own fiction, in the schism that develops in her invented protagonist in the novel about a suicide. Later, after the relationship with Paul has ended, Ella becomes sexually (but not emotionally) involved with a shallow but affable American brain surgeon, Cy Maitland. The antithesis of her psychiatrist-lover Paul Tanner, Cy has no inner schism, and finds no moral conflict in the form of surgery he practices in which self-division is simply eliminated by the radical approach of pre-frontal leucotomy. In the episode between Ella and Cy, Anna Wulf oversimplifies the problem of her own sexual and psychic dilemmas, approaching self-parody.

While the relationship explored in "The Shadow of the Third" is complicated enough within its own fictional reality, it assumes another level of complexity and narrative tension as Anna Wulf's invention. In the Yellow notebook Anna confronts and examines the psychological complexity not only of the male/female relationship but of the artistic process itself. As she observes, "The moment I, Anna, write: Ella rings up Julia to announce, etc., then Ella floats away from me and becomes someone else. I don't understand what happens at the moment Ella separates herself from me and becomes Ella. No one does. It's enough to call her Ella, instead of Anna" (p. 393). Moreover, in analyzing her fictionalization of the relationship with Michael, Anna discovers that retrospect and aesthetic distance distort its inner truth, just as fictionalizing the past events at Mashopi in either *Frontiers of War* or the Black notebook had altered them. She admits, "The trouble with this story is that it is written in terms of analysis of the laws of dissolution of the relationship between Paul and Ella. . . . As soon as one has lived through something, it falls into a pattern" (p. 196). She skirts the realization that there is no objective form for verbalized experience, since there is no way to step outside the subjectivity of her own consciousness, or to alter the effect of time on memory. "Pattern" itself is a distortion. As she later comes to accept, there are no "facts," only interpretations from different perspectives. Yet transposing her relationship with Michael into Ella's story enables her to objectify and to examine the inner dynamic of her own self-division.

Certainly the disillusionments of Anna's own domestic life—her earlier sterile marriage described in her Black notebook and in her novel, *Frontiers of War*, and later the dissolution of the totally involving relationship with Michael—are instrumental in her breakdown. However, her sexual vulnerabilities are only the most acute manifestations of self-dividing patterns that permeate all of her involvements with her world.[12] As Ernest Becker has pointed out, sexuality is the central expression of the existential paradox of human nature, for "the person is both a self and a body, and from the beginning there is the confusion about where 'he' really 'is'— in the symbolic inner self or in the physical body. Each phenomenological realm is different. The inner self represents the freedom of thought, imagination, and the infinite reach of symbolism. The body represents determinism and boundness."[13]

One form of fusion of these aspects of being is sexual intercourse itself. Anna's disillusionments about erotic relationships reinforce this existential dichotomy, however, for the deterioration of her relationship with Michael—examined through the Ella/Paul fiction—manifests itself in the deterioration of the quality of their lovemaking. The experience of genuine vaginal orgasm, the physical expression (for a woman) of erotic and ecstatic union, is, for Anna/Ella, "a dissolving in a vague, dark generalized sensation like being swirled in a warm whirlpool . . . there is only one real female orgasm and that is when a man, from the whole of his need and desire takes a woman and wants all her response" (p. 186). As that experience becomes elusive in her relationship with Paul, Ella feels the truth of the impending end before she faces it intellectually.

Eventually Anna's own psychic fragmentation overtakes her ability to analyze disillusionment from the aesthetic distance of fiction. While her fiction-making tendency is a means for holding off psychic breakdown, as the splitting process advances the words themselves lose their magical ability. "The Shadow of the Third" gives way in the last segment of the Yellow notebook (dated 1957) to numbered outlines and fragments of ideas for unwritten stories about frustrated or mismatched love affairs, neurotic or dependent attachments, futility, negation, and loss. The sources for these stories and their significance are only later understood from the segments that follow the final installment of the Yellow notebook —the last installment of the Blue notebook, the Golden notebook, and the final portion of *Free Women*.

The insinuating progress of breakdown is narratively divided, further, between the projected Ella and the direct account of Anna's experiences recorded in the Blue notebook. Anna had begun the latter notebook as a discipline against her tendency to turn everything into fiction, which she recognizes as a form of self-concealment. As she later observes, "Something strange happens when one writes about oneself. That is, one's self direct, not one's self projected. The result is cold, pitiless, judging" (p. 488). In the first segment of it (covering the years 1950–54) she has not yet broken with Michael, but she already senses her own inner division and consults a psychoanalyst because, she explains, "'I've had experiences that should have touched me and they haven't'" (p. 200). Psychoanalysis fails to resolve her inner conflicts, however, because her analyst, Mrs. Marks (whom Anna and Molly nickname Mother Sugar) is too much a representative of what Anna has come to reject. As Anna phrases it in *Free Women*, psychoanalysis is "traditional, rooted, conservative, in spite of its scandalous familiarity with everything amoral" (p. 10). Implicitly, Anna's abnormal anxiety is partly shaped and created by the times themselves. An analyst grounded in the orthodoxy of the establishment is unable to assist Anna in overcoming her fragmented condition, since the political and social norms themselves are part of the flux that creates Anna's inner chaos.

Mother Sugar tries to nudge Anna toward integration through her creative capacity—an application of Jungian therapy that, much later and on her own terms, Anna does accomplish. (Lessing's own more recent description of her experience with Jungian psychoanalysis is instructive here.[14]) At the time, however, the analyst's approach seems to Anna to reduce her anxiety to the "writer's block," an identification of the symptom rather than the source of her psychic paralysis. The analysis thus runs counter to her conviction that "the raw unfinished quality in my life was precisely what was valuable in it and I should hold fast to it" (p. 203). Furthermore, Anna believes that anxiety itself is a result of being "'highly conscious and developed. The essence of neurosis is conflict. But the essence of living now, fully, not blocking off to what goes on, is conflict. . . . People stay sane by blocking off, by limiting themselves. . . . Sometimes I meet people, and it seems to me the fact they're cracked across, they're split, means they are keeping themselves open for something'" (pp. 402, 405).

Like the later segments of the Black and Red notebooks, entries in the early installments of the Blue notebook are interspersed with insertions of several years of newspaper clippings describing the various manifestations of chaos raging in the external world. Symbolically the reports of war, violence, and repression that Anna selects as evidence of the condition of the external world appear first in her most personal notebook as analogues of her own incipient fragmentation. The clippings also indicate Anna's inability to face her internal chaos directly, for during that period of her life (1950–53) she writes in the other notebooks but not in the diary.

Anna's identification with the chaos of the external world to such a marked degree is an aspect of her abnormal consciousness in formation. Edgar D. Mitchell describes that capacity of "field consciousness" (also understood in the anthropology of primitive cultures as "participation mystique") as "an altered state of consciousness in which an individual seems to experience an enlargement of the ordinary boundaries of self, so that part or all of the individual's environment becomes merged with his awareness of self." [15] The sense of the term is generally positive, as in the mystic's feeling of union with the objects of his world; but the dissolution of the sense of ego may also be experienced negatively. In 1969 Lessing herself described this correspondence between mental experiences and the state of the external world: "'I feel as if the Bomb has gone off inside myself, and in people around me. That's what I mean by the cracking up. It's as if the structure of the mind is being battered from inside. Some terrible new thing is happening. Maybe it'll be marvelous. Who knows?'" [16] Late in *The Golden Notebook* Anna Wulf fantasizes the Bomb going off inside her (p. 538).

As the relationship with Michael unravels in 1954, Anna feels an encroaching unreality, as if "the substance of myself were thinning and dissolving. And then I thought how ironical it was that in order to recover myself I had to use precisely that Anna which Michael dislikes most; the critical and thinking Anna" (p. 283). Still able to marshal different aspects of herself to forestall chaos, she sees her fragmenting condition as partly a product of the conflict between her maternal and sexual selves: "The two personalities—Janet's mother, Michael's mistress, are happier separated. It is a strain having to be both at once" (p. 287).

Other aspects of Anna's experience assume dichotomous form as well, including her political awareness that the Communist party will inevitably crystallize into a ruling power and its opponents, in a dynamic process inimical to any group solidarity. The interchangeability of such positions makes a mockery of ideology, most acutely symbolized for Anna in a dream (reported in the second segment of the Blue notebook) in which the prisoner before a firing squad is replaced at the last moment by his political opposite as the leaders at the top flip-flop (p. 295). The two men in Anna's life at this time who understand her best—Michael and comrade Jack—themselves represent politically opposite positions, thus further embodying Anna's inner division; the party itself accepts "splitness" in a way that she intellectually rejects but emotionally exemplifies. She argues with Jack that "being split" is the "'moral side, so to speak[,] of the communist message. And . . . we must be content to not even try to understand things as a whole?'" (p. 307). Ironically, in the context of the Marxian dialectic that shapes its philosophy, the party furthers only antithesis, not synthesis.

Late in 1954 Anna separates from both Michael and the party, thus loosening her connection to two of the central dimensions of her reality. During that time her incipient breakdown begins in earnest as she senses "an awful black whirling chaos . . . just outside me, waiting to move into me" (p. 313). Mirroring her desperate need to pull the fragmenting pieces of her personality together, the Blue notebook evolves from its original purpose of resisting her fictionalizing tendency to become her one defense against chaos. For words themselves are her anchor on "reality," and as they increasingly detach themselves from the feeling and meaning of the experiences Anna tries to objectify, her disintegration accelerates:

> So I can't write any longer. Or only when I write fast, without looking back at what I have written. For if I look back, then the words swim and have no sense and I am conscious only of me, Anna, as a pulse in a great darkness, and the words that I, Anna, write down are nothing, or like the secretions of a caterpillar that are forced out in ribbons to harden in the air.
>
> It occurs to me that what is happening is a breakdown of me, Anna, and this is how I am becoming aware of it. For words are form, and if I am at a pitch where shape, form, expression, are nothing, then I am nothing, for it has become clear to me, reading the notebooks, that I remain Anna because of a certain kind of intelligence. This intelligence is dissolving and I am very frightened. (Pp. 407–8)

As Ernst Cassirer has observed in describing the phenomenology of mythical thinking and the important identity between language and the reality it describes,

> It seems that the true inner connection between the language world on the one hand and the world of perception and intuition on the other can only be apprehended clearly when, because of special conditions, the bond between the two begins to slacken . . . only then does it become evident how much the world of perception, which one tends at first sight to interpret as a datum of the senses, owes to the spiritual medium of language, and how every impediment of the process of spiritual communication effected in language also affects the immediate nature and character of perception.[17]

Anna's dissolution of ego-consciousness manifests itself not only in her detachment from language but in the figurative language of her dreams—one of the important narrative devices (beginning with Mary Turner's nightmares) by which Lessing represents the deeper, unrationalized dimensions of her characters' consciousnesses. One of Anna's recurring dreams, later described in *Free*

Women, symbolizes her sense that an inner spring or well has gone dry and that she must "touch some source somewhere . . ." (p. 336). Interestingly, Anna's Black notebook contains the heading "Source"; in her dreams she ultimately confronts one source of her present inner schism—the memories of Africa—as part of her later reintegration. The motif of separation from the fructifying source of life and regeneration carries over into the novel that follows this one: its title, *Landlocked*, describes Martha Quest's continuing geographical and psychic isolation as confirmed in her dreams. The theme modulates further in the dreamlike fantasies of Charles Watkins's sea voyage in *Briefing for a Descent into Hell*, and in Kate Brown's struggle to carry her wounded seal back to water in the dream sequence of *The Summer before the Dark*.

Another dream motif recurs in different forms in the Blue note-book, tracking the progress of Anna's breakdown.[18] It begins as a maliciously smiling crocodile that emerges from among the fragments and broken pieces she finds in a jeweled casket—symbolically, her own deadened, fragmented state and the ambivalent figure to which her deeper unconscious gives rise (p. 216). Later Anna comes to call this sardonic image the principle of "joy-in-spite." It always embodies an antithetical combination of vitality and malice. Esther Harding has pointed out that "in the archetypes the urges of the unconscious have not as yet been differentiated, for differentiation is a function of consciousness. Therefore they appear in ambiguous or dual form, in fact as pairs of opposites —as good-bad, favourable-harmful, spiritual-demonic, and so on through the whole range of possible dichotomies."[19] In the earliest occurrences of the dream the figure is embodied in nonhuman forms, as a vase or an elf or pixie conveying "something anarchistic and uncontrollable" (p. 408). As Anna's breakdown proceeds, the figure assumes progressively more human forms, both in dreams and in images and figures from her actual experiences. "The element took a variety of shapes, usually that of a very old man or woman (yet there was a suggestion of a double sex, or even sexlessness) and the figure was always very lively, in spite of having a wooden leg, or a crutch, or a hump, or being deformed in some way" (p. 408).

Once the joy-in-spite principle becomes manifest in distinctly human forms, as it does in the dreams reported in the third segment of the Blue notebook, Anna is frightened for her own sanity. As she reflects, ". . . if the element is now outside of myth, and inside another human being, then it can only mean it is loose in me also, or can only too easily be evoked" (p. 409). Eventually that is what happens, for Anna accepts the identification of herself with the dream figure. Acknowledging her own ambivalence, however, does not halt the inner process which now must run its entire course.

The last four parts of the novel—the final segments of the Yellow and Blue notebooks, the singular Golden notebook, and the final *Free Women* installment—trace the furthest extremes of Anna's "crackup" and the reversal into a positive reintegration. Like the most subjective chapters in *The Grass Is Singing* and brief sections in *Retreat to Innocence* and the several volumes of *Children of Violence*, the point of view in all but the *Free Women* section is that of the abnormal consciousness itself, the totally subjective experience of psychic distortion of perception and dissolution of the boundary lines between internal and external events. Just as the joy-in-spite principle evolves from nonhuman to human form in her dreams, so the irrational consciousness in Anna evolves to embrace more and more of her waking experience. As she loses control of her aesthetic and intellectual distance—her ability to externalize her inner chaos by transforming it into fictional form—Lessing (the controlling narrator behind Anna as narrator) gives the same weight of realism to her protagonist's distortions of perception and interpretation of events that she has given to every other formulation of Anna's experiences. From Anna's perspective the experiences are artistically formless and subjective. Lessing, of course, creates a deliberate aesthetic shape for their unfolding, using the recurring motifs of schism, duality, chaos, breakdown, and dream imagery as organizing principles.

The last segment of the Blue notebook opens with Anna's assertion that her daughter Janet is her anchor to what is normal in herself (p. 464); Janet leaves for boarding school and, symbolically, Anna's normality vacates her.[20] Shortly afterward Saul Green, a visiting American communist who needs a place to stay, arrives. Anna instantly perceives a split in his personality which in fact parallels that schism in her own: a jarring, wary, hostile physical presence juxtaposed with an intelligent, sensitive, candid aspect. Her immediate perception of bifurcation condenses the much more gradual split Anna had projected and experienced in her earlier relationship with Michael, as examined through Ella's relationship with Paul Tanner. Anna and Saul begin to "name" each other—a repetition of Anna's desperate need to impose order on her world by verbalizing all of her experiences. The reader subsequently discovers, by matching the parenthetical numbered asterisks in the Blue notebook with the numbered story outlines in the Yellow notebook, that Anna's projections onto Saul (whose name resembles that of the invented Paul—in turn echoing Paul Blackenhurst, whose death Anna describes early in the Black notebook) also begin at this moment.

This series of correspondences between notebooks is one of the most significant expressions of the tension between the linear and cyclic organizations of the novel and of modes of experience. We encounter the story outlines of the Yellow notebook first, only later recognizing them as adaptations of Anna's experiences with Saul Green recorded in the Blue notebook segment that follows. Like the intercalations of *Free Women* between groupings of the notebook sequence, this arrangement breaks up chronology, reinforcing the layering of experience and the necessity for the reader to consider the simultaneity of events described from several perspectives as if at once. The course of Anna Wulf's breakdown percolates through the novel both vertically and horizontally, moving forward in time and in the narrative unfolding of the novel, while turning back on itself both in the repetition of images and themes and in the circularity of the organization. To use the analogy of a stone dropped into a pool of water, the novel expresses both the pattern of the horizontal ripples moving outward in concentric circles from the single break in the water's surface, and the path of the stone itself as it travels vertically to the bottom of the pool. *The Golden Notebook* is a verbal hologram.

Anna's fiction-making tendency manifests itself more than ever as an aspect of her self-division: it is simultaneously her imaginative artistic talent and her strongest psychic defense against chaos. The very first story outline entered in the last segment of the Yellow notebook discloses the transforming process at work, as Anna outlines a story in which "a woman, starved for love, meets a man rather younger than herself, younger perhaps in emotional experience than in years; or perhaps in depth of his emotional experience. She deludes herself about the nature of the man; for him, another love affair merely" (p. 455). In this, as in most of the other story outlines, Anna articulates in fictional form emotions and ambiguities that she cannot face directly in herself.

The processes of splitting and projection, both far advanced by this point, permeate all of Anna's perceptions of Saul. She notes that he talks "two different languages" to her at the same time (p. 473), and that he is at least two different men whom she cannot connect (p. 480). In herself she finds "two other Annas, separate from the obedient child—Anna, the snubbed woman in love, cold and miserable in some corner of myself, and a curious detached sardonic Anna, looking on . . ." (p. 481). Despite the feelings of painful anxiety that Saul evokes in her, Anna allows herself, almost *wills* herself, to fall in love with him. The ensuing relationship retraces the emotional pattern already manifested in Anna's relationship with Michael and its projection into the fictional Ella's relationship with Paul. Like Ella, and thus like Anna who loved Michael (and also like Martha Quest), this Anna repeats the characteristic projection and splitting-off processes, denying the negative shadow in both Saul and herself in order to fulfill her ambivalent emotional needs. Though something in Saul terrifies Anna, she feels compelled to embrace it: the only way out of breakdown is further in.

Shortly after Anna and Saul begin sleeping together, she has the recurring dream about the dwarfed, malicious man who, this time, menaces her with an enormous protruding penis (p. 481). Saul is thus equated with her negative animus—the joy-in-spite principle with its strong sexual implications. At the same time the relationship between them develops a distinctly sadomasochistic rhythm, a "cycle of bullying and tenderness" (p. 496) corresponding to the self-division in both of them, in which hurt and submission alternate. Anna feels Saul turning her into a mother figure—a suspicion enacted by her own complicity in that emotional dynamic. Earlier, when Saul had awakened in fear as Anna checked on him in his sleep the way she would a child, Saul had put his arms up around her as might a frightened child (p. 475). Beneath her accusation that Saul has made her a mother figure is Anna's projection onto him of the dependent child she herself has become, as well as her intense ambivalence about her maternal role. This aspect of their relationship is Lessing's deeper dramatization of the bifurcation in the earlier Martha Quest's relationships with her two husbands as well as her ambivalent feelings about her own mother and her daughter. That particular cluster of conflicts is sharpened further by Anna's self-division into mother and mistress. As she admits to herself, "In a month Janet will be home and this Anna will cease to exist. If I know I can switch off this helpless sufferer because it is necessary for Janet, then I can do it now. Why don't I? Because I don't want to, that's why. Something has to be played out, some pattern has to be worked through . . ." (p. 498). What must be worked through is, in fact, the pattern of Anna's own psychic complexes: the ambivalent joy-in-spite principle, her masochism, her writer's block, her splits into mother, lover, artist, and socialist.

Because Saul's own schisms dovetail so closely with Anna's, and because each projects onto the other the aspects of themselves that they have not yet assimilated, they enter into a psychic process that resembles a mutual dissociation or breakdown.[21] Subjectively, Anna realizes that they are both mad. From the reader's point of view, if Saul's personality is in part a creation or projection of Anna's own inner fragmentation—the "sick person who inhabited my body for a while" (p. 480)—then the course of her breakdown is the denial and then progressive recognition and assimilation of Saul as the "other"—her emotional and artistic twin as well as her sexual opposite.

When the elements of Anna have dissolved into a chaos of qualities that are difficult to identify as either Saul or Anna, the slow process of reintegration of the personality begins. Anna acknowledges the message of her dream of the dwarf figure embodied in Saul Green, noting, "I was the old man, the old man had become me, but I was also the old woman, so that I was sexless" (p. 481). Thus the unresolved dualism of consciousness—the dialectical tensions of psychological reality dramatized by Lessing in each of her preceding novels—for the first time moves toward synthesis at a deeper level of the psyche, as Anna begins to make conscious and assimilate the alien other within herself. As she had anticipated in a sketch written by Ella that becomes Anna and Saul's story,

"A man and a woman—yes. Both at the end of their tether. Both cracking up because of a deliberate attempt to transcend their own limits. And out of the chaos, a new kind of strength" (pp. 399–400).

In expressing the radical disintegration of the elements of personality, Lessing describes her protagonist's consciousness in a variety of states in which the relationships between internal and external events, self and world, are altered. The distinctions between the two modalities blur as Anna loses her sense of time, space, and causality. Some of these altered states of consciousness are under Anna's control, others are not. One of her deliberate strategies to reduce her anxiety is a mental exercise she has practiced since childhood, which she calls "the game."

> First I created the room I sat in, object by object, "naming" everything, bed, chair, curtains, till it was whole in my mind, then move out of the room, creating the house, then out of the house, slowly creating the street, then rise into the air, looking down on London, at the enormous sprawling wastes of London, but holding at the same time the room, and the house and the street in my mind, and then England, and shape of England in Britain, then the little group of islands lying against the continent, then slowly, slowly, I would create the world, continent by continent, ocean by ocean (but the point of "the game" was to create this vastness while holding the bedroom, the house, the street in their littleness in my mind at the same time) until the point was reached where I moved out into space, and watched the world, a sunlit ball in the sky, turning and rolling beneath me. Then, having reached that point, with the stars around me, and the little earth turning underneath me, I'd try to imagine at the same time, a drop of water, swarming with life, or a green leaf. Sometimes I could reach what I wanted, a simultaneous knowledge of vastness and of smallness. (P. 469)

"The game" reveals several crucial aspects of Anna's consciousness: the importance of "naming" or maintaining a verbal control over the objects of her world, and of discovering a kind of hierarchy of organization in her physical and psychic space as she gains greater detachment and distance from her anxiety. Anna describes the end point as "a calm and delightful ecstasy, a oneness with everything, so that a flower in a vase is oneself, and the slow stretch of a muscle is the confident energy that drives the universe" (p. 480). Her game, recalling the field consciousness described above, parallels the technique of achieving a state of relaxed concentration practiced in many forms of contemplative meditation, in which the goal is a "deep passivity, combined with awareness." [22] Evelyn Underhill describes it in its specifically mystic manifestation as

> a psychic gateway; a method of going from one level of consciousness to another. In technical language it is the condition under which [the mystic] shifts his "field of perception" and obtains his characteristic outlook on the universe. That there is such a characteristic outlook, peculiar to no creed or race, is proved by the history of mysticism; which demonstrates plainly enough that in some men another sort of consciousness, another "sense," may be liberated beyond the normal powers. . . . [23]

Like Martha Quest, Anna has a kind of intuitive capacity that is almost too acute to bear, and that accounts in part for her psychic paralysis. As she observes, "It frightens me that when I'm writing I seem to have some awful second sight, or something like it, an intuition of some kind; a kind of intelligence is at work that is much too painful to use in ordinary life" (p. 489). Moreover, Anna's identification of her own self with the macrocosm reinforces the correspondence between private and collective breakdown, for later she experiences the game in the terrible immediacy of painful knowledge:

> I was experiencing the fear of war as one does in nightmares, not the intellectual balancing of probabilities, possibilities, but knowing, with my nerves and imagination, the fear of war. What I was reading in the newspapers strewn all around me became real, not an abstract intellectual fear. There was a kind of shifting of the balances of my brain. . . . I felt this, like a vision, in a new kind of knowing. And I knew that the cruelty and the spite and the I, I, I, I of Saul and of Anna were part of the logic of war; and I knew . . . in a way that would never leave me, would become part of how I saw the world . . . but the knowledge isn't in the words I write down now. (P. 503)

This particular kind of awareness functions not as an intellectual or analytical knowledge but as a fusion of levels of consciousness involving, as the mystical literature would phrase it, a direct perception of reality. Thus, intermittently but increasingly often, Anna's dissociated consciousness approaches that area of mental experience characterized by William James, Evelyn Underhill, and other commentators as mystical[24]—a mode of awareness in which the perceiver knows himself as identical with what he perceives.[25]

The sense of merging with the All is an equivocal one, however, for it typifies the loss of boundaries of the ego that characterizes both mystical vision and insanity. Significantly, as Anna's personality fragments, she finds it more difficult to play "the game." While the positive form of abnormal consciousness approaches the state of transcendental union, the negative form resembles the schizophrenic condition experienced as terrifying dissociation.[26] Those alternative forms describe the parameters of unconventional mental experience that recur in Lessing's fiction again and again— the poles of Heaven and Hell of the psychological universe—as the author traces the gradual conversion of the divided and fragmented consciousness into a more positive reintegration, synthesis of opposites, and unity of vision. *The Golden Notebook* is pivotal, dramatizing (among other themes) the crucial transition from breakdown to breakthrough.

One extreme form of the altered states of consciousness through which Anna Wulf passes on her way to a reintegration of her personality is the experience of dissolving into other people's identities. The most extended aspect of the phenomenon is the interpenetration (described above) of Anna and Saul into each other's personalities, emotions, psychic spaces. As Lessing explains in the introduction to the novel (written ten years after its original publication), Anna and Saul "'break down' into each other, into other people, break through the false patterns they have made of their pasts, the patterns and formulas they have made to shore up themselves and each other, dissolve. They hear each other's thoughts, recognise each other in themselves" (p. vii). Anna identifies herself so totally with Saul that when he leaves the flat to go for a walk, her "nerves seem to stretch out and follow him, as if tied to him" (p. 492).

In dreams Anna also enters the personality of the African nationalist Charlie Themba, an Algerian prisoner being tortured, and a number of other revolutionaries of various nationalities (pp. 506–9). In one dream she leaves her own body completely and watches from a distance as figures from her past try to enter her sleeping form. In the context of altered states of consciousness, that experience corresponds rather closely to the state variously identified as the "lucid dream," in which the dreamer knows he is dreaming and is often even aware of himself lying asleep in bed,[27] and the "out-of-body" experience, central to certain esoteric and sacred traditions, in which a person "experiences his consciousness existing outside his physical body."[28]

Throughout *The Golden Notebook*, in every layer of the narrative of Anna's experience, Lessing emphasizes Anna's self-division: in the separations between mind and body, between artistic objectivity and emotional subjectivity, and between the self and the outer world of other people and objects. These bifurcations suggest R. D. Laing's description of the schizoid personality,

> the totality of whose experience is split in two main ways: in the first place, there is a rent in his relation with his world and, in the second, there is a disruption of his relation with himself. Such a person is not able to experience himself "together with" others or "at home in" the world, but, on the contrary, he experiences himself in despairing aloneness and isolation; moreover, he does not experience himself as a complete person but rather as "split" in various ways, perhaps as a mind more or less tenuously linked to a body, as two or more selves, and so on.[29]

Though these divisions are the symptoms of Anna's breakdown, the alternative manifestation, in which such boundary lines between subject and object are blurred, is equally terrifying, for then the chaos which she controls by objectifying her experiences in various ways and maintaining some distance from them, rushes in to overwhelm her. Though she reaches the same area in the abnormal consciousness where the earlier Mary Turner had succumbed completely, for Anna these altered forms of consciousness become essential stages in the eventual reintegration of her personality.

In tracing the equivocal, shifting relationship between physical and psychic space in Anna's experiences, Lessing adapts a metaphor from the earlier novels: the analogue of rooms to states of consciousness. Not only does *The Golden Notebook* open with "the two women . . . alone in the London flat" (p. 9), but nearly all of the rest of the novel is circumscribed by Anna's rooms and flat, just as it is circumscribed by Anna's consciousness in its various stages and divisions. Quite early in the linear narrative (though formulated much later in time by Anna), in the opening segment of *Free Women*, one learns that "it was only alone, in the big room, that [Anna] was herself" (p. 52). As her breakdown advances, that self shatters into multiple fragments, and the room itself changes correspondingly. By that point Anna has separated from Molly, moving into a larger flat of her own to give "room to the notebooks" (p. 407), that is, to give her fragmenting personality space to play out that process without interruption. Through Ella, Anna admits that the choice of a flat much too large for her child and herself was unconsciously to leave space for a man: "for Paul [Michael], in fact . . ." (p. 195). Also through Ella, Anna narrates a dream that defines the state of her own splintering consciousness, projected through Ella before she confronts it in herself:

> She was in the ugly little house, with its little rooms that were all different from each other. She was Paul's wife, and only by an effort of will could she prevent the house from disintegrating, and flying off in all directions because of the conflict between the rooms. She decided she must furnish the whole house again, in one style, hers. But as soon as she hung new curtains or painted a room out, Muriel's [Paul's wife's] room was recreated. Ella was like a ghost in this house. . . . (P. 194)

Much later, after Anna and Saul have begun their joint breakdown into each other, Anna observes that "the walls of this flat close in on us. Day after day we're alone here. I'm conscious that we are both mad" (p. 491); she tells Saul, "'We're inside a cocoon of madness'" (p. 497). Even when she feels a temporary relief from chaos, she describes the flat as "a ship floating on a dark sea . . . isolated from life, self-contained. We played the new records, and made love, and the two people, Saul and Anna, who were mad, were somewhere else, in another room somewhere" (p. 498). Still later, when Anna feels invaded by alien personalities, the room is the analogue of her disorientation (recalling the occasional free-floating periods experienced by others of Lessing's characters): "The floor between me and the bed was bulging and heaving. The walls seemed to bulge inwards, then float out and away into space.

For a moment I stood in space, the walls gone, as if I stood above ruined buildings. I knew I had to get to the bed, so I walked carefully over the heaving floors towards it, and lay down. But I, Anna, was not there" (p. 512).

Following a particularly intense exchange with Saul, Anna experiences another attack of what she calls vertigo, as her room corroborates her paranoia: "My big room, like the kitchen, had become, not the comfortable shell which held me, but an insistent attack on my attention from a hundred different points, as if a hundred enemies were waiting for my attention to be deflected so that they might creep up behind me and attack me" (p. 541). A plant on her windowsill suggests "a little hostile animal or a dwarf, imprisoned in the earthenware pot" (p. 506), recalling the dwarf-vase embodying the joy-in-spite principle about which she has dreamed earlier.

During rare interludes in Anna's breakdown the flat corresponds to positive, rather than negative, states of consciousness. At the beginning of the Golden notebook section, after "the devils [her daemons] had gone out of the flat" (p. 523), Saul comes to Anna in affection and observes, before they make love, "'This is an extraordinary room . . . it's like a world'" (p. 523). But when Saul leaves her room, Anna perceives the walls, like her mind, again "losing their density" (p. 525), and finds herself moving further than ever from sanity. Items in the room transmogrify into elements of frightening fantasies: "areas of light on the ceiling had become great watchful eyes" (p. 525), and the curtains become "shreds of stinking sour flesh left by the animal. I realised I was inside a cage into which the animal could leap when it wished" (p. 525).

Thus her room and her flat become objective correlatives for the various forms of her consciousness during the dissolution of her personality, as Lessing fuses inner and outer worlds so totally that their indistinctness is both source and metaphor for Anna's confusion. As Anna's room assumes the shapes of prison, cage, cocoon, world, the reader is a silent prisoner in the containments of Anna's consciousness, locked into her subjectivity and unable to see any other reality than the one Anna projects.

During the days she spends "inside" madness—inside other people's identities and her own fantasies—Anna confronts the underside of her own personality. In identifying the shadow aspect of her self variously projected onto Saul Green and other figures in her experience, as well as through dreams and other altered states of consciousness, she ultimately accomplishes the assimilation of her negative self, and breaks out of the closed circle of her emotionally blocked personality. Her dream cycle finally reflects that conversion from a disintegrating to a reintegrating state: "This time there was no disguise anywhere. I was the malicious male-female dwarf figure, the principle of joy-in-destruction; and Saul was my counter-part, male-female, my brother and my sister. . . . In the dream, he and I, or she and I, were friendly, we were not hostile, we were together in spiteful malice" (p. 508). By acknowledging that the principle of joy-in-destruction and the way she experiences Saul are generated from within herself, Anna accepts that she has for the first time "dreamed the dream 'positively,'" in Mother Sugar's terms (p. 508). The androgynous quality of all of the figures in the dream, including Anna herself, suggests the synthesis of opposites toward which her consciousness moves.

Not long after this identification of the "enemy alien" within herself, Anna looks at her notebooks and remarks to Saul, in answer to his curiosity about why she needs four of them, "'Obviously, because it's been necessary to split myself up, but from now on I shall be using one only'" (p. 511). She concludes that until she says this to Saul, she had not been aware of the shift within herself, or that she had been suffering from what she now names as a "writer's block." To mark her progress, she determines to write "all of myself in one book" (p. 519), and purchases a new golden-covered notebook for that purpose. Saul lays claim to the Golden notebook, but Anna, at least temporarily in control, resists his pressure and seizes the notebook for herself. That act of self-assertion concludes the final segment of the Blue notebook.

The Golden notebook that follows narratively is a continuation of Anna and Saul's mutual breakdown. Significantly, however, Saul's function as a projection of Anna's psyche assumes a positive valence. The last Blue notebook and the Golden notebook thus form two complementary movements in Anna's breakdown and breakthrough. Despite the insights she has achieved into herself, she is still far from wholeness and sanity, but at least one aspect of her consciousness (Saul, whose name in Hebrew means "asked for") has developed to guide her away from further disintegration. In a dream that contains images of hostile animals, Anna sees a tiger that represents Saul. At first she fears it, but later she overcomes her terror and realizes that she does not want the tiger to be subdued or caged. The dream symbolizes her gradual acceptance of her own sexuality, after the long frigid period following her break from Michael.

Anna remarks to herself as she recalls the dream, "I must write a play about Anna and Saul and the tiger" (p. 527). In this particular image Lessing enters her own fiction by glossing her drama, *Play with a Tiger*, in much the same way that Anna's various narrative versions of her experience in *The Golden Notebook* resonate with one another.[30] In the dramatic version Anna and her tiger, Dave, break down into each other as they fight out the terms of their attraction to and possession of one another. Their sadomasochistic sparring challenges the intellectual, sexual, and psychological boundaries between them; the play dramatizes variations on the same emotional dynamics that bind Anna and Saul in the novel. These correspondences further emphasize the way in which various pieces of Lessing's own work, like Anna's several notebooks, reformulate and recast some of the same clusters of experience, image, and idea.

The remainder of Anna's dream in the Golden notebook takes the form of a "film" of her life, presented to her by an invisible projectionist whom she eventually identifies as Saul Green. Certainly Saul's partial function as a *projection* of Anna's self is nowhere more clearly suggested. Moreover, the fact that Anna's reintegration is accomplished through visual rather than verbal images is a way around the writer's block which had choked her psyche with intellectualizations of her experience. The film "corrects" and changes some of her own earlier perceptions. Antithetical elements become synthesized into new wholes: Paul Tanner (Anna's fictional creation) and Michael (her ex-lover) fuse into one person, reversing the earlier splitting process. The projectionist suggests that Anna had distorted the events of her past by not "directing" them appropriately. Anna is faced with the confusion she herself has created between, as she phrases it, "what I had invented and what I had known, and I knew that what I had invented was all false" (p. 530). Yet this is not entirely accurate either, since Anna ultimately recognizes that her "inventions" express psychic truths that are part of the way she shapes and interprets her experience. The film is a metaphor for her reconsideration of aspects of her past that she "had still to work on" (p. 529) in order to overcome the "lying nostalgia" of her memory and assimilate its meaning into her consciousness. Such salvaging operations on the past form an important element in the enlargement of consciousness (a process that Lessing pursues again later through Martha Quest's efforts to rescue certain painful experiences of her earlier life).

When that segment of the dream ends, Anna tells Saul that she has identified him as the dream projectionist, acknowledging, "'You've become a sort of inner conscience or critic'" (p. 531). Having assimilated the negative aspect of Saul as the destructive principle (recorded in the Blue notebook), Anna now projects onto him the positive role that will lead her to rediscover the sources of her own creative energy, critical intelligence, and wholeness. Yet at the same time she is also preparing to tell Saul that he must leave her. Despite their total fusion with each other, symbolically she must relinquish what Saul stands for in order to gain access to those elements of her own personality and integrate both the negative and positive aspects of her projection. Literally, she must dismiss Saul because he evokes the pleasure/pain pattern that otherwise will continue to fuel her self-division.

The beginning of Anna's new autonomy has been prefigured in the final film sequence in her dream, in which she is recreated as a whole being rather than a collection of fragments and compartments. In the film, "instead of seeing separate scenes, people, faces, movements, glances, they were all together" (p. 543). As certain kinds of awareness occupy Anna's consciousness, she acknowledges the limitations of language itself to express them—just as Lessing struggled with the limitations of both language and form to communicate the nature of her protagonist's extraordinary consciousness. Recognizing her compulsive writing as an escape from, not a way of seizing and comprehending, her self, she admits, "The fact is, the real experience can't be described. I think, bitterly, that a row of asterisks, like an old-fashioned novel, might be better. Or a symbol of some kind, a circle, perhaps, or a square. Anything at all, but not words" (p. 542). As she discovers (and as the novel itself mirrors), the deeper truths of experience resist labeling and can only be alluded to through metaphor and symbol.

Ironically, while Anna frees herself as a writer by purging her work-choked consciousness, she finds herself thinking about writing a new novel. She and Saul exchange first sentences for each other's novels, as hopeful catalysts to start each other writing. Saul "names" Anna's self-division as the logical theme for her novel, suggesting, "'There are the two women you are, Anna. Write down: The two women were alone in the London flat'" (p. 547) —which becomes the first sentence of Anna's novel, *Free Women*.

In this sentence the larger circle of the structure of *The Golden Notebook* is revealed. If the shape of *The Grass Is Singing* suggests the end in the beginning, in *The Golden Notebook* the beginning is in the end; the circle becomes a completion or renewal rather than a repetition. The reader, given the knowledge that Anna Wulf is the author not only of the notebooks but of the apparently "objective" *Free Women* sections, must reconsider both *The Golden Notebook* and the novel within the novel as fictional variations on equivalent themes. The distinction between subjective and objective reality is revealed to be totally nonexistent, for all perception is interpretation; there is no single authoritative view of events. In this sense the novel perfectly "makes its own comment, a wordless statement: to talk through the way it is shaped" (p. xiii), for Anna herself does not always know the difference between the fiction and the reality of her experience, and Lessing places the reader in no more privileged position in relation to the novel as a whole.

However, at some point the narrative must establish a trust for the reader; otherwise even the fictions-within-fictions would fail to convince, either within their respective contexts or as parts of the larger design of a novel in which the controlling artist "remains within or behind or above [her] handiwork, invisible, refined out of existence . . ." (to borrow from James Joyce). If Anna herself dissolves into the flat fiction of *Free Women*, the reader is momentarily left wondering whether there is a consistent mimetic reality supporting any of the major characters of the novel. Since the dialectic between Anna's projections and her self-cancelations is formally expressed through the self-canceling fictions that comprise the layerings of the narrative, the question is ultimately both psychological and formal: even the most subjective and distorted descriptions contained in the final segment of the Blue notebook and the Golden notebook are *written by* Anna Wulf. That is, despite their immediacy and apparent direct mimesis of Anna's consciousness, they are not articulated by a narrator granted privileged omniscience (as in Joyce's or Woolf's or Faulkner's renderings of their characters' interior monologues). Rather, as Lessing has shaped the novel, the narrator is Anna—who is necessarily once removed from the experiences she describes, since she cannot be simultaneously living and recording them.[31]

Moreover, though written after Anna's recovery and thus chronologically last, *Free Women* is as much a fictionalization of her experiences as are *Frontiers of War*, "The Shadow of the Third," and each of the other notebooks. Just as various sections of *The Golden Notebook* are Anna's self-parody, *Free Women* is Lessing's own self-parody: a pastiche of the flat, somewhat pedestrian style and chronological omniscient narrative form of the earlier volumes of *Children of Violence*. The most detached rendering of Anna's experience, *Free Women* is also the least absorbing or convincing version of them, reinforcing Lessing's point that the traditional novel form is inadequate to communicate the meaning of such experiences. In its "objective" rendering of events—a perspective created primarily by Anna's reference to herself in the third person rather than through the first-person point of view used throughout the notebooks—*Free Women* provides a balance for the highly subjective and abnormal consciousness given expression in the final segments. In the "novel" Anna admits to Tommy that her four notebooks contain "chaos" (p. 41), and confesses to Molly that she has been close to madness. In response to Tommy's challenge of her notebooks, in which she brackets off certain kinds of experiences, Anna dispassionately describes her flashes of madness (p. 232). Here Tommy is Anna's projected inner critic (the role played by Saul Green in the Blue and Golden notebooks), criticizing her for not being "'honest enough to let yourself be what you are—everything's divided off and split up. . . . You take care to divide yourself up into compartments'" (p. 234). Saul Green's occasional blind looks (p. 480) resonate with Tommy's self-created blindness; Tommy's attempted suicide resonates with Ella's novel about a suicidal young man.

In the third and fourth segments of *Free Women* Anna admits that the crackup is not just in the outer world but in herself. She knows she is mad by that point because "for some days she had been observing ideas and images pass through her mind, unconnected with any emotion, and did not recognize them as her own" (p. 433). She cries and observes herself crying—split into two separate entities, one experiencing emotion and the other dispassionately observing it. In the fifth and final segment of the novel within the novel, Anna describes the American named Milt who stayed in her flat for five days (not several weeks as did Saul Green or five years as did Michael/Paul). Milt fulfills Anna's acute need for a man to occupy the empty space in her flat/psyche, which she had "prescribed . . . for herself like a medicine" (p. 554). He is in good physical health, while Saul was cold, sickly, and wan —the projections of Anna's own illness and psychic frigidity. Milt's main dimensions are sexual bluntness and an uncomplicated personality; he thus bears the same relationship to Saul that Cy Maitland (Ella's casual American brain surgeon–lover) does to Michael/Paul. Milt is also "a feeder on women, a sucker of other people's vitality" (p. 563), a variation of Anna's sadomasochistic emotional entanglement with Saul.

The resonances and discrepancies between Saul and Milt obviously press most urgently the question of Saul Green's "status" as a character, particularly given the fact that one has only Anna's construction of the events that include his parallel breakdown. What initially distinguishes Saul from the other male characters who appear in the variations of Anna's story is that Saul exists on the same mimetic plane of the narrative—in time and in place —as Anna herself, in her most "recently" written and undisplaced version of events. Yet she has already conceded that even in the Blue notebook/diary she fictionalizes her experiences. As the angle of distortion increases during the course of her breakdown, Saul's function as a projection of her own inner schism also increases, so that his independent existence as a "character" narratively equivalent to Molly or Tommy becomes more problematic. Anna's "naming" of Saul provides both a psychological and a narrative rationale for his status; he, too, is one of her creations—or, at least, he participates in that blurring of the distinctions between "reality" and "fiction," one of the consistent subversions of narrative convention upon which the novel depends.

Saul Green is "real" within the layer of mimetic reality invented by Anna in the Blue and Golden notebooks, but he becomes part of her own invention as soon as one moves back from that frame. For if Anna Wulf is the author of everything in the larger work entitled *The Golden Notebook*, then the novel described as Saul Green's in the inner Golden notebook is ultimately *Anna's creation*. Though the "editor" tells us (in brackets) that Anna's handwriting ends and the story about the Algerian and French soldiers is in Saul's writing, we know from references elsewhere in the novel that Anna's own handwriting changes (p. 314). Moreover, at least two entries recorded earlier form the thematic material for "Saul's" novel: Anna's dream of the execution of the interchangeable prisoners (p. 295) resonates with the plot of Saul's Algerian story in which both soldiers are shot for fraternizing across enemy ideological positions; in the final segment of the Blue notebook Anna dreams that she is an Algerian soldier herself (p. 513). In the inner Golden notebook she even protests to Saul that one source of her writer's block is her conflict between artistic vocation and political conscience: her feeling that freedom fighters of various nationalities (including Algerian) are always watching over her shoulder as she writes, demanding her more useful political involvement.

Thus the outline of the "novel" about the two soldiers that concludes the inner Golden notebook—written by Anna through her alter ego of Saul Green—is the fiction that springs her loose from her own fragmented introspection, marks the resolution of her writer's block, and enables her at last to write about what has happened more directly to the "two women" in the conventional novel that "frames" the rest of Anna's fictions.

What is established by the multiple narrative frames is that all versions of Anna's experiences are fictions, though each is true in its own way, with varying degrees of aesthetic distance and psychic detachment. As Ernst Cassirer has said in another context, "It is not a question of what we see in a certain perspective, but of the perspective itself."[32] The "truth" is not in any one version of Anna's experiences but in what she—and we—understand by imaginatively fusing the various fragments and perspectives together. If anything, those experiences recorded in the Blue notebook, artistically unshaped by Anna (though shaped by Lessing), contain the essential raw material of her experiences, but knowable only through her perception and interpretation of them. At the opposite end of the spectrum, the *Free Women* fiction fails in its very selective and "objective" focus to convey the complexity of Anna's emotional life. Consistent with the formal issues raised by the larger novel's subversion of narrative conventions, Anna's "traditional" novel must be seen as an unsatisfactory work of art. But the fictional Ella's idea for writing a novel about "people who deliberately try to be something else, try to break their own form as it were" (p. 399), is the successful novel by Lessing that contains her.

Accordingly, the meaning of *The Golden Notebook* is not in any one version of Anna's fictions but in the composite. Just as Anna's reintegration is achieved by fusing the partial truths of each of her experiences in a process that is visual rather than verbal, a visual analogy most clearly expresses the structural design of *The Golden Notebook*. In making color plates, transparencies of several different colors are superimposed upon the basic black outline. In this novel the "outline" is the past contained in Anna's Black notebook. To it are added the three primary colors represented in the novel by the various perspectives of the Red, Yellow, and Blue notebooks—the combination of which yields additional colors—and the synthesizing transformation of the Golden notebook. All five are incomplete by themselves; only when they are superimposed does the complete picture emerge. The picture is "framed" by the *Free Women* story that provides a literal shape but not the essential content of Anna Wulf's experiences.

In thematic terms Anna's way out of the impasses of her own repetitive psychic patterns is to accommodate all of the partial perspectives of her experiences, to assimilate them into a composite whole that transforms and transcends its parts, and, finally, to organize them into the design and sequence that the reader confronts as *The Golden Notebook*. Though Lessing presses us to accept that there is no reliable version of the variations of experience described in the various fictional forms throughout the novel (or, that *all* are reliable), we must ultimately assume that Anna Wulf is in fact the "editor" of the entire work, interposed between the fragmented Anna of the notebooks and fictions and Doris Lessing herself. It is that invisible Anna who collates and organizes the pieces of her story into a nonchronological but shaped whole. Though in *Free Women* she may have failed in her desire to write "a book powered with an intellectual or moral passion strong enough to create order, to create a new way of looking at life" (p. 59), in *The Golden Notebook* she (and, of course, Lessing) accomplishes her goal. Recording the breakdown and reintegration of her political, aesthetic, emotional, and psychic life as she melds the past and the present, the "facts" and the "fictions," Anna affirms her life as a creator of order in herself and in her art.

The figures that Anna names (p. 542) when she admits the inadequacy of language to symbolize experience—the circle and the square—are important visual analogues for the forms of consciousness as well as the novel in which they are examined. Not only is the "beginning in the end," but the circular structure reflects a shift in Lessing's conception of the psychic universe and the meaning of the narrative shape, modulating from enclosure and entrapment toward wholeness and integration. The symmetrical repetition of the *Free Women* sections followed four times by the sequence of four notebooks is broken by the appearance of the synthesizing vision of the Golden notebook—the one that records Anna's reintegration.

Moreover, the square—which in a Jungian context reflects the activity of the conscious dimension of the psyche—complements the figure of the circle.[33] The major divisions of the novel into four groups of four are abstractions of the square, as is the room that symbolizes Anna Wulf's consciousness. The synthesis of the circle and the square is an abstract analogue for the fusion of the linear and cyclic patterns of narrative development that have paralleled the development of consciousness in Lessing's fiction. In both life and art, wholeness comes from reconciling the formulations of the rational intellect with the mythic or nonrational potentialities of the deeper strata of the psyche.

Though there are a number of forms in which Anna Wulf's experiences are expressed, there is only one form that contains all of them. As Lessing phrases it, "I understood that the shape of this book should be enclosed and claustrophobic—so narcissistic that the subject matter must break through the form. This novel, then, is an attempt to break a form; to break certain forms of consciousness and go beyond them." [34] In "breaking the forms of consciousness" Lessing demonstrates that there is no adequate verbal statement of psychic reality; the novelist's dilemma is the paradox of falsifying experience in the very act of trying to articulate its truth (just as the literary critic inevitably falsifies the experience of the novel in attempting to describe it).

In *The Golden Notebook*, the crucial turning point in the author's work in both formal and thematic terms, the challenge of conventional values and assumptions that has preoccupied each of her previous protagonists is widened to embrace an inquiry into the limitations of narrative form and, even more radically, of the description of "reality" itself. Anna's breakdown and breakthrough are both the meaning and the shape of the novel: Lessing's most innovative rendering of the way in which the mind not only confronts but creates its own reality.

Ultimately, then, *The Golden Notebook* is one story with one major character, split, divided, and refracted through a variety of invented personas, situations, and experiences. The extraordinary multiplicity of the novel is revealed to be an even more remarkable unity at base. Anna Wulf is almost a creation of her own imagination, split into an entire cast of characters who, as Lessing instructs, "*are* each other, [who] form wholes. In the inner Golden notebook, things have come together, the divisions have broken down, there is formlessness with the end of fragmentation—the triumph of the second theme, which is that of unity" (p. vii). Anna and Saul, Anna and Molly, Anna and Ella, Anna and Michael, Anna and Janet, Anna and Tommy: these are various pairings of the dialectical splits that resolve into wholes on the level of character, when Anna synthesizes those divisions in her consciousness. Simultaneously the juxtapositions of fact/fiction, past/present, sane/mad, male/female, objective/subjective, reason/emotion, conscious/unconscious, and a variety of other antinomies on the thematic level can finally be reconciled through the synthesizing capacity of the reader's own imagination.

The final statement of the shape of Anna Wulf's consciousness is reported in the last segment of *Free Women*, which also concludes *The Golden Notebook*. There Anna describes her search for "another, smaller flat" (p. 567), suggesting that her breakdown and later reintegration have enabled her to contain the fluidity of her consciousness in a more condensed and less fragmented form; she has also stopped waiting for the man who will "create" her by occupying the empty space in her personality. This is the real beginning of Anna Wulf's life as a "free woman." But her advance in consciousness is still a tenuous one. If she is to be "integrated with British life at its roots" (p. 568), as she ironically phrases it, her psychic integration implies a personal synthesis achieved within a fragmented and still chaotic outer reality: the final word of the novel is "separated." Consistent with the dialectical model of the growth of consciousness, each reconciliation of opposites inevitably gives way to the tension of new antinomies.[35]

Despite this equivocal ending to *The Golden Notebook*, Lessing charts the future course for the expansion of consciousness in the final section of the novel. From her aesthetic detachment Anna describes her entry into that new and terrifying area of her own mind as

> a reality different from anything she had known before as reality, and it came from a country of feeling she had never visited. It was not being "depressed"; or being "unhappy"; of feeling "discouraged"; the essence of the experience was that such words, like joy or happiness, were meaningless. Coming around from this illumination—which was timeless; so that Anna did not know how long it had lasted, she knew she had had an experience for which there were no words—it was beyond the region where words could be made to have sense. (P. 557)

It is the return visits to map the new "country of feeling" disclosed during that illumination that form the subject of each of Lessing's subsequent novels, as the elements of reality initially confronted through breakdown or schism are identified more positively as part of the totality of human consciousness. Increasingly, beginning with the breakthrough of *The Golden Notebook*, the author's focus evolves away from psychological realism altogether, taking shape in the symbolic, mythopoeic, and mystical dimensions of experience that go beyond language—the "new forms of consciousness" exposed through Anna Wulf's crackup.

NOTES

1. Some sections of this chapter originally appeared in slightly different form as an article entitled "Doris Lessing's *The Golden Notebook*: The Meaning of Its Shape," in *American Imago* 32, no. 1 (1975), 40–58.

2. In this context, the novel belongs in the company of other twentieth-century experimental fictions in which the central character challenges realism by writing —or unwriting—the novel in which he also appears as a writer; André Gide's *The Counterfeiters* and Aldous Huxley's *Point Counterpoint* come to mind. As Robert Alter has pointed out, the "self-conscious" novel is not actually a modern development in the form, having its source as far back as the fictional layerings of *Don Quixote* and other novels in the tradition that exploits the dialectical interface between deliberate artifice and illusory "reality." See *Partial Magic: The Novel as a Self-Conscious Genre* (Berkeley and Los Angeles: University of California Press, 1975).

3. Florence Howe, "A Conversation with Doris Lessing" (1966), in *Doris Lessing: Critical Essays*, ed. Annis Pratt and L. S. Dembo (Madison: University of Wisconsin Press, 1974), p. 11.

4. "Interview with Doris Lessing by Roy Newquist" (1964), in *A Small Personal Voice*, ed. Paul Schlueter (New York: Alfred A. Knopf, 1974), p. 60.

5. *The Golden Notebook* (1962; rpt. London: Michael Joseph, 1972), p. 9. All subsequent page references will be indicated in the text.

6. See Chapter I, pp. 22–24.

7. For further discussions of the double figure in literature, see Ralph Tymms, *Doubles in Literary Psychology* (Cambridge: Bowes and Bowes, 1949), and Robert Rogers, *The Double in Literature* (Detroit: Wayne State University Press, 1970).

8. Charles Brenner, *An Elementary Textbook of Psychoanalysis*, rev. ed. (New York: International Universities Press, 1973), pp. 50–56.

9. Letter from Doris Lessing to Roberta Rubenstein dated 28 Mar. 1977.

10. In a story that predates *The Golden Notebook* by several years, Lessing writes of a psychiatrist who voluntarily commits himself for six months of each year as an inmate in the mental hospital that he supervises. Through the medium of finger-painting he expresses the bifurcated vision that haunts him. See "The Eye of God in Paradise," in *The Habit of Loving* (New York: Ballantine Books, 1957).

11. Jung, *Aion*, trans. R. F. C. Hull, vol. 9 of *The Collected Works*, Bollingen Series XX (New York: Pantheon Books, 1959), p. 22.

12. For elaboration on the sexual politics implicit in *The Golden Notebook*, see Ellen Morgan, "Alienation of the Woman Writer in *The Golden Notebook*," and Lynn Sukenick, "Feeling and Reason in Doris Lessing's Fiction," in *Doris Lessing*, ed. Pratt and Dembo, pp. 54–63 and 98–118; and Annis Pratt, "The Contrary Structure of Doris Lessing's *The Golden Notebook*," *World Literature Written in English* 12, no. 2 (1973), 150–60. Pratt also views the pattern of relationship between the women and men in the novel as a dialectical one, corresponding with the vision of balanced opposites expressed in the poetry of William Blake.

13. Becker, *The Denial of Death* (New York: Free Press, 1973), pp. 41–42.

14. Lessing describes her therapist as "a Jungian Roman Catholic lady [who remarkably, converted from Judaism], a very good woman indeed. My views of

what I was doing, then, and now, are different. Then I thought I was becoming 'individuated.' But I do not think becoming individuated is so easily paid for as by talking to a person, good or not. And my subsequent behavior showed and shows that whatever else I was doing it was not becoming individuated. Now I think I was paying for a friend, which I needed desperately, to counterbalance certain very destructive things in my life. I think usually what people are doing when they are in analysis or therapy or whatever, is paying for a friend. There is nothing wrong with it! But it is not through words one learns, it is through situations, what one goes through. I did not, and do not now, much agree with what my therapist *said*—her analyses of what was going on, in my life, or between her and myself; though sometimes she was right. What I learned from was the interaction between us, and that was not necessarily what *she* saw.

"... I learned from her all right. Perhaps the chief thing was this: that one doesn't learn from people telling one things!

"She was a good, kind, infinitely generous woman." Letter from Doris Lessing to Roberta Rubenstein dated 28 Mar. 1977.

15. Mitchell, *Psychic Exploration*, ed. John White (New York: G. P. Putnam's Sons, 1974), p. 690.

16. "Doris Lessing at Stony Brook: An Interview by Jonah Raskin" (1969), in *A Small Personal Voice*, ed. Schlueter, pp. 65–66.

17. Cassirer, *The Philosophy of Symbolic Forms*, trans. Ralph Manheim, vol. 3: *The Phenomenology of Knowledge* (New Haven, Conn.: Yale University Press, 1957), p. 208.

18. Elsewhere I have discussed the cumulative rhythm of the dream motifs: their formal placement within the structure of the novel, and within the progress of Anna's breakdown and reintegration. See citation under n. 1 above.

19. Harding, *Psychic Energy: Its Source and Its Transformation*. Bollingen Series X (1948; rpt. New York: Random House, 1963), p. 367.

20. The suggestive connection between the name Janet and the two-faced Janus figure in mythology may or may not be intentional.

21. The pattern of psychic breakdown as the initial phase of a process that may ultimately lead to reintegration if allowed to run its full course parallels the therapeutic hypothesis of R. D. Laing outlined in *The Politics of Experience* (1967; rpt. Middlesex, England: Penguin Books, 1970), pp. 104–37; see Chapter VII—on *Briefing for a Descent into Hell*—in this study for a fuller discussion. Apropos Laing's suggestions that the schizophrenic member of a family group often is revealed to be the scapegoat for the other family members' acknowledged contradictions of value, expectation, and behavior (Laing and A. Esterson, *Sanity, Madness, and the Family* [1964; rpt. Middlesex, England: Penguin Books, 1970]), Anna Wulf sketches a plot outline in the last segment of the Yellow notebook: "Two people together, in any kind of relationship—mother, son; father, daughter; lovers; it doesn't matter. One of them acutely neurotic. The neurotic hands on his or her state to the other, who takes it over, leaving the sick one well, the well one sick. I remember Mother Sugar telling me a story about a patient. A young man had come to see her convinced he was in desperate psychological trouble. She could find nothing wrong with him. She asked him to send along his father to her. One by one, all the family, five of them, arrived in her consulting room. She found them all normal. Then the mother came. She, apparently 'normal,' was in fact extremely neurotic, but maintaining her balance by passing it on to her family, particularly to the youngest son. ... I remember [Mother

Sugar] saying: Yes, often it's the most 'normal' member of a family or a group who is really sick, but simply because they have strong personalities, they survive, because other, weaker personalities, express their illness for them" (p. 459).

22. Edward Maupin, "On Meditation," in *Altered States of Consciousness*, ed. Charles T. Tart, 2nd ed. (New York: Doubleday, 1972), p. 180.

23. Underhill, *Mysticism* (1910; rpt. New York: E. P. Dutton, 1930), p. 49.

24. See p. 47 above, n. 5. William James identifies the elements of mystical consciousness as ineffability, noetic quality, transiency, and passivity. See *The Varieties of Religious Experience* (1902; rpt. New York and London: Longmans, Green, 1929), pp. 380–81.

25. Kenneth Walker, "The Supraconscious State," in *The Highest State of Consciousness*, ed. John White (New York: Doubleday, 1972), p. 16.

26. R. D. Laing, *The Divided Self* (1960; rpt. Middlesex, England: Penguin Books, 1965), p. 79.

27. Frederick Van Eeden, "A Study of Dreams," in *Altered States of Consciousness*, ed. Tart, pp. 152–58.

28. Charles T. Tart, "Out-of-the-Body Experiences," in Mitchell, *Psychic Exploration*, p. 349.

29. Laing, *The Divided Self*, p. 17. Again, Lessing's novel precedes by two years Laing's phenomenological descriptions of those states. See Lessing's comments on Laing in Chapter VII below, pp. 196–99.

30. *Play with a Tiger: A Play in Three Acts* (London: Michael Joseph, 1962), was written in 1958 and published the same year as *The Golden Notebook*.

31. In his sensitive analysis of the relation of *Free Women* to the notebooks, John Carey arrives at some of the same conclusions I do concerning the relation of the structure of the novel to its meaning. Carey focuses primarily on the aesthetic rather than the psychological aspects of Anna's narration of her experiences. His discussion of the function that "naming" plays in Anna's various verbal reconstructions and the ultimate resolution of her writer's block is particularly illuminating. See "Art and Reality in *The Golden Notebook*" in *Doris Lessing*, ed. Pratt and Dembo, pp. 20–39.

32. Cassirer, *Language and Myth*, trans. Susanne K. Langer (New York: Dover, 1946), p. 11.

33. As Esther Harding notes, "The relation between the square and the circle has symbolized for many people through many centuries the problem of the relation of two incompatible values. The square represents the earth, which is, as we say, foursquare reality; it is the indisputable fact, the logical or rational principle, and symbolizes human consciousness and understanding. The circle is complete in itself, without beginning and without end; it represents the heavens, the cosmos, and symbolizes the sphere or the absolute, the divine" (*Psychic Energy*, p. 388).

34. From the dust jacket of the original British edition (London: Michael Joseph, 1962).

35. In the Hegelian terminology "the synthesis . . . will reveal itself as again thesis and develop itself to a new self-contradiction in antithesis and so be sublated in a fresh synthesis. . . ." See G. R. C. Mure, *The Philosophy of Hegel* (London: Oxford University Press, 1965), p. 36.

5

Landlocked

The two volumes of *Children of Violence* published after *The Golden Notebook*, like the volume published after *Retreat to Innocence*, show the clear impact of Lessing's digression from the series. In each case she has interrupted her own dramatization of Martha Quest's development in order to explore a particular group of ideas and concerns more completely; their meaning and implications later resonate in the ongoing life experiences of Martha Quest, the child of this century. Just as the antitheses between Julia Barr and Jan Brod (*Retreat to Innocence*) disclose the possibilities and disillusionments of Leftist political commitments—Lessing's exploration of a problem in the political sphere that is incorporated into Martha Quest's and Anna Wulf's moral dilemmas—so Anna Wulf's breakdown and eventual discovery of the larger country of consciousness on its other side reappear in Martha's equally complex growth of consciousness in the remaining volumes of *Children of Violence*. In working through the implications of Anna Wulf's fragmentation, Lessing found a way to carry Martha Quest beyond the point of impasse described at the conclusion of *A Ripple from the Storm*, while at the same time resolving her own aesthetic impasse.

With *Landlocked*, the form of the novel itself resumes the more conventional narrative shape of the previous volumes of the series. This formal retreat from the innovations of the preceding novel is inevitably disappointing, though one accepts the necessity dictated by the series of retaining the continuity and open-ended structure. Though the design of the work does not, like that of

The Golden Notebook, corroborate the process it describes, Anna Wulf's struggle to become a "free woman" spills over into Lessing's portrayal of the further stages in Martha Quest's developing consciousness.

While not as fragmented as Anna Wulf finally becomes, the Martha Quest of *Landlocked* initially retains the self-divisions that have described her consciousness since early in the *Children of Violence* series. By now the veteran of two different but equally unsuccessful marriages, she has identified the schism within herself between the outwardly attractive, socially compliant Matty, and "what was real in her, underneath these metamorphoses of style or shape or—even, apparently—personality. . . ."[1] In keeping with Lessing's overall conception of the series, *Landlocked* continues the history of the children born of violence: the insidious emotional tyrannies of family life and social roles as well as the larger collective violence of two wars and the sexual, racial, economic, and political inequities that frame them.

Much of the six-year time period covered in the novel[2] concerns Martha's efforts to maintain her personal equilibrium during a time of political and social as well as private upheaval: her stalemated marriage of convenience to Anton Hesse; the illnesses and deaths of her father and a political friend, Johnny Lindsay; the difficulties of another friend, Maisie Gale; her gradual disillusionment with the communist myth as the cycle of political belief runs its course and—typical of the dynamic of Lessing's universe—turns "into its own opposite" (p. 353); the further dispersal of friends who leave for their own countries as the war in Europe ends. From the greater emotional detachment of her present relationship to Anton, Martha admits to herself that both of her marriages had been false because the partners had never really touched each other. Moreover, as she subordinates her stale personal life to her party activities, she feels an even greater pressure to "[keep] things separate" (p. 286), holding the different aspects of her being apart from one another in order to avoid the very kind of breakdown that Anna Wulf had eventually experienced when such compartmentalization failed.

Lessing resumes her exploration of Martha's quest by enlarging upon two metaphors introduced in earlier novels and repeated in various forms throughout her fiction. Both are expressed through visual images, and both reflect the growing breach between Martha's public roles and her true self or center during this period of her life. One is an increasingly insistent dream of isolation and psychic drought. Reminiscent of Anna Wulf's dreams of sterility in *The Golden Notebook*, she dreams of herself "on a high dry rocky place and around it washed long shoreless seas. Across this sea, which she could not reach, no matter how much she leaned and stretched her hands, sailed people she had known. All the people she knew" (p. 397). That dream recurs twice more in *Landlocked*, figuratively defining the state of Martha's being. She watches from a "high dry place while ships sailed away in all directions, leaving her behind. On this high dry plateau where Martha was imprisoned, forever, it seemed, everything was dry and brittle, its quality was drought. Far away, a long way below, was water. She dreamed, night after night, of water, of the sea" (p. 466). At their most literal level the dreams reflect her actual geographical isolation in the interior of Zambesia: not only physically landlocked but also morally dehydrated by its racial and political divisions. The next stage in Martha's quest is her departure for England, across a sea she has never seen to the country of her own family's historical roots.

The other major, and related, dream image of *Landlocked* builds from the correspondences between rooms and psychic states introduced in *The Grass Is Singing* and repeated in different configurations throughout Lessing's fiction.

> [Martha's] dream at this time, the one which recurred, like a thermometer, or gauge, from which she could check herself, was of a large house, a bungalow, with half a dozen different rooms in it, and she, Martha (the person who held herself together, who watched, who must preserve wholeness through a time of dryness and disintegration) moved from one room to the next, on guard. These rooms, each furnished differently, had to be kept separate—*had* to be, it was Martha's task for this time. (Emphasis in original, p. 286)

In *Landlocked* the image varies in both time (past and future) and form, sometimes appearing as a townhouse, other times as a mud-and-grass farm hut. But, regardless of its architecture, it comes to represent for Martha the shape of her own psyche: the mental balancing act she must perform in maintaining the separate compartments of her experience (analogous also to Anna Wulf's four notebooks reflecting the divisions within herself). Martha admits that the maintenance of such partitions is a negative effort, for "keeping separate meant defeating, or at least, holding at bay, what was best in her" (p. 287). She is still waiting for the man who can create her as a whole person:

> If she lived, precariously, in a house with half a dozen rooms, each room full of people (they being unable to leave the rooms they were in to visit the others, unable even to understand them, since they did not know the languages spoken in the other rooms) then what was she waiting for, in waiting for (as she knew she did) a man? Why, someone who would unify her elements, a man would be like a roof, or like a fire burning in the centre of the empty space. (P. 302)

Eventually that man appears, in the form of Thomas Stern, a Polish Jew whom Martha meets in the course of her party activities. For the first time in her life she experiences a genuinely profound emotional and erotic relationship with a man, one so penetrating that it changes the shape of her consciousness and incidentally discloses to her how emotionally destructive for both partners her previous marriages had been. Significantly, Thomas Stern's vocation in southern Africa is as a gardener. Martha's discovery of whole new areas of her being through Thomas unfolds in a lush, fecund atmosphere—a variant of the image of Eden that symbolizes the idea of wholeness and creative life energies in Lessing's fiction. In Thomas Stern's nursery Martha Quest is reborn.[3] Her involvement with Thomas permeates her being in all of its dimensions—emotional, intellectual, and sexual—and accomplishes the fusion of her disparate selves.

> Adding a new room to her house had ended the division. From this centre she now lived—a loft of aromatic wood from whose crooked window could be seen only sky and the boughs of trees, above a brick floor hissing sweetly from the slow drippings and wellings from a hundred growing plants, in a shed whose wooden walls grew from lawns where the swinging arc of a water sprayer flung rainbows all day long, although, being January, it rained most afternoons. (P. 367)

The new energy that they generate between them is not only exhilarating but somewhat frightening. While Anton Hesse had provoked in Martha "only the enemy, feelings so ancient and, it seemed, autonomous, they were beyond her control" (p. 381), Thomas drives her more ecstatically "back and back into regions of herself she had not known existed" (p. 370). Martha's previous marriages had involved a closing off, a separation of areas of the self in order to maintain a precarious balance between opposing forces of the personality, or between herself and the antithetical male. In contrast, the terrifying force of union itself is exposed by the depth of her involvement with Thomas. Martha feels herself being wrenched away from her arid self-containment, drawn by his energy into a state of being that dissolves the boundary lines of her own personality. The expansion of herself activated by their "sinking deeper and deeper into light" (p. 422) is the positive form of the breaking-down process that takes place between Anna Wulf and Saul Green in the immediately preceding novel. Martha describes the fusion of the separate consciousnesses of Thomas and herself as "the long process of breaking-down—as they both learned to put it—for the other; of learning to expose oneself, was something they did together, acknowledging they had to do it" (pp. 482–83).

In *Landlocked* both potentialities of consciousness formulated in Lessing's previous novels—dissolution into schism and breakdown, and dissolution into self-transcendence and mystical union—assume renewed attention at deeper levels of experience. The process has modulated from its utterly destructive form in Mary Turner to the tenuous equilibrium between divided aspects of the self in Julia Barr and in the Martha Quest of the earlier volumes of *Children of Violence*. The transformation from sterile fragmentation to liberating psychic integration in Anna Wulf evolves further to the positive reorganization of Martha Quest's consciousness in this novel. Finally, both the psychological and physical demands of Martha's being are equally met in her total communion with Thomas Stern.

Ironically, it is not Martha Quest but her lover Thomas who succumbs to the destructive potentiality inherent in such profound psychic upheavals. The fusion of their personalities transforms both of them, regenerating Martha while exacerbating Thomas's inner split. The clues to his eventual breakdown are provided early in *Landlocked*, couched initially in the figurative terminology of abnormal mental states: at the beginning of their relationship he declares that he is "insane" with love for Martha (p. 371). She responds to his pleasure in her mere physical being with some confusion, wondering, "What was she to think, to feel—if Thomas loved, to such lengths, the temporary delicacy of a curve of flesh, if he had singled out, with the eye of an insane artist" (p. 371), certain pure lines in her body. Because of his own guilt at his infidelity to his wife, Thomas identifies himself for Martha as a split person, part of whom loves each of the women completely. When he comes to her in an agitated state some months after their relationship has begun, he speaks for her—as if he could read her mind—announcing, "'You're thinking: I came here to be with my lover, not with this madman. . . . More and more often I look at you and you are thinking: How did I land myself with this maniac?'" (p. 434); or, again, "'You're thinking: Thomas is paranoiac'" (p. 454).

In these passages Lessing not only indicates Thomas's acute self-awareness but suggests that he actually "hears" Martha's thoughts and articulates them for her. Later, when Thomas goes away to Israel (partly to escape the conflict of his divided emotional loyalties), Martha experiences a similar telepathic sensitivity to Thomas's thoughts. She understands the phenomenon quite unremarkably as a kind of imaginative sympathy that creates channels of profound emotional communion between personalities. She observes that "a person who has gone away is still here as long as one can hear what he says. . . . Ten times a day she caught herself in discussion with Thomas" (p. 460). By contrast, Martha and her husband, Anton Hesse, are so out of sympathy emotionally and psychically (besides physically) that she had to "cut Anton out of her consciousness, had to bring down a curtain in herself and shut him out. Otherwise she would get ill" (p. 382). She knows that once they separate, "they would not even be able to hear what the other said, even for a short time" (p. 482).

Time affects those channels of receptive telepathy, however; by the time Thomas returns to Zambesia, the quality of emotional communion with Martha has deteriorated. Unable to reconcile his inner division or cope with the extraordinary energy released by their union, he flees it a second time by going to live with a primitive tribe in the Zambesi Valley. When Martha sees him again, the split has so permeated his being that two Thomases compete for expression. In several flashes of conversation "an old Thomas came to life, briefly . . . a blunt, aggressive, obstinate man, very different from the solitary silent person he almost at once became" (p. 492). The Thomas Martha had loved has been overwhelmed by his darker shadow; when, later, she learns of his death in the bush from blackwater fever, she is not surprised that she "certainly was not able to hear what he said" (p. 512).

What he had been trying to communicate ultimately comes to her in written form, in a journal that documents the extent of his psychic fragmentation and a hint of its misdirected vision. In it, observations on conditions in the rural areas alternate with anecdotes from his Jewish childhood in Poland; obituaries of tribal members and facts about the tribe's daily life alternate with nonsense sayings, illogical annotations, recipes, and private jokes. It is the written record of an abnormal consciousness even more radically splintered than Anna Wulf's, but similarly trying to marshal written language as a defense against increasing internal chaos. Painstakingly copying Thomas's journal from the damp, stained original, Martha gradually discerns a pattern in his "last testament"; the journal reflects the psychic split that, perhaps more than the fever, had driven him to his death:

> One version [of the journal] consisted of the short biographies and obituaries and the recipes and the charms and the tales and anecdotes. The other, typed out on flimsy sheets which could be inserted over the heavier sheets of the first version, made a whole roughly like the original—more or less common sense, as a foundation, with a layer of nonsense over it. But even in the first version, the "sensible" one, was a note of something harsh and repellent. Martha sat holding this extraordinary document, fitting the leaves in between each other, separating them, so that sense and nonsense met each other, as in a dance, and left each other. . . . (Pp. 535–36)

These combinations, rearrangements, and merging boundaries of the layers of comprehensible meaning in the journal recall the partial truths of Anna's several notebooks, though Thomas's papers lack even their visible organization. It is a measure of Martha's own sensitive consciousness that any pattern at all can be discerned.

The entire document reveals the acute self-divisions that had precipitated Thomas's breakdown, including his projection of his inner "enemy" upon the outer world. At one point in the journal Thomas articulates his subjective distortion through a parable reminiscent of John O'Hara's *Appointment in Samarra*, but with an unexpected reversal of the tag: "'Once there was a man who travelled to a distant country. When he got there, the enemy he had fled from was waiting for him. Although he had proved the usefulness [sic] of travelling, he went to yet another country. No, his enemy was *not* there.' (Surprised, are you! said the red pencil.) 'So he killed himself'" (p. 534). While primitive tribal life had appealed to him as a way of simplifying his experience, it actually compounds it, facilitating his entry into the primitive dimension of his own consciousness. Finally like Mary Turner, but unlike Anna Wulf and Martha, both of whom find ways to meld the fragments of their divided selves, Thomas submits to what he sees as the only possible escape from his tortured vision: annihilation. The bush cooperates with him in his death-wish.

Thomas's breakdown into madness is another formulation in Lessing's fiction of the dialectic between mind and world: of mind imposing its construction of reality upon outer events, and of outer events impinging upon and shaping that inner reality. His experience dramatizes the potentiality of dissolution that Martha Quest has always contained within herself, carried to its negative extreme. Moreover, the connection of madness to visionary capacities is emphasized in Thomas's earlier observation to Martha that people like themselves, split between nerves and principles (p. 385), are transitional beings in the evolution of consciousness. "'Perhaps there'll be a mutation though. Perhaps that's why we are all so sick. Something new is trying to get born through our thick skins. I tell you, Martha, if I see a sane person, then I know he's mad'" (p. 385).

The recognition that the conventional definition of sanity excludes the visionary angle of perception (and vice versa) is the bridge between Lessing's ongoing preoccupation with atypical consciousness and her then-developing interest in Sufi thought, in which the possibility of heightened awareness is a central premise.[4] Lessing credits the works of Idries Shah (one of Sufism's most instructive interpreters, about whom she has since written at some length) with influencing her thinking in a major and radical way. As she notes, "When I read it [Shah's book called *The Sufis*, published in 1964], I found that it answered many questions that I had learned—I feel too belatedly—to ask of life. Though that book was only the beginning of a different approach."[5] In *Landlocked*, the first novel Lessing published following her introduction to Sufi thought, the author reveals her new orientation by using quotations from Sufi teachings as epigraphs to two of the four sections of the novel, including the final one that describes Thomas Stern's death and his journal. The sensitivity that ultimately drives Thomas mad is the same capacity that, if directed positively, may lead to a higher synthesis of being.

Sufi teaching not only accepts but assumes an unconventional consciousness as a prerequisite for further inner growth; one of its central premises, as Lessing interprets it, is that "man has the possibility of conscious self-development, becoming able—with his own efforts and under a certain kind of expert guidance—to transcend ordinary limitations: this not for 'kicks' or for self-aggrandizement, but to serve mankind on its path of planned evolution."[6] Seen in its broadest context, Sufism is a body of teachings and wisdom stressing the individual's growth toward a greater unity of vision—the gnosis that transcends the apparent contradictions produced by more conventional logical thinking. Its mystical tradition is ancient, embracing ten or more centuries of practice and expression, most extensively transmitted through Islamic and Arabic texts. However, its esoteric teaching is not attached to the form or language in which it appears, but maintains that "there is only one underlying truth within everything that is called religion."[7] Its kernel is thus common to a number of mystical and sacred traditions whose central assumption is the larger unity of all forms of being and beings.

As Idries Shah points out, the Sufi conception of the self is "in one sense the personality of man, which is used to handle outside impacts and employ them for gratification. But it also means the inner or essential quality of the individual."[8] That dual focus permeates the teachings as a way of acknowledging the separation between inner and outer spheres of being that must be overcome to achieve wholeness of vision. The scholar Nasrollah S. Fatemi explains that "Sufis divided the works of God into two kinds—the perceived world and the conceived world. The former was the material visible world, familiar to man; the latter the invisible, spiritual world. The Sufis tried to show that in the relation existing between them could be found the means whereby man might ascend to perfection. The one watchword in his philosophy is continuity or evolution." [9]

This orientation of Sufism is easily compatible with the already clear preoccupations and patterns in Doris Lessing's previous fiction: her interest in breaking through the conventional ways of thinking and being, the urge to understand and extend the parameters of consciousness, the mystical intimations expressed in her characters, the desire to overcome the dialectical antitheses of perceived experience in favor of a synthesizing vision of wholeness. As Lessing herself has phrased it,

> [F]or people like myself, unable to admire organized religions of any kind, this philosophy [Sufism] shows where to look for answers to questions put by society and by experience—questions not answered by the official purveyors of knowledge, secular or sacred.
>
> "Man has had the possibility of conscious development for ten thousand years," say the Sufis. . . . [M]an is woefully underused and undervalued and does not know his own capacities. I have believed this all my life, and that the idea is central to Sufism is one reason I was attracted to it. [10]

The quest toward self-definition implicit in the protagonists of Lessing's earlier novels assumes another dimension of meaning when considered in the context of Sufi thought: the vision of human enlightenment modulates from that of the realization of the Golden Age through collective political action to a more private and inward path toward the same ideal. Concurrently, the aim is to escape from the blinders of convention, self-interest, and subjectivity to achieve a direct perception of truth or reality—the goal of all mystical traditions. Lessing has observed, however, that in contemporary society one is unaccustomed to believe in the compatibility of the mystical and the practical, and may resist the truth that Sufism is not an esoteric system so much as a way of living in the ordinary world. Its interpreters (she writes) insist that "you cannot approach Sufism until you are able to think that a person quite ordinary in appearance and in life can experience higher states of mind. Sufism believes itself to be the substance of that current which can develop man to a higher stage in his evolution. It is not contemptuous of the world. 'Be in the world, but not of it,' is the aim." [11]

The view of the unfolding development of the self is also central to psychological systems concerned with the full realization of the personality. Thus the Sufi inflection of Lessing's work, beginning noticeably with this novel, is actually an intensification of what has been present in her work from the beginning, rather than a discontinuous tangent from it. The gnosis of being is the end point shared by a psychology of self-realization and a metaphysics of mystical truth.

The message that Thomas Stern communicates to Martha through their physical and psychic union, and later through his posthumous journal, carries forward Lessing's theme of the evolution of consciousness toward higher and more unified manifestations. Though Thomas is ultimately a victim rather than a successful mutation himself, his insights significantly influence Martha's future life. Recognizing that his madness had been a desperate attempt to "get messages out" (p. 536), she has perceived meaning and sense in the apparent chaos of his raging mind. As she packs her suitcase for departure to England—the sea journey that ends her landlocked state both literally and symbolically—she throws Thomas's manuscript in with her baggage. Not only does that sea voyage initiate Martha's movement away from what Africa has come to represent for her—the pulls of convention, schism, emotional stasis, and loss. Her northward orientation also recalls the direction opening to the "hinterland to the imagination we cannot do without" (Martha Quest, p. 13): the promise of the future, the unactualized, and even the transcendent that Lessing details in the final volume of the series. Thus does Thomas's account of the journey of the abnormal consciousness accompany Martha to London, where she eventually enters the same chaos of the mind by choice and becomes a conduit for the evolutionary psychic mutations that Thomas had envisioned.

NOTES

1. *Landlocked* [*Children of Violence*, vol. 4] (1965; rpt. New York: Simon and Schuster, 1966), pp. 285–86. All subsequent page references will be indicated in the text.

2. Nancy Porter points out the various proportions of time encompassed by the several volumes of the series, observing that "fictional time is foreshortened in the early part of *Martha Quest* and lengthened gradually in the rest of the novels." See "Silenced History—*Children of Violence* and *The Golden Notebook*," *World Literature Written in English* 12, no. 2 (1973), 166.

3. Given Lessing's sexual politics, a comparison with D. H. Lawrence may seem incongruous—but the image brings to mind the illicit but profound emotional and sexual baptism of Connie Chatterly by the game-keeper Mellors in *Lady Chatterly's Lover*. Lessing acknowledges that Lawrence is one literary influence on her work in general (see letter from Lessing to Roberta Rubenstein in the concluding chapter of this study). Mark Spilka has elaborated on their approaches to sexual politics by focusing on *The Golden Notebook* and *The Four-Gated City* in particular. See "Lessing and Lawrence: The Battle of the Sexes," *Contemporary Literature* 16, no. 2 (1975), 218–40.

4. I am indebted to the ground-breaking scholarship of Nancy Shields Hardin and Dee Seligman on the Sufi influence in Lessing's work. See Hardin, "Doris Lessing and the Sufi Way," in *Doris Lessing: Critical Studies*, ed. Annis Pratt and L. S. Dembo (Madison: University of Wisconsin Press, 1974), pp. 148–64; and Seligman, "The Sufi Quest," *World Literature Written in English* 12, no. 2 (1973), 190–206.

5. Letter from Doris Lessing to Roberta Rubenstein dated 28 Mar. 1977.

6. Lessing, "A Revolution," *New York Times*, 22 Aug. 1975, p. 31.

7. Idries Shah, *The Sufis* (1964; rpt. New York: Doubleday, 1971), p. 55.

8. Ibid., p. 182.

9. Fatemi, "A Message and Method of Love, Harmony, and Brotherhood," in *Sufi Studies: East and West*, ed. L. F. Rushbrook Williams (New York: E. P. Dutton, 1973), pp. 58–59.

10. Lessing, "An Ancient Way to a New Freedom," in *The Elephant in the Dark*, ed. Leonard Lewin (1972; rpt. New York: E. P. Dutton, 1976), p. 78.

11. Lessing, "In the World, Not of It" (1972), in *A Small Personal Voice*, ed. Paul Schlueter (New York: Alfred A. Knopf, 1974), p. 133.

6

The Four-Gated City

As the final volume of *Children of Violence*, *The Four-Gated City* is the most comprehensive synthesis of the ideas and narrative techniques that have steadily evolved in Doris Lessing's fiction. Since the series as a whole traces Martha Quest's evolution through the various stages of her life from youth through adolescence, womanhood, maturity, and death—and since it was written and published during a time period embracing two decades—it is not surprising that the theme itself evolved from its original premises. In 1957, when only the first two volumes had appeared, Lessing described the series as "a study of the individual conscience in its relations with the collective";[1] its modulation in the final volume might be paraphrased as a study of the individual consciousness in its relations with the collective consciousness. The realization that both life itself and its symbolic transformation into fiction are organic, evolutionary processes is the shaping structure as well as the visionary theme of *The Four-Gated City*. Concurrently the series as a whole, framed by acts of collective violence, suggests more pessimistically that even the highly developed individual consciousness cannot finally influence the self-destructive potentiality and the inertia of the collective.

A number of other ideas in Lessing's fiction (considered earlier in this study) are also assimilated into the larger spectrum of *The Four-Gated City*: the forms of relationships (between men and women, women and women, parents and children, private and public selves, artists and society); the functions of politics, the arts, institutions (psychiatry, government, journalism), and others. In its scope the novel goes far beyond the traditional *Bildungsroman* convention that Lessing has identified as the form in which the series is cast.[2] Martha Quest matures beyond the young adult's first strong claim on his/her identity to embrace a more collective and transpersonal sense of her own being. At the same time the final volume of *Children of Violence* asserts most clearly the Hegelian underpinnings of the form: Martha not only mirrors the education and progress of consciousness, directed by reason, toward a spiritual plane, but also embodies the assumption that "the individual, child of [her] time, possesses within [herself] the whole substance of the spirit of that time. [She] needs only to appropriate it to [herself], make it present to [herself] again. . . ."[3]

While unorthodox narrative elements are not as apparent in *The Four-Gated City* as in *The Golden Notebook*, the novel is still formally innovative in its synthesis and further extension of conventions from the divergent narrative traditions of realism and romance. As Northrop Frye has proposed, the realistic tendency "moves in the direction of the representational and the displaced," whereas the romantic mode moves toward the "formulaic units of myth and metaphor."[4] Moreover, romance more often tends to dichotomize the ideal and the abhorrent, to assimilate the individual quest with the social one, and to depend upon cyclical patterns in both the universe it describes and in its own formal design. The antithetical tensions in Lessing's fiction, understood as functions of consciousness, may also be understood as functions of an essentially romantic orientation within the formal design of the narrative.

Structurally, this concluding volume of the series bears the same relationship to the earlier four that the "Golden notebook" section bears to the novel of the same name: that of encompassing, reconciling, and transforming the spectrum of ideas that lead up to it—like the white light that results from the fusion of the colors of the spectrum. Moreover, the structural organization of fourness which Jung and others have identified as the image of rational wholeness and completion functions in the shape of *The Four-Gated City* itself.[5] Like *The Golden Notebook* with its structure of repeating fours, there are four major sections of the novel, each of which contains four chapters. The Appendix, analogous to the

Golden notebook, is a separate section that forms a synthesizing conclusion and returns the open-ended ambiguity of the whole.[6]

Quaternity is an integral image within the novel's thematic development as well. Martha inhabits four houses during the course of the novel: the flat over Iris's restaurant at the beginning, and subsequently Jack's, Mark Coldridge's, and Paul Coldridge's houses, in each of which Martha discovers different aspects and capacities of her personality.[7] The more obvious image is that of the mythical four-gated city which resonates throughout *Children of Violence*, with its great roads approaching "from north and south, east and west. When they had fairly entered it, they divided it into arcs, making a circling street, inside which were smaller ones: a web of arcs intersected by streets running into a centre" (p. 133).

The image of the city also reproduces the configuration of the sacred city, laid out with four cardinal orientations whose center symbolizes the sacred center of the universe. As Erich Neumann (after Jung) describes the symbolic significance of the circle-and-square configuration,

> The symbol of the circular mandala stands at the beginning as at the end [of collective and individual consciousness]. In the beginning it takes the mythological form of paradise; in the end, of the Heavenly Jerusalem. The perfect figure of the circle from whose center radiate the four arms of a cross, in which the opposites are at rest, is a very early and a very late symbol historically. . . . [The mandala] is the place of transfiguration and illumination, of finality, as well as the place of mythological origination.[8]

What is remarkable about this multivalent symbol is the fact that, though Martha Quest (and Lessing) has obviously matured and changed, the image itself has remained more or less constant, though its metaphoric significance has deepened during the unfolding of *Children of Violence*. In the final volume of the series its symbolic meaning percolates through all levels of the novel and becomes an emblem for the consciousness of Martha Quest herself.

Without pressing the correspondences too closely, one can observe that the four sections of *The Four-Gated City* have, like *The Golden Notebook*, a circular as well as a linear design. To a certain extent, each first section charts a set of events characterized by flux; the second sections in each larger unit focus on the "growing point"—experimentation with alternatives—leading to each third section, in which significant changes and transformations within either characters or situations, or both, occur; and finally, in each fourth section, a tentative transition to a new stage of comprehension (which then spills over into the next stage of flux). That the four larger units of the novel also reflect organic growth or transformation is suggested through Lessing's choice of opening epigraphs. The "Dedication" of the novel is a Sufi teaching story which alludes not only to a foolish man's misunderstanding of the obvious but to the loss that results from categorization, from trying to keep substances separate. The epigraph to Part One (from Rachel Carson's *The Edge of the Sea*) concerns the earth in its capacity as an evolving entity, changed by its relationship to bodies of water and the organic life they contain. The epigraph to Part Two (from Robert Musil's *The Man without Qualities*) addresses itself to the multivalent qualities and different perceptions of water. Part Three is preceded by quotations from school textbooks about weather, viewed in terms of the interrelationships of earth, water, air, and fire.

The several epigraphs to Part Four (from a school broadcast and from Sufi teachings) again concern organic evolution as both a biological and a spiritual process. Thus, using the mystical or esoteric symbols of transformation from one level of consciousness to another, Lessing makes explicit the central theme of *The Four-Gated City*. It is most completely formulated in the last of the epigraphs, an explanation of the Sufi belief that

> expressed in one way, humanity is evolving towards a certain destiny. We are all taking part in that evolution. Organs come into being as a result of a need for specific organs. The human being's organism is producing a new complex of organs in response to such a need. In this age of the transcending of time and space, the complex of organs is concerned with the transcending of time and space. What ordinary people regard as sporadic and occasional bursts of telepathic and prophetic power are seen by the Sufi as nothing less than the first stirrings of these same organs. The difference between all evolution up to date and the present need for evolution is that for the past ten thousand years or so we have been given

the possibility of a conscious evolution. So essential is this more rarefied evolution that our future depends on it. (P. 426)[9]

The evolution of the *theme* of the evolution of consciousness in Lessing's fiction becomes visible when one reconsiders the preceding novels: the Martha Quest who emerges "after" *The Golden Notebook* carries with her not only the seeds of Thomas Stern's inner division but echoes of Anna Wulf's. Like Anna, Martha must find a way to accommodate fragmentation perceived in the phenomenal world as well as the inner one. The bipolar potential for breaking down into madness on the one side, and breaking through to psychic growth on the other side of the painful splits in consciousness, is carried over into the alternative fragmentary and unitive potentialities of the mind. The quest motif itself culminates with several "descents" into the demonic unconscious and an apocalyptic "ascent" into the idyllic dimension—the characteristic antithetical movements of the romance genre.[10] Further, like the writers she has created—Anna and the projected alter egos Ella and Saul Green—Lessing continues to dramatize complementary or opposing valences of personality or psychic energy in the form of significantly grouped characters; the psychological triad examined in Anna's fiction, "The Shadow of the Third" of *The Golden Notebook* resonates in the fluid *ménage à trois* of Martha Quest and Mark and Lynda Coldridge of *The Four-Gated City*.[11]

Other characters, analogous to the supporting cast of characters in *The Golden Notebook*, may be understood psychologically as split-off aspects, doubles, or opposites of the major triad of characters. For example, the younger Coldridges, the cousins Francis and Paul, complement each other and mirror their elders in their opposing temperaments; later they both assume Mark's role as nurturers of dependent women. Mark and Martha each cope with the children (the future) as well as their respective mothers (the past), who threaten or complicate their lives further. At various points in the novel Martha's complementary doubles are reflected in Patty Samuels (who, desperate for marriage and children, competes with her for Mark), Phoebe Coldridge (whose sincere but rigid left-wing political position prevents her from seeing the alarming changes going on before her eyes), and others. Such correspondences are temporary and shifting, since the novel covers a long time period and traces a number of significant changes in Martha Quest's own personality and in the social order. Moreover, the correspondences suggested here are neither consistent nor comprehensive, since the characters function on the literal plane of the novel in ways that cannot always be correlated with aspects of Martha's inner experience.

Since the mind is the mediator between inner and outer modalities of experience, the role of consciousness is, in this novel, more than ever that of the central transformer of "objective" or public reality into the subjective and personal reality that Martha creates out of her experiences. When the society itself is seen to be in flux the mind mirrors it and must either capitulate to that chaos or transcend it within its own structures. During the course of Lessing's fiction the form that such struggles take shifts from external to internal: from political and social involvements to psychological, philosophical, and finally mystical apprehensions of the nature of reality and personality. Despite this shift, the realism of detail sustained throughout the earlier fiction is not abandoned in *The Four-Gated City*. Rather, the narrative maintains the essential plane of social interaction and event in its documentation of the fifties and sixties, intensified by the parallel and more surely developed exploration of Martha Quest's own consciousness on the symbolic level.

Whereas in *The Golden Notebook* there is only Anna Wulf's point(s) of view, narrated from different fictional perspectives, in *The Four-Gated City* the story is told through a central intelligence who describes the world as seen and interpreted by Martha Quest. Though this narrative shape seems simpler, the content of the novel actually discloses an equally complex fictional universe. The novel unfolds on two levels simultaneously: the literal or phenomenal plane traces the development of events in the macrocosm, the world of other people, while the symbolic plane connects those events to the microcosm of Martha Quest's own consciousness. The characters who populate the external reality that Martha inhabits thus double as personifications or projections of Martha's inner reality. Through this technique Lessing formulates the mythic or psychological truth that the macrocosm and the microcosm are merely two aspects of the same reality. She has described that correspondence emerging in her thinking and writing:

Writing about oneself, one is writing about others, since your problems, pains, pleasures, emotions—and your extraordinary and remarkable ideas—can't be yours alone. The way to deal with the
problem of "subjectivity," that shocking business of being preoccupied with the tiny individual who is at the same time caught up
in such an explosion of terrible and marvelous possibilities, is to see
him as a microcosm and in this way to break through the personal,
the subjective, making the personal general, as indeed life always
does, transforming a private experience . . . into something much
larger. . . .[12]

What makes this truism about the representative nature of all genuine art more salient is Lessing's concurrent interest in the Sufi
view, which—like all mystical traditions and many other philosophies going back to the Greeks—identifies the microcosm with the
macrocosm. As the medieval Sufi alchemist Jafar Sadiq wrote,
"Man is the microcosm, creation the macrocosm—the unity. . . .
Start with yourself, end with all. Before man, beyond man, transformation." [13] The pattern of *The Four-Gated City* is the alternating focus upon these two worlds as they reflect, contrast with, and
shape one another, and finally are understood as the same.

Martha Quest is thirty when *The Four-Gated City* opens. Now
twice divorced and an emigrant from Zambesia facing a new geographical setting (London) which rapidly transmogrifies into a
new inner landscape, she confronts her further capacities for emotional, sexual, intellectual, and psychological growth. As she
muses during an apparently dormant interlude in her psychic life,
"In every life there is a curve of growth, or a falling away from
it; there is a central pressure, like sap forcing up a trunk, along
a branch, into last year's wood, and there, from a dead-looking
eye, or knot, it bursts again in a new branch, in a shape that is
inevitable, but known only to itself until it becomes visible" (p.
192). This process describes the ongoing course of inner growth
that shapes the further explorations of Martha Quest's consciousness in this final volume of *Children of Violence*.

The theme of self-division is brought forward from Lessing's
earlier protagonists as well as from Martha's own previous self-
discoveries and conflicts in the earlier volumes, as Lessing continues to dramatize the mind's inherent dualism—that "something

131

in the human mind that separated, and divided" (p. 79). In the opening chapter of *The Four-Gated City*, as Martha tries to find her bearings in the chaos of London and in herself, she is both "Matty" and Martha—"Matty" being variously her old socially malleable self, "the enemy" (p. 6), her "imp" (pp. 25 and 27), and "an aspect of hysteria" (p. 68). She enjoys her experience as the "open-pored receptive being who hadn't a name," but also confronts its negative aspect, "that inner shrinking which was the result of surroundings that did not know her, until, fought, it became the strength which set free" (p. 47). All of these aspects of Martha's personality provide the focus for her more thorough exploration of her inner opposite later in the novel, and underline, once again, the inherent self-division of consciousness.

As she drifts through London, Martha discovers that by mini-mizing her sleep and controlling her food intake she can induce a kind of "high" mental state and so reach a new area in her self. Beneath the several more familiar identities she discovers a "soft dark receptive intelligence" (p. 36) that is without gender, sensi-tive to the "wavelengths" of other dimensions of consciousness, and unaware of time. One of the crucial problems both within Martha's inner world and in the collective is the difficulty of "remembering"—in this case, of recalling the experiences them-selves as well as the technique for returning to that fluid area within the self. Because human beings cannot maintain the state of abnormally aware consciousness for long, the individual (like the collective) continues to repeat the same mistakes over and over again. The fact that Martha herself does not return to that area within her consciousness for further exploration until some years later—just as she has rarely returned to it since her epiphanies on the African veld in childhood—emphasizes the difficulty that Lessing repeatedly stresses.

Encountering her own characteristic ambivalence once again at this turning point in her life, Martha Quest "crosses the river" to the other side of the Thames. She quickly finds herself facing a choice between the disorder and freedom she has indulged in since her arrival in London, embodied by a man named Jack, with whom she has become sexually involved, and the more orthodox values of order and responsibility offered (and represented) by Phoebe Coldridge.

Jack's primary mode of existence is physical, but his immersion in sexuality is, at this point, a way of reaching the same "high" state leading to a transpersonal level of consciousness that Martha reaches by another route. With Jack she learns that the "wavelengths" she had discovered through Thomas Stern have different valences; Jack has the same ability to tune in to that area in the psyche, to "go into it, as if it were a *place*" (p. 57). But the wavelength he enters also contains his inner enemy, and bears the negative valence of hatred. Martha speculates that every person has a ruling passion, a driving need that in its extreme form unbalances his personality, producing the inner enemy that may become his madness. This truth, given its basic form by Lessing in Mary Turner and its more multifaceted one in Anna Wulf, is the psychological basis for breakdown. If not recognized as part of the self, the emotional energy of the shadow is projected into the outer world, and may result in the acute form of self-division that drives one mad. Later Martha realizes that "madness" is itself not so much a personal disorder as something "in the air" that a person may "hook into" quite accidentally (p. 380); the demonic shadow has a collective aspect as well.

That Jack is also, symbolically, an aspect of Martha's many-sided self is suggested in several ways. Not only must she (like Anna Wulf) come to terms with her own sexuality through her male opposite before she can reach a kind of androgynous wholeness; but the inner enemy that manifests itself in Jack is the same shadow or self-hater that Martha carries within herself. Further, Jack's house, like Mark Coldridge's house later, has a lower level occupied by a "crazy" person: metaphorically, the deeply buried irrational aspect of the self that must be confronted and integrated into the whole personality.[14] For Jack that assimilation ultimately takes a negative form. Ten years later, when Martha returns to visit him again, she sees how his inner enemy has utterly possessed his entire personality, transforming him from an erotically vibrant being to a master of psychological degradation who breaks young girls in for careers as accomplices in sexual perversion. This sadistic Jack, Martha finds, is really an inversion of his former self, the "old Jack's shadow side, turned outwards" (p. 471). Martha later confronts her own self-hater and experiences a similar, though temporary, inversion, becoming "turned inside out like a glove or a dress . . ." (p. 524). Unlike Jack, however, she remains "the watcher, the listener" (p. 524), observing both aspects and resisting total identification with the inner enemy.

At the earlier stage of her psychic journey when she is still actively involved with Jack, however, Martha's vision is still clouded and ambivalent. Her erotic relationship with him is more specifically physical, lacking the sense of total emotional fusion that she had experienced with Thomas Stern. The disillusionments of erotic love eventually press Lessing's later female protagonists to find alternative psychic routes into the experience of union. Martha's sexual intimacy with Jack anticipates that development, culminating in two opposing precognitions that correspond to the recurring split consciousness of Lessing's fiction. One vision is the "golden age" dream—a variant of the archetype of Eden,[15] of the psychic wholeness of the human family (and the self) before the Fall (p. 59). The other is a nightmare, a more immediate foreknowledge of the Coldridge family that Martha will soon join, with its inner schisms and problems. Both dreams have the family unit as their central image, and are accompanied by the emotion of pain: the first in the acknowledged loss of perfection, the second in the disillusionments of ordinary life.

Here, as elsewhere in her fiction, Lessing stresses the failure of the family as a social institution: "A baby is born with infinite possibilities. But there's no escaping it, it's like having to go down into a pit, a terrible dark blind pit, and then you fight your way up and out: and your parents are part of it, of what you fight out of. The mistake is, to think there is a way of not having to fight your way out. Everyone has to" (pp. 68–69). Much later Martha amends that recognition with the further knowledge that "you start growing on your own account when you've worked through what you're landed with. Until then, you're paying off debts" (p. 432). The symbolic human journey from innocence through ignorance or corruption to experience and then—for the intrepid only—backward/forward (or down/up) to a state of wholeness and reintegration of the self is the circular path of the mythic and spiritual journey that shapes Martha's quest for wholeness. The obvious weak link in this process is (for Lessing) the family unit. Significantly, the Martha Quest of The Four-Gated City is without a family or a country, a position that facilitates her leap from the private to the transpersonal.

Despite her ambivalence, Martha decides to remain at the Coldridges rather than with Jack; symbolically, she wakes up in the Coldridge house "rising towards light" (p. 100). The last chapter of Part One thus opens with the clue to Martha's location on the right path toward awareness and eventual spiritual illumination. In the context of the correspondence between rooms or houses and the state of the protagonist's consciousness, Martha has settled in the more "respectable" but by no means conventional house within which she will grow for most of the rest of her life.

During the first part of the novel other corollary themes are introduced and consolidated. Though Martha is initially employed as Mark Coldridge's temporary secretary, she soon becomes a permanent friend and indispensable member of the household. Early in their relationship she confides to Mark her dream of the four-gated city, and he contributes to her fantasy. As they invent the details of the mythical place together, the image evolves, becoming more complex; the city eventually develops "a shadow city of poverty and beastliness. . . . And one day the people of the outer city overran the inner one, and destroyed it" (p. 134). The archetypal image of the four-gated city thus ramifies to reflect the tension between the ideal (the positive potentiality of the self or the collective) and the demonic (symbolized by the negative shadow) —a dialectic that shapes the novel's central themes.

Two further important characters are introduced in the final section of Part One: Lynda Coldridge, Mark's "mad" wife, and Jimmy Wood, his business partner. Only later do their complementary qualities become clearer on the novel's symbolic level. For years Lynda has been in and out of mental hospitals and on and off of prescription drugs, her heightened sensitivity long ago pathologized by doctors as schizophrenia and thus converted into her own uncontrollable self-hater. Jimmy Wood is also "a human being constructed on a different model from most" (p. 163). But, like his name, he is made of wood; "where other people resounded, he did not" (p. 163). While Lynda has a supernormal sensitivity, Jimmy Wood is an ethical and emotional moron with an "almost pathological indifference to any ordinary ideas of decency" (p. 506). Both Lynda and Jimmy can "tune in" to a reality which falls outside the parameter of the norm, through telepathy as well as what is labeled by conventional minds as "the occult." But Jimmy's interest is an abstract, emotionless one, eventually translated into the technology of brain machinery and science fiction novels; Lynda's psychic ability ultimately becomes one of the vehicles for recognizing and escaping collective cataclysm. Lynda and Jimmy thus embody complementary aspects of the abnormal consciousness. Both are carriers of the psychic mutation (proposed by Thomas Stern in *Landlocked*) that develops around the edges of the conventional human consciousness and extends the parameters of the internal geography that Martha subsequently explores.

Part One also introduces the several generations of the Coldridge family: Mark's social-hostess mother, Margaret Patten; Francis, the silent son of Lynda and Mark; and Paul, the orphaned child of Mark's brother Colin (who defects to Russia) and Sarah/ Sally (Colin's self-divided Jewish wife who kills herself only partly in response to her husband's flight). These characters, ideas, themes, and relationships multiply and recombine in Part Two, in which the general mood is one of pervasive "bad times." The claustrophobic, reactionary political atmosphere of Britain during the 1950's is the external dimension of the private reality that the members of the Coldridge household generate and explore. The macrocosm interpenetrates with, creates, and reflects the state of the microcosm; Martha later makes this correspondence explicit, reflecting that "an interior experience had matched the exterior, the bad time" (p. 285). Even while it is taking place, Martha feels she has "been here before" (p. 149).

Whereas in Part One the social macrocosm is projected through the various members of the Coldridge household, in Part Two the psychic microcosm is conceptualized through the stratification of the house itself. Most significantly, Lynda Coldridge moves from a mental hospital into a flat in the basement (designed and prepared by Martha) and brings with her a friend named Dorothy as a defense against the marital relationship she cannot bear to experience. Dorothy and Lynda are themselves an incongruous, complementary pair, Lynda's introverted sensitivity contrasting with Dorothy's coarse possessiveness.

Two floors up, Mark and Martha are engaged in "working" on Mark's writing, but are more immediately involved in the process of absorbing one another's personality characteristics. Their relationship recalls Anna Wulf and Saul Green's mutual "breakdown" into each other's personalities in *The Golden Notebook*, the condensed positive form of which process takes place between Martha and Thomas Stern in *Landlocked*. Mark, under the pressures of being spied upon because he refuses to repudiate his defector-brother, develops half a dozen new personas, including the "defender" personality that Martha identifies as a quality of her own earlier self in the more politically active phase of her life (delineated in earlier volumes of *Children of Violence*). Indicative of the psychic symbiosis that has temporarily developed between them, Mark writes a novel based on Martha's imaginary four-gated city. However, the draft shows the strains of his warring personalities; the heavily annotated manuscript pulls in two directions, much like the journal that documents Thomas Stern's divided psyche. In fact, Martha unearths her copy of Thomas's journal and compares it with Mark's novel draft, finding that "the insertions into the original manuscript made by Mark . . . were the same in 'feel' as a good part of Thomas' writing. They had come from the same place, the same wavelength. Somewhere, those two extraordinarily different people, Mark, Thomas, inhabited the same place, made contact there" (p. 176).

In "absorbing" Martha's past, Mark also absorbs the aspects of Thomas Stern that had become part of her own consciousness. Martha identifies elements in Mark's present identity as aspects of her self, "as if her past had become fused with Mark's present. Almost; or as if Mark was herself, or she Mark . . . she was not able to put herself back there, in that place in herself where she had been; for that place was inhabited by Mark" (p. 178). Lessing's further exploration of the geography of consciousness is in the direction of the transpersonal, the collective substratum of the psyche proposed by Jung. Each person must find his own entrance into that area of the unconscious, and the outcome is predictable. "From here, this place [wavelength], Thomas had gone down into madness and to death. . . . She had understood once before that the new, an opening up, had to be through a region of chaos, of conflict. There was no other way of doing it" (p. 176).

The children in the house are also part of the process taking place in the adults, participating symbolically as "the pasts and the futures of the adult people" (p. 191). Moreover, though Paul and Francis also suffer from their own inner divisions (partly because of their unconventional parenting), only the then-six-year-old Paul —who is tuned in to the "truth-teller" in Lynda—has (for a time) free access to the basement. Figuratively, children experience the irrational more easily than adults, bridging the gap that later develops as the process of compartmentalization closes it off from awareness. Since the stratifications of the house come to symbolize the constantly shifting aspects and divisions of Martha's consciousness, the children correspond on that metaphoric level to the "children" within her: one who is obedient and quiet (Francis), reminiscent of the socially compliant "Matty"; and his opposite (Paul), who has "no sense of right and wrong" (p. 340). The latter quality, while potentially dangerous, also accounts for Martha's capacity to test conventional limits, to suspend moral judgment and thus learn from her unorthodox experiences.

During this particular time (Part Two) Martha finds herself in a dormant phase—a slump of exhaustion caused, she later sees, by the effort of holding together the currents of the personalities inhabiting the house. That the house is an objective correlative of the stratified levels of the personality becomes more explicit; Martha glimpses "a view of life where the house and people in it could be seen as a whole, making a whole" (p. 191). In fact, the two planes of reality—macrocosm and microcosm—described earlier (p. 130) actually realign slightly into three spheres of experience, corresponding to the three dimensions of psychic and physical life delineated by Erich Neumann. The three domains,

> although interconnected, are nonetheless clearly marked off from one another. The world as the outside world of extrahuman events, the community as the sphere of interhuman relationships, the psyche as the world of interior human experience—these are the three basic factors which govern human life, and man's creative en-

counter with each of them is decisive for the development of the individual. . . . Contents of this kind are recognized readily enough as projections when they derive from earlier epochs, from alien spheres of culture, or from other people, but it becomes increasingly difficult for us to do so the more closely they approximate to the unconscious conditions of our own time, our own culture, and our own personality.[16]

In *The Four-Gated City* these three domains are the outside world (political events, London, the social fabric, "the times"), the community (the Coldridge household with its network of interrelationships), and the psyche of Martha Quest that interpenetrates with the two other spheres. If envisioned as concentric circles, these three spheres metaphorically define the complex structure of the novel, for the "four-gated city"—the ideal center of the macrocosm—corresponds to Martha as the center of energy of the Coldridge house, as well as to the center of private consciousness that Martha seeks and ultimately achieves within herself. At various points in the novel the major narrative movement occurs within one, two, or all three spheres at once. Since change itself is revealed as a cyclic process, fads, movements, and ideas in the political, communal, and personal spheres keep recurring in the novel. The image of the circle resonates at every level, suggesting the organizing symbol of the mandala that expresses wholeness and unity.[17]

While the "bad time" in Martha herself and in the Coldridge house is a period of sluggishness and mental torpor, its counterpart in the macrocosm is the repressive political and social atmosphere. The Coldridge family, with its known connection to a defector to Russia, is suspiciously perceived as one of the "'enemies within our gates'" (p. 201) by the British media. The fear of the "inner enemy," the collective shadow of hatred, is the personal shadow projected on a larger scale: "Whole nations went mad overnight" (p. 201). Thus are the individual and collective consciousnesses inextricably meshed. Despite the prevailing atmosphere of bad times, several positive things do happen in the Coldridge household. Mark's novel, *A City in the Desert*, inspired by Martha's vision of the four-gated city, is published, and his personal reputation salvaged. Ironically, Mark's own principles and values remain nearly constant throughout the novel (one of the obstacles to his psychic growth); only the fickle societal perception of him changes.

Though the surface of Martha's life is calm, her inner growth continues, metaphorically, in the basement. The news of a visit from her mother from Zambesia, after the long separation since Martha had left there for England, propels her into a state of panic, during which she gradually realizes that the painful quality of her past relationship with her mother has blocked off whole areas of herself. That recognition is the necessary catalyst for growth out of the dormant phase, leading to communication with the buried dimension of herself. Lynda and her companions in the basement represent the irrational and repressed levels of her own being that she must confront in order to dissolve the pain she has carried within her for years.

First, Rosa Mellendip, a fortune-telling friend of Lynda's and Dorothy's, comes up from the basement to Martha's room and advises her that even bad times can carry the possibility of something good, of changes resulting from the "deepening of experience, if properly used" (p. 209). Lessing reiterates the correspondence between the literal and symbolic dimension of events by describing Martha's reaction to the advice: "The basement flat, its occupants, were isolating themselves in her mind, as if it was a territory full of alien people from whom she had to protect herself, with whom she could have no connection. . . . For two pins now she could switch into an enemy of the shadow world of the basement" (p. 211). Once before, during her first weeks in the Coldridge house, Martha had experienced a similar defensive reaction which, if followed through, would have insulated her from further growth. Instead she accepts (as she had before) the call to her deeper self, by returning the visit with the tenants of the basement.

Once there, she questions Lynda about psychoanalysis, wondering if it can help her to deal with the inner pain precipitated by her mother's impending visit. Her panic is so great that she feels her past becoming inaccessible again, encapsulated by psychic pain; she approaches an amnesiac state, "like a person who wakes up in a strange city, not knowing who he, she, is" (p. 215). (Lessing pursues this experience more centrally in her next novel, *Briefing for a Descent into Hell,* in which the male protagonist in fact suffers from a stress-induced amnesia.) As soon as she begins to explore that pain, she understands that "for years she had been listening, half listening, to talk in the basement which she had thought was too crazy to take as more than pitiable. Now she was understanding it—or a lot of it. She was even learning the language" (p. 216). These small openings into the basement and into her self are parallel processes: literally, mental illness loses its alien quality; metaphorically, the "crazy" language of her own deeper psyche also becomes more comprehensible.

Through what proves to be a fortuitous postponement, Martha cannot see Lynda's psychiatrist, Dr. Lamb, for some weeks, during which her own psyche literally rises to the occasion. Tapping the process of inner concentration that she had stumbled on several times before, she slowly re-enters her past as if it were a location in space rather than time. When she finally meets with Dr. Lamb, she has taught herself what her sessions with him only reinforce: "One talked, one did this or that: finally, one 'heard' for the first time what one's life had been saying over and over again, in various ways, for years. One hadn't heard before, because one had had nothing to 'hear' with. Living was simply a process of developing different 'ears,' senses, with which one 'heard,' experienced, what one couldn't before" (p. 225). That discovery marks the beginning of the next stage of Martha's psychic and spiritual evolution toward wholeness, consistent with the Sufi belief that human consciousness generates the appropriate organs to facilitate its further development.

Perhaps here, as elsewhere in Lessing's fiction, the reader might pause to question the ultimate relationship between the author's ideas and their aesthetic formulation: to what degree does the artistic merit of Lessing's work depend upon the reader's willingness to accept her ideological premises? For a writer whose ideological commitments range over systems of belief as dissimilar as Marxism and Sufism, this is indeed a central question. I would suggest that we can value the persuasive social realism along with the symbolic layerings of Lessing's fictional worlds without literally endorsing (though we may) her views on socialism, the assumptions of radical psychiatry, mental telepathy, or the ascending path of spiritual development. Increasingly in her fiction Lessing adapts narrative strategies and symbolic motifs that have

persisted through centuries of story-telling as ways of conceptualizing private visions of transcendent and universal experiences.
What we must assess in Lessing's particular variations is the con-
vincingness of the literal level of the narrative, the coherence of
its symbolism, and the author's control over elements that condition our willingness to suspend disbelief. The last demand—one
that is necessarily greater from a writer whose presentation of
visionary goals and prophetic judgments is so impassioned—may
challenge our own assumptions about the nature of consciousness
or social realities, while still allowing for our appreciation of their
narrative expressions.

Martha's new telepathic abilities open a new dimension of her
relationship with Mark, in an intimacy that creates not only a
sexual communion absent before but also engages him as a sympathetic partner in what she calls her "work" on the area of
herself sealed off by the anxiety, pity, and pain generated by
her mother. (The word "work" appears throughout esoteric and
hermetic traditions, including Sufism, as the term for the discipline
facilitating greater spiritual development.) Mark is, psychologically, the reasonable and rational self against which she tests the
insights about the way one relearns what she already knows. As
an aspect of her own intelligence (comparable to the role Saul
Green eventually enacts for Anna Wulf), Mark thus assists Martha
at her growing point—"the furthest point she had reached in her
life" (p. 230).

The final chapter of Part Two is narrated from the visiting Mrs.
Quest's point of view and, in addition to providing some wry
comic relief in a novel weighty with serious ideas, reveals the distortions of May Quest's own conventional consciousness. Her perceptions—largely unexamined dogmatic prejudices about blacks
and liberal principles—are further distorted by self-pity, vanity,
and repressed sexuality. The description of a belated and halting
initiation into a meaningful relationship with a young black servant shortly before her departure from Zambesia reveals the furthest extent of her limited capacity for growth and self-awareness.
But in London she and Martha are too much for each other. They
sap each other's psychic energies and reach impasse after impasse
of noncommunication, as if they were magnets with north poles
facing each other. Though objectively Martha can see her mother

as a pathetic old woman, subjectively she experiences her as the perpetrator of extensive psychic damage in the past, and a heavy drain on her present inner resources. The patterns of their relationship are stubbornly fixed, and Martha's efforts to reach her mother at a level below pretense and falsity are consistently rebuffed.

Significantly, in terms of the symbolism of the Coldridge house, Mrs. Quest stays in a room on the top level and descends to the basement only once. That visit, however, is without meaning for her, since she is unable to "hear" what is told her there. She interprets Mrs. Mellendip's remark that old age is a valuable time for reflection as offensive and impertinent, coming as it does from a woman twenty years her junior. Mrs. Quest experiences a temporary mental breakdown while staying with Martha, during which, obsessed by the sexuality and filth she projects onto the Coldridge household, she talks hysterically to herself. Finally, Martha arranges for them to consult Dr. Lamb separately, for neither can cope with the pain they inflict upon one another (the source of which Martha identifies and her mother does not).

Mrs. Quest eventually departs for Africa, having learned little herself but having left (as Rose Mellendip had predicted) one positive result: Martha's inadvertent introduction to the salvaging process—the conscious "work" on her own mind that, beginning with restoration of access to the most painful dimension of her past, continues to occupy her for the rest of her life. Symbolically, she has finally stripped off (by identifying) the part of herself that her "inner" mother had controlled. As Lessing has said elsewhere, "We use our parents like recurring dreams, to be entered into when needed; they are always there for love or for hate. . . ."[18]

The second half of *The Four-Gated City* opens with a change in the *Zeitgeist* corresponding in importance to the inner change in Martha: the year 1956 is a watershed year, both in the world and in the smaller microcosms of the Coldridge house and Martha Quest's consciousness. The "bad times" invisibly recede, but Lynda and Mark are both still "split people" (p. 285); the children of the house, Paul and Francis, create new kinds of pressures upon the adults. Lynda, having given up prescription drugs a year earlier, backslides into madness and returns to the hospital; Dorothy

attempts suicide (which Martha had "seen" in advance) and ultimately succeeds in her next attempt. The basement world is thus
in a state of flux, analogous to the intense activity taking place
in Martha's own psyche. As the narrator rather bluntly phrases
it, "Living with the mentally 'upset' is a lesson in our own splits,
discords, contradictions" (p. 300).

For Martha, the salvaging operation continues, reinforced by
her successful reclamation of certain areas of herself. "She had
found doors she had not known existed. She had wrestled herself
out of the dark because she had had to, and had entered places
in herself she had not known were there" (p. 286). Beginning
with her foreknowledge of Dorothy's suicide attempt, she starts to
"pick up" voices and visions more regularly, and consults Dr.
Lamb because she wonders if she is also going "mad." The psychiatrist's failure to explain to Martha's satisfaction the distinction
between schizophrenic hallucinations and the experiences she reports implies their proximity. As Lessing has emphasized before,
consciousness is not so easily compartmentalized into madness
and sanity.

The author's affinity with R. D. Laing and other radical theore-
ticians of psychopathology rests in the shared assumption that
the images of madness, dreams, and visionary experiences originate in the same dimension of the psyche. What distinguishes
between their effects is the reception by the conscious personality
and the perceptual mode of the experience. As Jung wrote (many
years before Laing developed his radical approach to schizophrenia),

> Anyone who observes himself, carefully and unsparingly, will know
> that there is something within him which would gladly hide and
> cover up all that is difficult and questionable in life, in order to
> smooth a path for himself. Insanity gives it a free hand. And once
> it has gained ascendancy, reality is veiled. . . . In insanity we do not
> discover anything new and unknown; we are looking at the founda-
> tions of our own being, the matrix of those vital problems on which
> we are all engaged.[19]

Besides hearing voices, Martha also begins to dream profusely.
"It was as if something in [her] that needed to talk, to express,
to speak, to advise, could use this channel or that—pictures or
voices, if she was able to sit quiet in her room, waiting, listening,

and if not, was quite prepared to use dreams instead" (p. 311). All of these experiences are channels or conduits to and from the deeper levels of the unconscious, which may be nurtured by conscious attention. As Lessing has elsewhere remarked, "The hidden domain of our mind communicates with us through dreams. I dream a great deal and I scrutinize my dreams. The more I scrutinize the more I dream. When I'm stuck in a book I deliberately dream. . . . I fill my brain with the material for a new book, go to sleep, and I usually come up with a dream which resolves the dilemma."[20]

As Martha becomes more sensitive to these extra wavelengths of consciousness, she recognizes the ordered microcosm of the Coldridge house and her function within it. The house is "separated with the people who inhabited it, into areas or climates, each with its own feel, or sense of individuality" (pp. 335–36). Her own personality, or room, functions as a "roomstat, adjusting from outside the house rather than in, setting the flow of air, moisture, heat, light" (p. 336). Later she understands her role in other terms: she is a conduit for the various currents of psychic energy generated by the house's inhabitants; her occasional periods of psychic exhaustion occur when that energy exchange is particularly intense. In this sense she is like Lynda, except that Martha is able to move freely among several levels, while Lynda—broken down by drugs, shock, and other abuses of her psychic sensitivities —can function as a receiver only in the basement.

At this point in the novel Martha Quest is a middle-aged woman who feels "herself (or rather, the surface of herself) to be a mass of fragments, or facets, or bits of mirror reflecting qualities embodied in other people . . ." (p. 336). Analogously, the house itself seems to be without a true center. "It was all a mass of small separate things, surfaces, shapes, all needing different attention, different kinds of repair" (p. 336). To emphasize the correspondences to Martha's interior state, the narrator adds, "This was the condition of being a middle-aged person, a deputy in the centre of the house, the person who runs things, keeps things going, conducts a holding operation. . . . Yet the house had been done up twice, thoroughly, since Martha had come into it—but still nothing was right, everything second-rate and shoddy" (pp. 336–37). That is, despite the "work" that has enabled Martha to retrieve the part of her past congealed into pain by her mother, and her partial identifications with Mark and Lynda (figuratively, the rational and irrational dimensions of her own self), Martha is still, psychically, a collection of imperfectly melded pieces—a woman "whose eighteen hours a day were filled with a million details, fragments, reflected off the faceted mirror that was one's personality, that responded all the time every second, to these past selves, past voices, temporary visitors" (p. 340).

Rather than ignoring the confusing voices she overhears, however, she learns to "tune in" more consciously, and is rewarded by a breakthrough in consciousness, symbolized by her new relationship with Lynda. She begins to descend to the basement nightly to work on her mind, to map the landscape of consciousness with Lynda as her corroborator. She stumbles once again upon the psychic truth she must continually forget and remember, that "one could never be told what one did not really know, though of course the 'knowing' might be hidden from oneself" (p. 353). Just as the conscious and unconscious domains of the psyche (in the Jungian schema) complement each other, the two women are reciprocally enriched by their partnership: "It was as if doors kept opening in their brains just far enough to admit a new sensation, or a glimmer of something. . . . What they wanted, looked for, searched for was everywhere, all around them, like a finer air shimmering in the flat air of every day" (pp. 356–57).[21] That finer air is Lessing's closest verbal equivalent for a heightened state of consciousness whose description defies language, since it exists as an interior state not under intellectual control.

Moreover, Martha acknowledges that because these extraordinary perceptions are beyond the parameters of experience conventionally accepted as "normal," they fall into the large category of unorthodox experiences arbitrarily grouped as "abnormal." As the psyche of Western culture is presently constituted, normality is the "condition of disparateness" (p. 61); the higher states of consciousness that transcend fragmentation and schism are thus perceived as "abnormal" and labeled "mad," as in Lynda Coldridge's case.[22] Yet,

Perhaps it was because if society is so organised, or rather has so grown, that it will not admit what one knows to be true, will not admit it, that is, except as it comes out perverted, through madness, then it is through madness and its variants it must be sought after.

An essential fact was that if Lynda had not been mad, had not tested certain limits, then some of the things they discovered would have frightened them so badly they would not have been able to go on. (P. 357)

"Testing certain limits" involves the genuine risk of never being able to return to the state in which inner and outer are held in some kind of balance. Though dreams, visions, hallucinations, and other experiences originating from deep within the psyche are different forms of communication from the same "basement" of consciousness, Lessing does distinguish among their manifestations: on the one hand, the shrinking of the self (as in Mary Turner's experience), and on the other, the form of breakdown that ultimately produces new awareness, further psychological integration, and growth (as in Anna Wulf's experiences). The difference is not in kind but in direction, depending upon the ability of the personality as a whole to accommodate rather than resist the frightening messages and images generated deep within the mind. Anna Wulf's breakthrough from one to the other is Lessing's artistic formulation of that shift in consciousness at the point of its transformation; Martha's communication with Lynda represents another breakthrough to a new form of consciousness that evolves beyond Anna's.

A disproportionately high number of the characters in *The Four-Gated City* suffer mental breakdowns in one or the other form during the course of the narrative: Mark Coldridge, Phoebe Coldridge, Elizabeth Coldridge, Martha's and Mark's mothers, Jimmy Wood's wife, Nicky Anderson (Paul's friend), Patty Cohen, Patty Samuels, and others. As in the biological phenomenon of mitosis or cell division, the selves in Lessing's fiction seem to grow by splitting. The catch-all phrase "mental breakdown" is the verbal label for the psyche's reshuffling of its own contents in the process of confronting new experiences and either synthesizing them and thus transforming them into positive form or, as in Lynda's case, having the deepest self pathologized by the orthodoxy of medical and social opinion. Elsewhere Lessing has described her own long involvement with mental illness, commenting,

For some reason, when you've finished a patch of your life you look back and you see that it has a pattern which you didn't notice

147

when you were living through it. For the last twenty years I have
been closely involved with psychiatrists and mentally ill people. I
did not make a deliberate choice in the matter, but I started a process which is now common. Twenty years ago it was considered
unusual to have a psychiatrist. Now, almost everyone I know has
had a breakdown, is in psychoanalysis, or pops in and out of mental
hospitals. Mental illness is part of the mainstream. People who are
classified as sick are becoming more and more important in England, the USA, and in socialist countries too. People who are called
mentally ill are often those who say to the society, "I'm not going
to live according to your rules. I'm not going to conform." Madness
can be a form of rebellion.[23]

That Martha's own psyche is in an ongoing state of upheaval
analogous in some ways to a mental breakdown, but held in check
through the stronger conscious control she exerts over it, is once
again symbolized by the house, which "continued, if not divided
against itself, at least layered in atmospheres or climates" (p.
358).[24] Moreover, "of all the times in her life she had never been
less Martha than now. . . . Even her room was not hers" (p. 369).
The demands and stresses created by Lynda's most recent relapse,
the problems of Paul and Francis and their cousins Gwen and
Jill, make Martha's roles as receiver and conduit even more
complex.

The frequent visits of Phoebe's teenage daughters enable Martha
to confront yet another aspect of her past younger self, the archetypal pattern she identifies as "A Young Girl"—one of several
life-roles that one puts on and takes off like parts in a play. That
recognition becomes another "setting-free into impersonality, a
setting-free also, from her personal past" (p. 369). Such recognitions also reinforce the consistent deepening of Lessing's vision
and the larger archetypal and circular patterns that inform the
Children of Violence series, for early in the first volume a much
younger Martha observes that she is expected to "play the part
'young girl'" for her elders (*Martha Quest*, p. 12).

If a large fraction of any personality is the series of life-roles
through which he or she inevitably evolves, then only beneath
these stereotyped scripts is the unique self to be found. Jung calls
these roles the "personas," each of which is a "compromise between individual and society as to what a man should appear to

be. . . . In relation to the essential individuality of the person concerned it is only a secondary reality, a product of compromise, in making which others often have a greater share than he."[25] Much of Martha Quest's life, in London and before, has been her education in "the exercise of holding on to what is permanent in people" (p. 382) beneath the personas, and—once these temporary roles have been identified and thus integrated into her consciousness—what is permanent in herself. The more Martha discovers the general in the particular, the more she becomes merged with that larger unity of experience and consciousness, reflecting Lessing's own development from realism toward myth. As the author has remarked elsewhere, "Since writing *The Golden Notebook* I've become less personal. I've floated away from the personal. I've stopped saying, 'this is *mine*, this is *my* experience.' . . . I don't believe any more that I have a thought. There is a thought around."[26]

The description of the Aldermaston march against nuclear proliferation that opens the final chapter of Part Three dramatizes this process on the communal and societal levels of Martha Quest's universe. The march provides the occasion not only for Lessing's observations about the frustrations of effecting change through political action (an evolution away from the political activism and idealism of the earlier volumes of *Children of Violence*) but also for her suggestion that "the revolution had gone inwards, was in the structure of life's substance" (p. 396).[27] Her comments in an essay on Sufism entitled "A Revolution" are instructive here. In her description of Idries Shah's role as commentator and transmitter of Sufi thought, Lessing notes, "It is our habits of mind that are being challenged. Politically, of course; in other ways as much."[28]

Several generations of Coldridges and others who participate in the Aldermaston demonstration become part of the mutation process that corresponds to the evolution taking place within Martha. The signs are multiple: Jimmy Wood's latest science fiction novel concerns a human mutant who looks and seems "normal" but whose capacities are superhuman; Martha overhears people discussing the inevitability of genetic mutation, wondering if there were already mutants among them, "for good or for bad, but one did not yet know it" (p. 396). Martha's growing ability to discern what is permanent beneath the assumed life-roles people play discloses repeated "variations on a theme" of herself, Lynda, and Mark throughout the crowds at the demonstration.

The significant symbolic aspect of the Coldridge house during this stage is not rooms or doors but walls. Mark begins to tack on the walls of his study news items and other "signs of the time" that describe various destructive events occurring around them. One wall is reserved for the "X-factor"—"that absolutely obvious, out-in-the-open, there-for-anybody-to-see fact which nobody was seeing yet . . ." (p. 414). In cataloging the insanities of contemporary life (pollution of the air, water, body, and mind; violence and the potential for nuclear holocaust; oppression and repression —the social issues that have always concerned her) Lessing describes an activity she has introduced earlier, in *The Golden Notebook*. But in that novel the newspaper clippings were emblematic of the growing fragmentation of Anna Wulf's consciousness. In *The Four-Gated City* they exemplify part of an opposite process, the development toward the larger group consciousness as a response to the public "signs of the time." At a meeting in Mark's study following the Aldermaston march, several people, including Lynda, begin to pick up each other's thoughts and ideas in the form of energy impulses, and build from one realization to the next. Since too few of the people present are able to "hear" what is going on, the process is short-lived. But the momentum of the struggle toward a collective "organ" of deeper psychic connections leading to a supernormal, transpersonal consciousness is clearly underway.

Lessing has noted that, years earlier in her own experience, her Jungian therapist had inferred the existence of this kind of sensitivity to the thoughts of others, but that she had not been ready then to understand its full significance:

> One of the things she said which at the time I could not understand but which now makes every kind of sense was this: "If you were sitting there for an hour, and neither you [n]or I said one word, we would still be exchanging thoughts and emotions." She did not mean what we now call "body language" or "the unconscious language." She meant much more. Now I agree with her. I think that the liveliest of "conversations" go on all the time between people even when they are not talking.[29]

The fourth major part of *The Four-Gated City* focuses on that development beyond private consciousness, tracing the culmination both of Martha's personal quest and the collective descent into hell and its aftermath. As noted before, this final segment of the novel is preceded by descriptions of evolution: its biological manifestations as well as the Sufi belief that humanity is evolving toward a certain destiny, developing organs that transcend time and space to facilitate the process (p. 426). From various psychic places Martha, Lynda, and Mark are working on their respective "growing points," submitting themselves to the process of "*being stripped*, being sharpened and sensitized, which uses the forms of ordinary life merely as tools, methods" (p. 428).

By contrast, the larger body of society in the 1960's—no longer a reflection of Martha's psychic space—slides back into unconsciousness and desensitization, unable even "to diagnose its own condition" (p. 430). The times are not "bad" like the phase just past, but frenzied, desperate, artificial—socially and politically in tremendous flux. Ironically, that instability favors the development, acceptance, and even imitation of the abnormal; one of the many "signs of the time" is that Lynda's behavior is no longer dismissed as madness but accepted as a form of charming eccentricity. Eventually the strain of trying to be "normal"—of surviving on the plane of ordinary life by imitating Martha's role as conduit for the Coldridge household—drains Lynda's psychic energies too much and she cracks up again. Martha concurrently enters another dormant stage.

Mark's growing point faces the external world rather than the interior one. Despite his otherwise admirable qualities, he is unable to "let go of ordinariness to sink himself into Lynda" (p. 461), suggesting the limits of rationality in the development of higher levels of consciousness. Martha, on the other hand, enters the basement world totally for a time. In a psychological sense both Mark and Lynda are aspects of Martha's journey to the center: Mark is upstairs, "trying to absorb what the walls said" (p. 463) —including a "new" wall containing facts about madness and mental hospitals; Lynda is down below, batting her head and moving her hands along the walls of her flat as if trying to escape. Martha realizes that it is "the walls of [Lynda's] own mind that she was exploring" (p. 469). Since Martha is, as the narrator states, "part of Lynda" (p. 466), she is clearly involved in the offensive on the walls herself, trying to break through the barriers of her own consciousness at both the rational (Mark) and the irrational (Lynda) levels. Martha and Lynda intermittently "become" each other, absorbing aspects of each other's personalities just as Martha and Mark had done earlier.

This merging of separate selves is a further extension of the mutual breakdown and interpenetration of personalities dramatized in *The Golden Notebook* and *Landlocked*. While Mark functions variously as Martha's somewhat circumscribed rational consciousness, her "defender" and nurturer aspects, and her sense of the past or memory, Lynda functions variously as her irrational, nonlogical, and visionary aspects, her self-hater (at times), and her sense of the future. Mark and Lynda thus represent complementary aspects of Martha's self, as Lessing dramatizes the effort of consciousness to overcome the chronic division between the rational and nonrational dimensions.[30]

Martha enters Lynda's basement world through a symbolic identification, by sipping milk from a broken piece of crockery that Lynda throws at her. In accepting Lynda's fractured reality, Martha steps across the figurative boundary line between sanity and madness—the rational and irrational dimensions that had formerly separated them. While the life of London continues overhead and outside, Martha temporarily relinquishes being "reasonable" and "sensible." Leaving Mark and what he represents behind, she stays in the basement with Lynda for a month, opening herself completely to what she can learn by "looking at ordinary life from another dimension" (p. 466).

She discovers that Lynda's psychic energy manifests itself as a lighter, finer capacity than hers. Slowly developing a finer receptivity herself, by finding in her consciousness a "listening space" (p. 470), she tunes in with more control to the stream of impulses from a dimension where time does not exist. This area of consciousness is described through images of water: currents, waves, rivulets, fountains, oceans of sound—suggesting the primordial matrix from which life (literally) and consciousness (symbolically) are generated. While Anna Wulf had feared drowning, Martha Quest voluntarily submerges herself. Having earlier broken out of her own landlocked state, she now descends deeply enough into the fluid area within her own psyche to move beyond the personal to the collective unconscious where such primordial images (or archetypes) originate.[31]

Her emergence from the basement after a month of exploration of those sounds and images is a euphoric rebirth.

> Everything was so much there, present, existing in an effulgence of delight, offering themselves to her, till she felt they were extensions of her and she of them, or at least, their joy and hers sang together, so that she felt they might almost cry out, Martha! Martha! for happiness, because she was seeing them, feeling them after so long an absence from them. She walked, she walked, looking, gazing, her eyes becoming cloud, trees, sky and the warm salutation of sunlight on the flank of a high glowing wall. (P. 480)

Her union with the natural world is a manifestation of that same "field consciousness" or "peak experience" that she had experienced intermittently as an adolescent on the African veld, and that Mary Turner and Anna Wulf reach momentarily during their breakdowns.[32] Its positive form is the mystical perception of identification with the universe, of "one's total union with the infinite. . . . The usual ego boundaries break down, and the ego passes beyond the limits of the body."[33]

However, in the characteristic dialectical process that permeates Martha's (and Lessing's) universe, the vision alternates with its negative form, as Martha observes other human shapes from her perspective of altered awareness. Lessing describes what Martha sees as if from the point of view of an extraterrestrial creature observing life on earth with all familiarity of objects stripped away —reminiscent of the negative insight into the nature of things expressed by Roquentin in Sartre's *Nausea*. Martha sees her fellow creatures as

> soft like pale slugs, or dark slugs, with their limp flabby flesh, with hair sprouting from it, and the things like hooves on their feet, and wads or fells of hair on the tops of their heads. There they were all around her, with their roundish bony heads, that had flaps of flesh sticking out on either side, then the protuberance in the middle, with the air vents in it, and the eyes, tinted-jelly eyes which had a swivelling movement that gave them a life of their own. . . . (P. 480)

Lessing elaborates this alien perspective of life on earth at some length. Such distinctly science-fiction-like passages reinforce the developing romantic strain of the author's narrative strategies, a movement away from the mimetic realism of Martha Quest's experiences in the earlier volumes of the series.[34]

The science fiction metaphor is explored in the novel in another sense as well. At various points Martha has been intrigued by the correspondences between what she and Lynda experience and what Jimmy Wood writes about in his science fiction novels. His plots often involve telepathic and other extrasensory phenomena, including psychic mutations: people who have "more senses than are considered normal" (p. 355) and beings who can plug into other people's energies like psychic vampires. Eventually Martha visits Jimmy's storeroom of ideas and finds there "books on Rosicrucianism and the old alchemists; Buddhist books and the dozen or so varieties of Yoga; . . . Zoroastrianism and esoteric Christianity; tracts on the I Ching; Zen, witchcraft, magic, astrology and vampirism; scholarly treatises on Sufism; the works of the Christian mystics. Here, in short, was a kind of potted library representing everything rejected by official culture and scholarship" (p. 486). (This is, incidentally, the storeroom of ideas that underpins Lessing's own gradual evolution from political to psychological reality, from the external to the internal world of change.) But Jimmy himself is insensitive to the psychological or spiritual significance of these maps of human consciousness. Though he can tune in to what is in the air, he is incapable of converting those messages or ideas into the personally meaningful context that Martha and Lynda explore.

Eventually Martha accepts that she and Jimmy use the same terms or labels for what are in fact vastly different experiences; while he is writing about outer space, Martha is voyaging in inner space. Jimmy's "center" is the psychological opposite of Martha's, just as Jack is Martha's opposite in his one-sided commitment to the body. Jimmy and Jack each become human machines, having pushed to the extreme one aspect of the self at the expense of all the rest.[35] Symbolically, they represent aspects of Martha herself which, if carried to their extreme, would deflect her from the center of her being and from her central task. Nonetheless, Jimmy's introduction to Martha of the enormous resources of the

"occult" leads her to search there for further entrances into herself, just as Jack's sexual "laboratory" had led her to important
insights about sexuality and the self-hater. Moreover, Martha
realizes that this material is the corpus of transpersonal knowledge
that the human race keeps forgetting and having to "remember"
over and over again in different forms, languages, and images. As
the narrator phrases it,

> The civilised human race knew that its primitive members (for in-
> stance, Bushmen) used all kinds of senses not used by itself, or not
> admitted: hunches, telepathy, "visions," etc. It knew that past civil-
> isations, some of them very highly developed, used these senses and
> capacities. It knew that members of its own kind claimed at certain
> times to experience these capacities. But it was apparently incapable
> of putting these facts together to suggest the possibility that they
> were calling people mad who merely possessed certain faculties in
> embryo. (P. 496)

Thus Lessing brings together ideas that have been evolving both
in this novel and in the larger unfolding of her fiction through the
vehicle of the abnormal or unconventional consciousness: that
psychic dimension shared by primitives, children, madmen, and
the sensitives in any population at any time, whose unorthodox
"sense of reality, that is, their sense of how to conform to the outside world" (p. 498) places them in a special category. What is
"abnormal" is the pathological labeling of such unorthodox perceptions; contemporary society's special form of blindness is to
persecute or incarcerate its own seers rather than be guided by
them. Elsewhere Lessing has observed, "Our culture has made an
enemy of the unconscious."[36] Neumann phrases it, "The very
things which the child has in common with the man of genius,
the creative artist, and the primitive, and which constitute the
magic and charm of his existence, must be sacrificed. The aim of
all education, and not in our culture alone, is to expel the child
from the paradise of his native genius and, through differentiation
and the renunciation of wholeness, to constrain the Old Adam
into the paths of collective usefulness."[37]

While Martha taps more and more of the knowledge preserved
in the collective unconscious, Mark evolves from his role as an
aspect of her personal past to become a sensor of the future of
the macrocosm. Analogically, Martha's rational consciousness is

focused less on the personal problems of her past (which have, through the course of the novel and her journey, been "worked through") than on the problems of the collective.[38] Mark's work of absorbing the messages on the walls evolves into an open-ended "Memorandum to Myself" in which he extrapolates from present signs an imminent catastrophe that will endanger the very survival of the race. Concurrently, Lynda envisions the same eventuality from her own extrasensory sources. Martha simultaneously makes one more descent into the collective unconscious. A room at the *top* of Paul Coldridge's house (suggesting both a new and higher location in the figurative landscape of Martha's consciousness) provides the setting for Martha's self-generated passage through the most difficult and dangerous stage of her journey.

Lessing pointedly emphasizes the spiritual nature of Martha's exploration by identifying her vigil in Paul's house as the "progress through the Stations of the Cross" (p. 502). Unlike Anna Wulf, who struggles to contain her inner chaos by resisting it, Martha deliberately seeks it. Using the techniques she has learned before of controlling her food intake and sleep, Martha sends herself "over the edge" on a "brief trip into a totally uncharted interior" (p. 507). Elsewhere Lessing has described her own exploration of that region:

> It's very easy to send oneself round the bend for a couple of days. I did it once out of curiosity. I do not recommend that anyone should do it. I'm a fairly tough character and I've been in contact with a very large number of people who've been crazy, and I know quite a lot about it, and I knew exactly what I was doing. I sent myself round the bend by the simple expedient of not eating and not sleeping for a bit. I instantly encountered this figure I call the self-hater.[39]

Though Martha's experiences are beyond language, she tries to capture their essence in journal form in order to "remember" for later the difficult terrain she travels and the truths she discovers about herself. Like Anna Wulf's notebooks and Thomas Stern's double-layered journal, this diary is Martha's record of the highly symbolic journey into the abnormal consciousness, transcribed into the inadequate language of ordinary discourse.

Rendered in alternating sections of stream-of-consciousness and more conventional narrative style, the journal is almost a digest of the various stages of the atypical dimensions of consciousness "worked through" in Lessing's previous works. As in the pattern of the archetypal journey,[40] Martha's path is impeded by obstacles —the dragons symbolizing fear that guard "the entrances and exits of each layer in the spectrum of belief" (p. 489). She encounters the self-hater that has already manifested itself as both the collective and personal shadow—the inner antagonist that every person must confront sooner or later in order to transcend the boundaries of limited self-awareness; the sadomasochistic pleasure/pain complex; and other antitheses already intimated as part of Martha's psychic life. She sees, as she had seen in smaller glimpses before, that her personality is multifaceted, divided into opposing tendencies; "*every attitude, emotion, thought, has its opposite held in balance out of sight but there all the time*" (p. 521). She confronts in its direct form the dialectical tension inherent in the structure of consciousness itself, which determines that "nothing can be defined or exist by itself, but only through its opposite: only when they are mutually supportive can there be a release of creative power between the perpetually generated polar forces."[41]

Finally Martha descends into the darkest circle of hell within her own being, the demonic underside of her acceptable self, represented by the deliberately archetypal figure of the Devil. Like Anna Wulf, who eventually recognizes herself in the projected figures of the dwarflike joy-in-spite figure, Martha recognizes herself in the horrifying underside of her being.

> *If all these subhuman creatures are aspects of me, then I'm a gallery of freaks and nature's rejects.*
>
> *See above. Fool. Don't you ever learn. These things are there. Always. I can choose to be them or not. I can collect them . . . or not.*
>
> . . .
>
> *Man understands the Devil very well. The Devil has taught him all he knows.* (Pp. 522–23, emphasis in original)

Facing the darkest aspect of her irrational self, Martha comprehends that she must not identify exclusively with her inner demons, for that is the route to the madness that has entrapped people like Lynda. Instead she "names" and thus makes conscious the knowledge of her shadow at its most deeply buried level.

As she perceives, the area she enters is an extension of aspects of consciousness she has touched on before:

> Defective though her experiments were, terrified though she was, totally inadequate in every way for what she was trying to do, she *was* encountering previously known states of mind (regions, boxes, areas, wavelengths, countries, places), and in them were recognisable features. So this was not all chaos, it was not just a jumble: one could, in fact, make some kind of sense of all this by using one's ordinary faculties of memory, judgment, comparison, understanding. In short, one could use one's common sense here, in this uncommon area, just as one could in ordinary life. (P. 508)

She also recognizes that the state she has deliberately invoked is different in only one sense from what is labeled madness and treated with shock treatment, drugs, and/or incarceration: she has retained control of the journey herself. She writes in her journal of her explorations:

> THE CENTRAL FACT. IF AT ANY TIME AT ALL I HAD GONE TO A DOCTOR OR TO A PSYCHIATRIST, THAT WOULD HAVE BEEN THAT. I'M OVER THE EDGE. BUT EVEN IF I STAY HERE I CAN MANAGE (LIKE LYNDA). WHY? BECAUSE I KNOW JUST THAT SMALL AMOUNT ABOUT IT NOT TO LET MYSELF BE STAMPEDED. IF AT ANY MOMENT I'D GIVEN IN DURING THIS SESSION I'D HAVE BEEN SWEPT AWAY. WITHOUT KNOWING WHAT I KNOW, THROUGH LYNDA, I'D NOT HAVE BEEN ABLE TO HOLD ON. (P. 524)

As Kenneth Wapnick has observed in his comparison of schizophrenic and mystical experiences, the crucial distinction lies in the individual's preparation for the experience of the Absolute. While the mystic gradually and consciously develops the ability to withdraw from surface attachments into an inner world where the connection to the cosmos is manifested, the schizophrenic experiences the domain of deep and overwhelming feelings suddenly and involuntarily. Further,

> Though the mystic and schizophrenic ostensibly share the same flight from the social world, the mystic's abandonment is merely of his own dependent attachments to it. . . . [For the schizophrenic] the flight into psychosis, if successful, restores his capacity to function as a productive member of society, but it does not necessarily prepare him for the lifelong process of movement between inner

experience and social functioning, nor for the elimination of those learned habits that preclude the development of his inner potential. . . . The mystic provides the example of the method whereby the inner and outer may be joined; the schizophrenic, the tragic result when they are separated.[42]

On the literal plane of the novel Martha has been fortified by her participation in and identification with Lynda's madness; on the psychological plane she has visited the "basement" or unconscious space in her self often enough to recognize its symbols and images and thus to know how to enter and leave the alien realm where less proficient voyagers have become permanent prisoners. Her reward is the total repossession of her own mind. At the same time Martha's journey provides the integration of the polar dimensions of abnormal consciousness maintained throughout Lessing's fiction, the negative self-annihilating experience of chaos and the positive reconciliation of opposites into a higher synthesis.

The fact that her own inner journey is nearly complete is symbolized on the novel's literal level by the dissolution of the "old order" of the Coldridge house and household. It is vacated because, since Martha has figuratively outgrown it by unifying the layers of her own personality, "no longer was this house her responsibility" (p. 556). Mark and Lynda have finally separated, and Mark's own new state is symbolized by his marriage to Rita, another person from Martha's African past. Mark and Rita (now pregnant, suggesting the generative incorporation of the past into the present) depart for northern Africa, to turn the "city in the desert" (envisioned first by Martha and then Mark) into a real asylum for people escaping the predicted destruction of England. Lynda returns briefly to the mental hospital, tormented by hallucinations which are in fact the prophetic revelations of the cataclysm.

Feeling somewhat at loose ends, Martha wonders whether she has relapsed into another dormant period (Lessing's suggestion that the journey of self-discovery is never complete; the cycle of forgetting and remembering continues). But the next stage is to be found by looking not around her but within herself again; psychic changes take place in the domain of the figurative, not literal, geography.

Where? . . . How? Who? No, but *where*, where. . . . Then silence
and the birth of a repetition: *Where?* Here. Here?

Here, where else, you fool, you poor fool, where else has it been,
ever. . . . (P. 559)

Martha's recognition that the next step is always just under one's
nose, where she can't see it without extraordinary effort, is the
symbolic conclusion to the journey of the abnormal consciousness
on the microcosmic level. As in the geometry of the mythic pattern Lessing invokes, the cycle inevitably returns to its beginning
as the circle closes upon itself and thus defines its center. However,
though this is virtually the end of Martha's personal quest initiated several decades earlier, it is not the end of the novel; the Devil/
shadow/self-hater must be confronted once more, in the macrocosm. The conclusion of that dimension of the journey is detailed
in the final section of the novel. Ironically called the Appendix to
The Four-Gated City, that extrapolation of events is actually the
necessary and symbolic completion to what has preceded it. Moreover, like the Golden notebook in the earlier novel in which it
appears, it synthesizes the patterns and themes through which the
novel has been shaped to that point.

Lessing's appropriation of the conventions of fantasy and speculative fiction—intimated earlier in *The Four-Gated City*—becomes clearly developed and explicit in the apocalyptic conclusion
to the entire series. Abandoning strict formal realism, Lessing
adopts the narrative perspective of the fabulist in order to extrapo-
late imagined, but altogether credible, consequences from the present trends and dangers already documented as part of everyday
reality. Her modulation to the speculative voice translates into
fictional form her conviction that "science fiction writers have
captured our culture's sense of the future. *The Four-Gated City* is
a prophetic novel. I think it's a true prophecy. . . . I believe the
future is going to be cataclysmic."[43]

In diagnosing the insanities of contemporary life earlier in the
novel (and in her previous fiction), Lessing always keeps one eye
on the evolution of the collective. Thus in her summation of the
future in this section she conceptualizes in fictional form the crisis
of values that has occurred at all levels of the larger macrocosm
she observes. In another context Jean Houston has described that

crisis in a way that reinforces the accuracy and comprehensiveness of Lessing's vision:

> From the perspective of the phenomenologist of consciousness and culture, it is important to suggest . . . that apart from the environmental stresses; the runaway technology; the hunger, crime, strife, and weapons of unprecedented destructiveness; the increasing withdrawal of human beings from their biorhythmic roots in nature; the sensory and existential overload; and the intensification of conflict as a way of life in practically every aspect of our social being —apart from these, we are faced with a shudder at the core of man's inwardness so profound that humanity seems threatened at its most basic level, that of the general consensus about what is real and what is not, perhaps the one consensus without which civilization is impossible.[44]

The Appendix of the novel elaborates upon the post-cataclysm era in a rhythm that recapitulates the patterns of destruction and transcendence of the earlier parts of the novel.

Communications sent by Martha Quest, Mark Coldridge's private notes found after his death, the letters of Francis Coldridge (biological son of Mark and Lynda, and spiritual offspring of Martha as well), and other lesser exchanges and correspondences describe the pre-catastrophe era and the twenty-five years following the destructive event whose cause is vague but traceable to some human-political accident. Francis's section emphasizes that the cataclysm results not from extraordinary events but from the cumulative momentum of ordinary ones.

In letters to his step-daughter Amanda, Francis describes the evolution of the core of group consciousness that began with the members of the Coldridge household and radiated outward into a kind of utopian community in the countryside, based not on stated principles but upon spontaneous pooling of energy, resources, responsibility, and affection. In retrospect, Francis realizes that this movement in the 1970s was a product of the group's dimly perceived sense of future events, "a shadow of foreknowledge" that "was in everyone, affected anyone: accounted for the fantastic character of that decade" (pp. 565–66). The collective shadow manifested itself in political repression, governmental invasion of privacy, increasing violence, and—the most ubiquitous symptom of impending collapse—the fact that *"nothing worked"* (p. 568). The bizarre behavior of "normal" people who intermittently took leave of their senses was another symptom of the propensity of the human race to drive itself mad. Such aberrations, the collective manifestation of the inner enemy, were partly explained by the increasing effects of man's self-created poisons: pollution, drugs, preservatives, noise.

During this time Lynda's prophetic visions of disaster had been interpreted by her family and by doctors as evidence of her further mental deterioration, one of the recurring obstacles of a life in which "accepting the evidence of her own senses against a climate of orthodoxy had cost her her health and, for long periods at a stretch, her sanity" (p. 587). But Martha—by then having educated her own sensibilities through Lynda's assistance, without the invalidations that had crippled Lynda's ability to function in the outer world—had begun to tune in on some of the same wavelengths. Later the two women were able to describe their knowledge to Francis in a way that he could finally "hear." Martha and Lynda had become part of a surreptitious group of "sensitives," including several psychiatrists who had the courage to buck the establishment view, dedicated to channeling their intuitions of the future in order to rescue civilization from impending annihilation.

On the psychological level this is analogous to the most developed dimension of the consciousness guiding the rest of the self through the potentially dangerous level of the irrational, in order to save the total personality from the self-hater and from psychic disintegration. In *The Golden Notebook* the same mechanism guides Anna Wulf toward reintegration at the level of the individual psyche. On the transpersonal level it suggests the Sufi role as transmitter of "that current which can develop man to a higher stage in his evolution."[45] The group was secretive about its activities, recognizing that the shock created by dissemination of the truth that "a significant proportion of the population had various kinds of extrasensory power—not as a theoretical possibility but as a fact" (p. 585)—would paralyze their efforts. As it transpired, even their elaborate preparations, and their eleventh-hour release of their foreknowledge of imminent catastrophe, failed to save the multitudes who were unable to "hear."

In the context of Lessing's larger theme in the series of *Children of Violence*, the individual's relation to the collective still functions at a moral level, but it has evolved from a political to a psychological dimension: "The old right of the individual human conscience which must know better than any authority, secular or religious, had been restored, but on a higher level, and in a new form which was untouchable by any legal formulas" (p. 586). Francis's aunt, Phoebe Coldridge, who throughout the novel embodies the well-meaning but rigidly dogmatic left-wing political position, reflects the conventional view from which such groups needed to protect their knowledge, for she had seen even the life of the Coldridge commune in the country as "a very selfish way of living" (p. 596).

While Francis's section recapitulates the events culminating with the Epoch of Destruction, Martha Quest's section—her final communication—describes the events that follow it. The corresponding psychic dimension of the evolved consciousness is not self-destruction but dissolution into the larger whole. Martha's group had managed to reach one of the rescue boats outfitted for hasty exodus, and had drifted westward to an uncontaminated island off the Scottish coast. Crusoe-like, the seventy-three members of the group had adapted to living off the resources of the land. But the physical renewal thus accomplished, including the new generation of healthy children born on the island, is less significant than their spiritual mutation. While Lynda and Martha (and even, to some extent, Jimmy Wood) had been nature's "experimental models" for increasing powers of consciousness, the new generation on Martha's island is the true evolutionary mutation containing the seeds for the psychic and spiritual renewal of the race. The youngest members of the new generation live on a higher plane of reality, having various forms of what, to the adults, are extrasensory capacities. Several of them even seem to have already matured psychologically, having assimilated the wisdom of the collective consciousness that Martha has needed a lifetime to accomplish. "They are beings who include that history [of what the human race is in this century] in themselves and who have transcended it. They include us in a comprehension we can't begin to imagine" (p. 608). Only in the isolated microcosm of the island, where the innate potentialities for "seeing" and "hearing" need not be conditioned out of human beings while they are still children, can these extrasensory capacities take hold and flourish.

The island itself is another form of the mythical four-gated city: the archetype of paradise or wholeness transported from an urban to a pastoral context. The final transformation in the consciousness of the protagonist of *Children of Violence* is effected not in Mark's landlocked city in the desert—the social-political realm—but in an island community surrounded by water—the more private, self-contained dimension toward which Martha has been evolving. During Martha's time on the island it becomes invested with rare qualities that defy precise description, such as "a sweet high loveliness somewhere, like a flute played only just within hearing" (p. 604). Several of the islanders actually communicate with beings not of their known company, as if the final veil between this world and another had fallen and divinity itself had been perceived. (The atmosphere and setting suggest the sea-changed world of Shakespeare's *The Tempest*.) In a striking emblem Lessing captures the sense of the mutation that symbolizes the interpenetrating dimensions of spirit and matter. Martha sees one of the younger (and pregnant) women looking at a fish that had washed ashore: "The fish was as it were double—no, not a Siamese-twin fish. It was one fish enclosed in another fish, the enclosing shape being of a finer subtler transparency, and it was hard to say whether the imprisoned fish was dying because of being shut in the embracing fish, or whether the delicate outer fish found its inner burden too much for it and so was dying" (p. 603). The relationship between the microcosm and the macrocosm, between the spiritual and phenomenal dimensions of reality, is conceptualized in the image of an imperfectly realized symbiosis.

In psychological terms, if the individual consciousness could actually incorporate all of its contents (both repressed and unrealized), thereby reaching totality, the boundaries of the private self would be congruent with the transpersonal consciousness. That utopian state exemplifies the mystic union with the infinite, where "what is most deeply personal is also most universal."[46] In *The Four-Gated City* the psychic journey culminates in a symbolic resolution of the dualities of the individual consciousness, in Martha's achievement of spiritual wholeness. Completing the cycle of individuation, or the mythic journey to the center that begins and ends with violence in the phenomenal world, she recovers the primary unity of being symbolized by her arrival at an island evolved out of her original fantasy of the four-gated city.

The conclusion of *The Four-Gated City* is, however, more ambiguous than Martha Quest's personal apotheosis. The larger macrocosm, still trapped by blindness and ignorance, has retreated from such a vision of wholeness. The notes left behind by Mark Coldridge in his city in the desert contain the frustrated observation that the collective, as distinct from some of its more enlightened individual members, is unable to learn from its mistakes and experiences. Civilization begins to recover from the ashes of destruction only to repeat the cycle yet again, for few have been able to learn that there is not, and never has been, an external enemy but only the inner one. In his function as the encapsulations of rational consciousness that Martha progressively sheds, Mark thus embodies the fact that the intellect cannot easily assimilate the truth of the larger consciousness. Mark himself has never been able to acknowledge the equal validity of the non-rational (Lynda's reality), for, as a product of the old order, he has never succeeded in transcending the categories of his own rationally conditioned perceptions of the world.

Concomitantly, the collective cannot easily assimilate the truth tapped by the abnormal individual, as the final section of the Appendix suggests. The emissary from Martha's island is one of the exceptional mutants, a black child named Joseph. Symbolically, he is both Martha's spiritual legacy to the next generation and, through her, the spiritual offspring of Thomas Stern (Martha's lover in *Landlocked*): not only the seer who had predicted the psychic mutations of the human race which in fact develop on Martha's island, but the loving man who had awakened in Martha the potentialities of higher, unitive vision. The young child Joseph is, predictably, not "recognized"; he is only provisionally admitted to the camps of Africa, reclassified as "subnormal" (p. 609). But, like Thomas Stern, he will become a gardener—on a vegetable farm in the new city. Like Martha Quest herself, Joseph is one of the new generation's children of violence, heir to the endless dialectic between collective cataclysm and extraordinary vision.

Despite the apocalyptic conclusion to *The Four-Gated City* and, by extension, *Children of Violence*, the ending suggests that the gap between individual and society increases rather than diminishes as the private consciousness evolves to greater awareness and finds itself increasingly at odds with orthodox values and perceptions. Even if the antidote to collective blindness or madness is in the private sphere, the regenerative and predictive powers of the exceptionally developed consciousness prove to have only limited influence upon larger events.

In the seventeen-year time period between the publication of the first and final volumes of *Children of Violence*, Lessing's own orientation modulated from a political ideal to a psychological and spiritual resolution of fragmentation, from material to psychological reality as the form of primary truth; her socialism has slowly evolved into a more inward transcendental vision. Yet the dynamic shape of her fiction has remained constant, for the structure of consciousness itself is dual. Her own dialectical imagination outlasts that of her protagonists, as she balances the optimistic hope of individual enlightenment against the pessimistic realization that the collective body cannot absorb and learn from its exceptional members. Moreover, while unity may be the goal of the individual consciousness, division and self-division form the dialectical pattern along which the curve of growth must occur, until it finally circles back upon itself. As the utopian vision inevitably recedes into the future, it comes to approximate the idealized past, for both are expressions of the original unity. The Sufi scholar Nasrollah Fatemi observes that "man is complete when he has gained gnosis, but gnosis is also the primal element; so it is the beginning and the end, the first and the last, and thus the mystic circle is perfect."[47]

Erich Neumann describes the psychological relationship of the individual to the collective unconscious as another idealized identity:

Humanity as a whole and the single individual have the same task, namely, to realize themselves as a unity. Both are cast forth into a reality, one half of which confronts them as nature and external

world, while the other half approaches them as psyche and the unconscious, spirit and daemonic power. Both must experience themselves as the center of this total reality.

. . . .

The collective unconscious of mankind must be experienced and
apprehended by the consciousness of mankind as the ground common to all men. Not until the differentiation into races, nations,
tribes, and groups has, by a process of integration, been resolved
in a new synthesis, will the danger of recurrent invasions from the
unconscious be averted. A future humanity will then realize the
center, which the individual personality today experiences as his
own self-center, to be one with humanity's very self. . . .[48]

At the end of *The Four-Gated City*, such an ideal state has not
been achieved at the collective level. But as Lessing's vision turns
more inward, she continues to frame, through the conceptualization of the exceptional consciousness, an increasingly mythical and
mystical solution to the problem of the individual's relation to the
world.

From this vantage point it is instructive to view *Children of
Violence* as a whole, and to assess the enormous distance that both
its protagonist and its author have traversed (literally and figuratively). Clearly the character of Martha Quest and the world she
inhabits in the final volume are appreciably more richly developed
than in the earlier novels. Lessing's narrative control of the elements of that world emerge most sharply when measured against
the commonplaces of the opening volumes. Yet what unifies the
series and ultimately justifies those initial volumes is the very
resonances that develop as the author amplifies possibilities present from the beginning, such as the fantasy of the four-gated city
or the quest framework itself. Concurrently, her introduction of
entirely unanticipated narrative directions and concerns—from
the more multi-layered psychological exploration to the extrapolation and social prophecy at the end—create the necessary elements
of surprise and variety. Young Martha Quest's quotidian experiences give way in the last volumes to ones that are less conventional but more convincingly portrayed.

It must be conceded that Lessing's use of language in this
monumental work is more suited to the panoramic than the po-

etic; at times the author seems to be deliberately resistant to the felicities of style. The tension between aesthetic and ideological demands of the fictional universe she creates is more frequently resolved in favor of the latter; even the absorbing events of the final volume are sometimes weighed down by prolixity. Lessing exacts from her readers a certain fee of patience in return for the comprehensive documentation of ordinary experience as it shades into the remarkable.

NOTES

1. Lessing, "The Small Personal Voice" (1957), in *A Small Personal Voice*, ed. Paul Schlueter (New York: Alfred A. Knopf, 1974), p. 14.

2. Lessing, "Author's Notes," *The Four-Gated City* [*Children of Violence*, vol. 5] (New York: Alfred A. Knopf, 1969), p. 615. All subsequent page references will be indicated in the text.

3. Jean Hyppolite, *Genesis and Structure of Hegel's Phenomenology of Spirit*, trans. Samuel Cherniak and John Heckman (Evanston, Ill.: Northwestern University Press, 1974), p. 39.

4. Northrop Frye, *The Secular Scripture* (Cambridge, Mass., and London: Harvard University Press, 1976), p. 37.

5. See p. 112 above, n. 33.

6. Each of the preceding volumes of *Children of Violence* contains four major sections. In *Martha Quest*, each is subdivided into three segments; in the remaining volumes, each is subdivided into four. Only beginning with *The Golden Notebook* does the organization of the novel corroborate its meaning.

7. F. R. Karl has also pointed out that the four houses in the novel are analogues of enclosure, though he draws different conclusions about the novel's meaning. See "Doris Lessing in the Sixties: The New Anatomy of Melancholy," *Contemporary Literature* 13 (1972), 15–33, esp. p. 28.

8. Erich Neumann, *The Origins and History of Consciousness*, trans. R. F. C. Hull, Bollingen Series XLII (1954; rpt. Princeton, N.J.: Princeton University Press, 1969), p. 37. See also Mircea Eliade, *The Sacred and the Profane*, trans. Willard R. Trask (New York: Harcourt, Brace, and World, 1969), pp. 46–47.

9. The quotation appears in Idries Shah, *The Sufis* (1964; rpt. New York: Doubleday, 1971), p. 448.

10. Frye, *Secular Scripture*, pp. 97–158.

11. In her analysis of the changes in theme and narrative approach from *The Golden Notebook* to *The Four-Gated City*, Dagmar Barnouw suggests that the protagonist of the latter novel is not Martha but "Martha, Mark, and Lynda together." Barnouw proposes that Lessing abandons her interest in form, in the tradition of Robert Musil and the twentieth-century formlessness of the *Bildungsroman*. See "Disorderly Company: From *The Golden Notebook* to *The Four-Gated City*," in *Doris Lessing: Critical Essays*, ed. Annis Pratt and L. S. Dembo (Madison: University of Wisconsin Press, 1974), pp. 74–97, esp. p. 90.

Lynn Sukenick states that Martha "loses most of the personality that has earmarked her as Martha and dissolves into the lives of those around her like some sort of intellectual Mary Worth." See "Feeling and Reason in Doris Lessing's Fiction," in *Doris Lessing*, ed. Pratt and Dembo, pp. 98–118, esp. p. 102.

12. Preface to *The Golden Notebook* (London: Michael Joseph, 1972), p. xii.

13. Shah, *The Sufis*, p. 223.

14. Adrienne Rich has pointed out the interesting parallel between this aspect of *The Four-Gated City* and *Jane Eyre*: the mad women who, residing in some part of the protagonists' houses (basement/attic), reflect an aspect of their respective personalities that must be symbolically integrated into the self. See "Jane Eyre: The Temptations of a Motherless Woman," *Ms.* 2, no. 4 (1973), 72. I would draw the further parallel between Martha Quest and Jane Eyre as visionaries who "hear voices" telepathically and have dreams that guide them beyond their sexual dependencies toward autonomy and self-knowledge.

15. Mircea Eliade identifies the "nostalgia for Paradise" as "the desire to be always, effortlessly, at the heart of the world, of reality, of the sacred, and, briefly, to transcend, by natural means, the human condition and regain a divine state of affairs. . . ." See *Patterns in Comparative Religion*, trans. Rosemary Sheed (1958; rpt. New York: New American Library, 1963), p. 383. In formal terms this is also one of the two thematic poles of myth and romance: the antithesis between the experience of primordial identity and its negation in the imperfect world.

16. Neumann, *Origins*, p. 267.

17. As Eliade also points out in discussing the multilayered potentiality of a symbol, "Whatever its context, a symbol always reveals the basic oneness of several zones of the real." See *Patterns in Comparative Religion*, p. 452.

18. "My Father" (1963), in *A Small Personal Voice*, ed. Schlueter, p. 83.

19. Jung, *The Psychogenesis of Mental Disease*, trans. R. F. C. Hull, vol. 3 of *The Collected Works*, Bollingen Series XX (Princeton, N.J.: Princeton University Press, 1960), pp. 177–78.

20. "Doris Lessing at Stony Brook: An Interview by Jonah Raskin" (1969), in *A Small Personal Voice*, ed. Schlueter, p. 67.

21. In a review of Idries Shah's various books on Sufism, Lessing comments in similar language, "I wish I could have the experience of reading [*The Way of the Sufi*] again for the first time: it was like a door opening where one least expects it." See "What Looks Like an Egg and Is an Egg?" *New York Times Book Review*, 7 May 1972, p. 41.

22. Interestingly, in view of the Hegelian drift of Lessing's fiction, Hegel suggests in his *Philosophy of Mind* that both insanity and clairvoyant powers are unremarkable and even predictable aspects of psychic activity in the evolution of consciousness. See *Hegel's Philosophy of Mind*, Part III of *Encyclopedia of the Philosophical Sciences* (1830), trans. William Wallace, together with *Zusätze* in Boumann's Text (1845), trans. A. V. Miller (Oxford: Clarendon Press, 1971), esp. pp. 92, 110–15, and 124–31.

23. "Doris Lessing at Stony Brook," p. 69.

24. Northrop Frye observes that when psychology enters the area of romance, "it is concerned mainly with the defensive devices that people use in trying to strengthen the barriers between the waking consciousness and the other parts of the mind. . . . [T]he actual world, as such, keeps dreaming and waking, play and work, in a continuous antithesis: each takes its turn in dominating our interests, yet remains separate from the other." But the world of art, as distinct from nature, is "a creative process informed by a vision" which, in romance, is indi-

cated by the polarization "between the world we want and the world we don't want. The process goes on in the actual world, but the vision which informs it is clear of that world, and must be kept unspotted from it." See *Secular Scripture*, p. 58.

25. Jung, *Two Essays on Analytical Psychology*, vol. 7 of *The Collected Works*, trans. R. F. C. Hull, Bollingen Series XX (New York: Pantheon Books, 1953), p. 156.

26. "Doris Lessing at Stony Brook," p. 68.

27. Frye contrasts the innate conservatism of realism that derives from its "acceptance of society in its present structure" with the more "revolutionary" quality of romance, in which what is regressive is equated with the demonic and clearly separated from the progressive elements of the story. See *Secular Scripture*, pp. 164 and 139.

28. "A Revolution," *New York Times*, 22 Aug. 1975, p. 31.

29. Letter from Doris Lessing to Roberta Rubenstein dated 28 Mar. 1977.

30. In the Freudian schema of the components of the psyche, Mark might be understood as the superego, Lynda as the id, and Martha herself as the ego mediating between their opposing configurations. However, this is a less satisfactory paradigm than the Jungian schema, since it cannot, as the latter can, suggest the unconscious as the source of embryonic future capacities of the personality.

31. As Erich Neumann describes it, "The cardinal discovery of transpersonal psychology is that the collective psyche, the deeper layer of the unconscious, is the living ground current from which is derived everything to do with a particularized ego possessing consciousness: upon this it is based, by this it is nourished, and without this it cannot exist." See *Origins*, p. 270.

32. See *The Grass Is Singing*, p. 277; *The Golden Notebook*, p. 469.

33. John White, ed., *The Highest State of Consciousness* (New York: Doubleday, 1972), p. vii.

34. The contemporary subgenre of science fiction or speculative fiction is in fact a development of the "didactic romance," the tradition of which precedes and runs parallel to that of the novel as a form. See Robert Scholes, *Structural Fabulation* (Notre Dame and London: University of Notre Dame Press, 1975), p. 102.

35. Sydney Janet Kaplan points out the use of images of machinery and technology as metaphors in *The Four-Gated City*, in contrast to the more organic metaphors of the earlier volumes of *Children of Violence*. See *Feminine Consciousness in the Modern British Novel* (Urbana: University of Illinois Press, 1975), p. 164.

36. "Doris Lessing at Stony Brook," p. 67.

37. Neumann, *Origins*, p. 400.

38. Patricia Meyer Spacks arrives at the opposite conclusion, suggesting that "as Martha concentrates more and more on her inner life, the outer world becomes (not only to her: to the reader) increasingly attenuated. Relationships multiply, but their complexities are stated rather than felt." See *The Female Imagination* (New York: Alfred A. Knopf, 1975), p. 313.

39. Quoted by Josephine Henden in "Doris Lessing: The Phoenix 'Midst Her Fires," *Harper's Magazine* (June 1973), p. 89.

40. See Neumann, *Origins*, esp. Part I (pp. 5–256); and Joseph Campbell,

The Hero with a Thousand Faces, 2nd ed., Bollingen Series XVII (Princeton, N.J.: Princeton University Press, 1968), esp. pp. 245–46.

41. José and Miriam Arguelles, *Mandala* (Berkeley and London: Shambhala, 1972), p. 92.

42. Wapnick, "Mysticism and Schizophrenia," in White, ed., *Highest State of Consciousness*, pp. 172–73.

43. "Doris Lessing at Stony Brook," p. 70. Lessing's shift to the speculative mode is consistent with what Robert Scholes and other critics of contemporary fiction see as a distinct trend; for a variety of reasons that encompass historical, ethical, and metaphysical changes in the tradition of fiction, "the most appropriate kind of fiction that can be written in the present and the immediate future is fiction that takes place in future time." See *Structural Fabulation*, pp. 17–18. Similarly, Northrop Frye observes that the apocalyptic stance in contemporary fiction is almost inevitable, in part because "fantasy is the normal technique for fiction writers who do not believe in the permanence or continuity of the society they belong to." See *Secular Scripture*, p. 138.

44. Houston, "Myth, Consciousness, and Psychic Research," in Edgar D. Mitchell, *Psychic Exploration*, ed. John White (New York: G. P. Putnam's Sons, 1974), p. 585.

45. Lessing, "In the World, Not of It" (1972), in *A Small Personal Voice*, ed. Schlueter, p. 133.

46. White, ed., *Highest State of Consciousness*, p. xiv.

47. Fatemi, "A Message and Method of Love, Harmony, and Brotherhood," in *Sufi Studies: East and West*, ed. L. F. Rushbrook Williams (New York: E. P. Dutton, 1973), p. 62.

48. Neumann, *Origins*, pp. 416, 417.

Returning to the Center

7

Briefing for a Descent into Hell

If *The Golden Notebook* and *The Four-Gated City* can be taken as the breakthroughs in Lessing's fiction in both structure and idea, each of the novels (to date) that comes after them carries echoes of the far-ranging nexus of issues, characterizations, and patterns embraced by those two works. Yet, despite the continuity of themes, *Briefing for a Descent into Hell* initiates new formal and narrative shifts in Lessing's fiction. For the first—and only—time, the protagonist of the novel is male.[1] Structurally, the novel is closer in conception to the experimental form of *The Golden Notebook*, with its inversion of chronology and multiple perspectives that reinforce the subjectivity of point of view. In fact, the story itself is adumbrated in the earlier work, in Ella's idea of writing a story about "a man whose 'sense of reality' has gone; and because of it, has a deeper sense of reality than 'normal' people" (*The Golden Notebook*, p. 458).

Like the latter novel, *Briefing for a Descent into Hell* depends on a basic pattern of theme and variations: the "theme" is Charles Watkins's deeper psychic urge to heal the schism of his present condition of self-division; the variations include his nostalgia for union and his recognition of separation, envisioned by Lessing through a series of metaphoric or symbolic journeys. In its paring down of the density of narrative description in favor of a flowing, more symbolically saturated language, it represents a new shape for Lessing's central vision.

In its particular exploration of the abnormal consciousness, this novel poses an even more radical critique of both "reality" and

narrative realism than the novels that precede it. It is worth reviewing here the way madness itself as a particular manifestation
of the abnormal consciousness has evolved thus far in Lessing's
fiction. In *The Grass Is Singing* fragmentation is the response of
Mary Turner's personality to the polarizations of reality along
sexual and racial lines—antitheses that do exist in the phenomenal
world and that are only catalysts for her own inner divisions. The
resulting breakdown emphasizes the disjunction between self and
world through the fact that oppression has both political and
psychological modalities, both of which are divisive. Julia Barr's
self-division in *Retreat to Innocence* is primarily represented
through ideological and sexual antitheses. Anna Wulf's breakdown is the most thorough "working through" of the manifold
implications of unconventional mental experience, with the begin-
nings of visionary intuition (adumbrated in the younger Martha
Quest of the early volumes of *Children of Violence*) taken further
until they lead to a reintegration of the personality. Thomas
Stern's madness in *Landlocked* presses that connection between
the dissolution of the self common to certain kinds of psychotic
and mystical perceptions still further. Martha Quest's later incorporation of the meaning of his and of Lynda Coldridge's schizophrenic visions and her own explorations in *The Four-Gated City*
are thus comprehensible as evolutionary stages in developing the
organs of spiritual perception.

Moreover, as the "inner enemy" or shadow aspect of the self
becomes more conscious and is integrated into the personality beginning with the character of Anna Wulf, breaking through rather
than breaking down assumes a more central thematic position in
Lessing's fiction. At the same time the emphasis begins to shift
from the personal to the collective aspects of consciousness. For,
while Anna Wulf wants, as she tells her therapist, to be "'able
to separate in myself what is old and cyclic, the recurring history,
the myth, from what is new, what I feel or think that might be
new . . .'" (*The Golden Notebook*, p. 404), Martha Quest understands her personal psychological growth as a function as much of
those recurring cycles as of unique events.

The changing function of "madness" thus expresses the author's
conception of both social-political realities and personal develop-

ment. Lessing has summarized her long involvement with abnormal consciousness in her own life, observing,

> I have spent nearly thirty years in close contact with mental illness, first through various brands of analyst and therapist and psychiatrist, and then through people who were "mad" in various ways, and with whom I had very close contact. And still have. All this was not by any conscious choice on my part: it happened, presumably because of unconscious needs of my own.
>
> . . . I have always been close to crazy people. My parents were, mildly, in their own ways. My father was done in by the [F]irst [W]orld [W]ar, from which he never really recovered, and my mother had what is known as an unfortunate upbringing, her mother dying when she was three or so, and she never got over that. Both were acutely neurotic people. But I do not regard this as any personal fate, far from it, I believe that the world gets madder and madder, and when I say that it is not rhetorical or because the words sound attractively eccentric.[2]

As Lessing's protagonists turn away from the Leftist ideological framework for effecting social change, the "revolution" goes inward; the dream evolves from political to psychological alterations of the structures of reality as the novel structure correspondingly incorporates more of the motifs and narrative conventions associated with myth, romance, and speculative fiction. Breaking through one's conventional perceptions remains the primary task, with attendant risks, though even successful accomplishment of that task rarely affects the macrocosm, which continues to poison and fragment itself through self-interest, ignorance, and limited vision.

From the beginning of this next work, Lessing alerts the reader to the dual schema, as well as to the underlying Sufi inflection of its meaning, by providing a context for the novel on the frontispiece: "Category: Inner-Space Fiction—For there is never anywhere to go but in."[3] Two epigraphs—one from the fourteenth-century Sufi Mahmoud Shabistari's poem *The Secret Garden,* and the other from Rachel Carson's *The Edge of the Sea*—describe the macrocosm encapsulated within a raindrop or a sand grain suspended in water. As in *The Four-Gated City,* the part not only represents the whole but paradoxically contains it. By analogy, the unnamed seafarer of the first pages of *Briefing for a Descent into Hell* is Everyman, rediscovering (remembering) through the exploration of the microcosm of his own consciousness the experience of the human race.

Characteristically, the protagonist of this novel is self-divided. As one subsequently learns, the stresses of middle age and personal problems have propelled Charles Watkins, a professor of classics at Cambridge, into a mental breakdown accompanied by a temporary loss of identity medically described as amnesia. The motif of amnesia is a central one in the romance tradition: the series of adventures of the protagonist may be precipitated by "some kind of break in consciousness, one which often involves actual forgetfulness of the previous state. . . . Such a catastrophe, which is what it normally is, may be internalized as a break in memory, or externalized as a change in fortunes or social context."[4]

In *Briefing for a Descent into Hell* alternating sections correspond to both ways of perceiving the psychic crisis of the central character: from within and without his own consciousness. Accordingly, the first long portion is narrated primarily from the more immediate and subjective focus of the perceiving consciousness, while the remaining portions are composed primarily of letters, dialogues, and more public communications from members of Watkins's milieu and "reminiscences" provided by Watkins himself. In the first section, however, doctors' evaluations juxtaposed with the directly recorded subjective experiences of the protagonist emphasize the perceptual antithesis further.

When the protagonist is most awake and aware within his own mental experience, he is most deeply asleep from the point of view of the medical observers. His being is split into two modes: while his body participates in one, his mind participates in the other; they are complementary and, much of the time, mutually exclusive. "Inner" and "outer" space become metaphors in the novel not only in the sense of the cosmic voyage doubling as the journey of the private self but, more immediately, in the sense of disjunction between the mental and physical spaces that a person simultaneously occupies.

Watkins is Lessing's most identifiably "schizophrenic" character. In fact, a number of parallels can be drawn between the experiences of her protagonist and the existential phenomenology of schizophrenia proposed by R. D. Laing, not the least of which is a ten-day psychotic journey described by one of Laing's ex-patients, coincidentally named Jesse Watkins.[5] One of Laing's central (and controversial) hypotheses is that the psychotic breakdown manifested in acute schizophrenia is a natural process of mind-healing which, if allowed to run its full course, will be therapeutic rather than destructive. Following Bateson and others, Laing describes the "inner space journey" of the schizophrenic as follows:

> The person who has entered this inner realm (if only he is allowed to experience this) will find himself going, or being conducted—one cannot clearly distinguish active from passive here—on a journey.
>
> This journey is experienced as going further "in," as going back through one's personal life, in and back and through and beyond into the experience of all mankind, of the primal man, of Adam and perhaps even further into the being of animals, vegetables and minerals.
>
> In this journey there are many occasions to lose one's way, for confusion, partial failure, even final shipwreck: many terrors, spirits, demons to be encountered, that may or may not be overcome.[6]

However, the inner journey described here is not unique to psychotic breakdown, and Lessing's apparent indebtedness to Laing accounts for only one of the multiple routes to the same archetypal experiences.[7] The comparative mythologist Joseph Campbell has observed that the pattern of experience generated during an acute schizophrenic crisis is "the universal formula also of the mythological hero journey. . . . Interpreted from this point of view, a schizophrenic breakdown is an inward and backward journey to recover something missed or lost, and to restore, thereby, a vital balance."[8] As Northrop Frye has pointed out, the motifs of ascent and descent are patterns in the romance tradition in literature, wherein the worlds of idyllic and demonic experience are characteristically polarized as the narrative movement alternates between the psychological representations of wish fulfillment and nightmare.[9] That same journey pattern also appears in esoteric traditions. The Sufis describe man's evolutionary course from the simplest form of matter through vegetable, animal, human, and suprahuman states of consciousness, to the achievement of the "total perception of the external phenomenal world." [10] Further, phenomenologists of consciousness document similar motifs in the classical experiences described throughout the centuries in mystical and occult literature, and in the more recent psychedelic (or psycholytic) drug-induced experiences. [11]

What all of these parallel formulations suggest is that the collective unconscious—whether reached by psychotic, psychoanalytic, psychedelic, or contemplative means—manifests itself in similar archetypal images and symbols. Regardless of the catalyst, the unconscious generates patterns which, under certain but diverse circumstances, become more readily accessible to the other layers of the psyche. That identity is central to the major motifs of *Briefing for a Descent into Hell*, the first movement of which may be read as the narrative of a spiritual, archetypal, psychotic, or even drug-induced inner journey. What determines its fullest symbolic meaning is not so much what stimulates the journey as what is attained through it, and whether or not the change in consciousness has long-reaching effects on the personality of the protagonist.

Throughout the first long portion of the novel, the images resonate on several levels of meaning. The protagonist initially finds himself "at sea," a figurative pun suggesting the nature of his personal crisis as well as the base-element that symbolizes the origin of individual and collective, organic and psychic, life. The protagonist's wanderings express other primary images and rhythms, including heat, light, and circles. His "anti-clock Wise" (p. 38) direction and his need to experience a birth in reverse (p. 33) suggest the circularity of his journey backward both in time and in the development of his own consciousness as he tries to locate the center of his being. [12] He is the archetypal seafarer, alternately Jason, Jonah, Odysseus, Sinbad, adrift in a ship that is inhabited temporarily by a strange unearthly light (called the Crystal) that incorporates his shipmates but leaves him behind. (One learns later in the novel that during Watkins's war experience he was twice the only survivor in a group of buddies; in this section he is twice left behind by the Crystal—an example of Lessing's refraction of events from later in the novel through the protagonist's altered consciousness.)

While the inner space journey traces the narrator's subsequent efforts to reach the Crystal again, it figuratively recapitulates the cumulative history of life on earth. The protagonist is identified with the first living organisms emerging from the slime as they become land creatures (p. 40); the psychological and spiritual parallel is the emergence of human consciousness and its growth toward enlightenment and wholeness. As in *The Four-Gated City*, evolution in *Briefing for a Descent into Hell* is conceived as a dual process, both biological and spiritual; in each context ontogeny recapitulates phylogeny. That progress of human evolution appears in the writings of the thirteenth-century Sufi teacher Jalaluddin Rumi as follows:

> He came, at first, into the inert world, and from minerality developed into the realm of vegetation. Years he lived thus. Then he passed into an animal state, bereft of memory of his having been vegetable—except for his attraction to Spring and flowers. This was like the innate desire of the infant for the mother's breast. . . .
>
> From realm to realm man went, reaching his present reasoning, knowledgeable, robust state—forgetting earlier forms of intelligence.
>
> So, too, shall he pass beyond the current forms of perception. . . . There are a thousand other forms of Mind. . . .[13]

Within his existential reality Lessing's protagonist accomplishes the evolutionary step from sea to land, literally and figuratively, with the aid of a dolphin. Once on land, he establishes an intuitive communication with two gentle cat-like creatures who guide him over an apparent impasse in his upward climb. He arrives at what is at first an uninhabited archaic city. Like the mythical four-gated city of *Children of Violence*, it is organized in a circle/square configuration suggesting a sacred dimension. Later the houses are noticeably "turned inwards, to the centre" (p. 77), and the city itself seems to acknowledge the protagonist's presence as if also possessed of consciousness.

At first the archaic Eden-like atmosphere of the surroundings is emphasized, "as if this was a country where hostility or dislike had not yet been born" (p. 42). The protagonist experiences a sense of harmony and unity analogous both to the state of undifferentiated wholeness in the generic individual's personal development, and to the hypothetical primitive pre-ego consciousness in the history of civilization. However, that state is soon interrupted by the appearance of the ubiquitous "enemy" that Lessing has shown consistently as a configuration of the dark side of the mind.

The protagonist accordingly feels himself under a lunar influence, a reference not only to the pull of that dark or irrational side of the self, with its multiple metaphoric meanings,[14] but also an ironic gloss on the "lunacy" that his rambling monologues represent to the medical staff. On the outskirts of the city he witnesses, and feels himself implicated in, a ritualistic blood-letting involving several male babies and three females whose identities are disturbingly familiar to him. He realizes that their rite destroys forever some fundamental innocence in nature by their introduction of carnality into the pure world; like Adam in the Garden, he acquires a knowledge of the flesh, and feels compelled to cover his nakedness. Just as his imagination had "invented" the city itself, "now I understood my fall away from what I had been when I landed, only three weeks before, into a land which had never known killing. I knew that I had arrived purged and salt-scoured and guiltless, but that between then and now I had drawn evil into my surroundings, into me . . ." (p. 66). The shadow further manifests itself in two species of ugly, rapacious animals—the negative (and further divided) counterparts of the benevolent beasts that had earlier guided him. From the first appearance of these rat-like dogs and monkeys, the protagonist watches their mutual antagonism build and then break into open warfare, and tacitly acknowledges his own complicity in their violence.

During the time he spends on land, the voyager sees as his task the preparation of a landing pad in the center of the city, in anticipation of the return of the Crystal. Significantly, both the Crystal and the landing area are images of wholeness; in archetypal symbolism crystals and the abstract circle/square configuration often represent "the union of extreme opposites—of matter and spirit."[15] After delays and failures in his effort to prepare himself for this crucial segment of his journey, he finally senses the presence of the Crystal. But, again, he is not ready for it: "Whatever it was that I could not quite see, but was there, belonged to a level of existence that my eyes were not evolved enough to see. . . . Beating out from that central point came waves of a finer substance, from a finer level of existence, which assaulted me, because I was not tuned in to them . . ." (p. 76). The equation of extrasensory perception with the evolving organs of consciousness described by Sufi mystics underlies the formulations of Watkins's experience. The metaphoric language parallels the Sufi chemist Fariduddin Attar's description of inner transformation: "Every fiber has been purified, raised to a higher state, vibrates to a higher tune, gives out a more direct, more penetrating note. . . ." [16] At the same time Watkins's inadequacy makes explicit the difficulty of achieving that elevated level of being.

Thus far the protagonist's journey has been on water or land. His nascent "lighter" state now enables him to move in air, through the assistance of a great white bird, and suggests his further ascent toward enlightenment. Finally, in an event that symbolically condenses the several levels of the meaning of his experience, the Crystal arrives at the center of the circle-in-the-square to receive him. His own body becomes "a shape in light" (p. 102) and the city changes correspondingly, "as if the city of stone and clay had dissolved, leaving a ghostly city, made in light . . ." (pp. 102–3). As the boundaries between self and world, inner and outer space, dissolve, the light is simultaneously "inner or outer as one chose to view it" (p. 109). The protagonist's inner being becomes congruent with the macrocosm; he understands that the mind of humanity is also a unified consciousness, of which he is an integral part. Even the war and blood-lust he has witnessed have been essential to his eventual transmutation, providing the "page in my passport for this stage of the journey . . . a door, a key, and an opening" (pp. 105, 107).

Formally, the movement toward a higher plane of mystical awareness suggests the ascent motif of romance and myth, in which "escape, remembrance, or discovery of one's real identity, growing freedom, and the breaking of enchantment" shape the narrative; the growth of identity through "the casting off of whatever conceals or frustrates it" typifies the positive metamorphosis of the protagonist.[17] Thus Lessing renders the fundamentally ineffable and self-transcending experience of spiritual illumination —the event that Evelyn Underhill has called the "crystallization" of consciousness at a higher level.[18] The Sufi teachings have it that "when apparent opposites are reconciled, the individuality is not only complete, it also transcends the bounds of ordinary humanity as we understand them. The individual becomes, as near as we can state it, immensely powerful." [19]

In one of a series of lectures given in 1972 at the New School for Social Research, Lessing alluded to her own conversion from the rationalist position to one accommodating the connections among extrasensory perception, elevations of consciousness, and the intensification of personal energy. As she phrased it, "Now the real question is this: Where do you get your energy from? What kind of energy is it? How do you husband it? How do you use it? . . ." [20] And, further, concerning the ESP phenomenon—the source of apparent coincidences of like thinking between people (such as the affinity, described later in *Briefing for a Descent into Hell*, of Rosemary Baines's and Charles Watkins's ideas on education)—Lessing added, "What energy is reaching you? We don't know why, do we? There is something there to be explored . . . if we don't get upset." [21]

Narratively, the description of this process of exploration unfolding in the consciousness of Lessing's inner space voyager is periodically interrupted by the medical staff's observations on their patient's mental condition, and their disagreements about appropriate treatment. Doctor X (deliberately nameless, like the patient) recommends extensive use of drugs and eventually electroconvulsive therapy (shock treatment), while Doctor Y is more restrained, arguing for a gradual approach with minimal intervention. Watkins perceives the doctors' different sensitivities: while he can scarcely "see" Doctor X, Doctor Y is more "visible," burning with a "small steady light" (p. 162). However, despite their different auras and their conflicting diagnoses, both doctors are primarily concerned to restore their patient to the same orthodox model of "normality." Monitoring his responses to the drugs, they interpret his mental condition through its physical manifestations, concentrating on such behavioral evidence as alertness, coherence, drowsiness, and other physiological signs. The reader, suspended between the image of the protagonist as Everyman journeying through the collective unconscious, and Charles Watkins as amnesiac patient, observes the same experiences as described from internal and external perspectives. To emphasize their radical disparity, Lessing juxtaposes the protagonist's approach to the pinnacle of his vision of unity with the medical records showing that he had "less grasp of reality than when he was admitted" (p. 101). The quintessential spiritual experience is, from the medical point of view, a religious delusion.

Consistent with the paradoxes possible at nonrational levels of consciousness, the protagonist's inner space journey is increasingly conceptualized as occurring in outer space. One recalls Anna Wulf's "game," in which the mind progressively distances itself in the direction of a more comprehensive and inclusive geography, a metaphorical statement of the cosmic perspective (*The Golden Notebook*, p. 469). From deep in inner/outer space the protagonist of this novel has a similar overview of all of the earth, with its petty wars, political schisms, social insanities, divisions. Yet the index of his psychic wholeness is his perception of the fundamental unity of all things, of the interrelatedness of matter and spirit in every dimension of the cosmos. The real madness of humanity, he comprehends, is the failure to remember that unity at the base of all life, instead pursuing the courses of separation and division.

The same identification of microcosm with macrocosm, of inner with outer space, extends still further, as the enlightened protagonist finds himself at a cosmic conference presided over by an illuminated deity (the Sun). There he learns that the troubled planet Earth is in a state of First Class Emergency. The cosmic spirits—including Merk Ury, Minna Erva, and other refractions of Watkins's intellectual familiarity with the Greek classics—are being "briefed" to carry the easily forgotten message of Harmony to its inhabitants once again before it self-destructs. Though the style in this section, occasionally verging on parody of the more classic fabulations of science fiction (and also of conference rhetoric), lightens the novel's tone, the straining after humor is somewhat jarring. While Lessing frequently depends on irony and even parody (as in Anna Wulf's self-parodies in *The Golden Notebook*), humor itself is rare in her work; where it does appear, it is somewhat self-conscious. Thus, of the stylistic variations within *Briefing for a Descent into Hell*, this section and the serious but rather pedestrian verses of the earlier phase of Watkins's journey are the least successful. However, while stylistically awkward, they are nonetheless consistent with the larger design: the creation of verbal equivalents for various kinds of perception and communication, ranging from deeply interior and nearly inarticulable mental experiences to the more public messages (both implicit and explicit) that govern interpersonal relationships. To this point, Lessing has her protagonist repeat several times during his reluctant interchanges with the medical staff, "'I gotta use words when I talk to you . . .'" (p. 162).

The Forecast for Earth made by the benevolent overseers echoes the extrapolated future envisioned at the end of *The Four-Gated City* but concludes more optimistically. The "film" of the planetary crisis ends with the appearance of a new breed born with an altered mental structure promoting increased powers of perception; its members are endowed with the heritage of the previous generations, "plus, this time, the mental equipment to use it" (p. 140). Through the apocalyptic perspective, Lessing continues to exploit the narrative liberties of speculative fiction.[22]

If the macrocosm and the microcosm are understood as congruent, then the anticipated cataclysm on earth that Watkins observes corresponds to the psychic crisis in his own personality; like Anna Wulf, he discovers the chaos in the outer world that is a projection of his inner state. Furthermore, for the cosmic beings who seek to revitalize the message of harmony and, analogously, for the vision of wholeness in the unconscious that seeks entry into consciousness, the obstacles are great. Even with the "brain-printed" message, the emissaries face a considerable risk of amnesia during their descent into Hell (earth); Watkins's descent into his own inner hell is manifested as amnesia to the medical observers.[23] Symbolically, though each human being is born ("brain-printed") with the experience of harmony and wholeness, subsequent experience erodes that primary knowledge and substitutes division. As he grows older, he is more and more like a victim of amnesia, increasingly self-estranged and forgetful of the knowledge of original unity as the deepest reality of his being. Literature of the romantic tradition consistently alludes to the transcendental state of innocence (as in Wordsworth's "Ode: Intimations of Immortality"), and all mystical traditions seek the way back (or forward) to that experience of undifferentiated wholeness. Idries Shah notes in the latter case that in the Sufi dervish tradition, "remembering" is an important aspect of psychic development, beginning with "'remembering oneself,' after which the function shifts to one of harmony with the greater consciousness."[24]

The problem given this particular symbolic form in *Briefing for a Descent into Hell* is the characteristic metaphysical one of Lessing's fictional protagonists. As Watkins formulates it, "Each individual of this species is locked up inside his own skull," unable to "see things except as facets and one at a time" (p. 142). Watkins himself is ironically the prime example of that propensity. Unlike Martha Quest, who ultimately fuses the opposites of her personality through diligent "work" on her self, the Watkins of the second part of the novel and the mind-voyaging protagonist of the first part do not constitute a *conscious* integrated whole personality. In his own "First Class Emergency," amnesia is the psychological manifestation of an ontological crisis, a breakdown or disintegration of his life-roles as husband, father, paramour, professor. Forgetting for a time who he "is" for others, he journeys within his own unconscious self in an effort to rescue some deeper knowledge from which his waking ego personality has become severed. Thus the hallucinations, fantasies, and visions of his inner space journey are—from the point of view of his total personality—"unconscious." His larger task is to bring the truths discovered in the collective memory to personal awareness, to fuse the split between the generic Everyman of the inner space journey and the individual self of waking life.

In the subsequent movements of the novel the emphasis shifts from cosmic to biological and social time and their corresponding metaphorical formulations. Formally, the narrative reverses from the pattern of ascent, with its impetus toward unity, to that of descent, with its impetus toward separation. Following the rebirth that expresses his spiritual gnosis, and his cosmic briefing on Harmony, the protagonist "returns to the beginning" again, this time reliving the primary biological separation of his own physical birth experience:

> Sucked into sound, sucked into sea, a swinging sea, *boom*, shhhh, *boooom*, shhhh, *boooom* . . . thud thud, thud thud . . . one two, and the three is me, the three is me, THE THREE IS ME. I in dark, I in pulsing dark, crouched, I holding on, clutching tight, boooom,

shhhh, boooom, shhh, rocked, rocking, somewhere behind the gate, somewhere in front the door, and a dark red clotting light and pressure and pain and then OUT into a flat white light where shapes move and things flash and glitter. (P. 148)

His first "personal" memory following birth is his initiation into the drugging of his awareness and the equation of sleeping with being a "good" baby, an expectation that prefigures the chronic spiritual torpor of adult life.[25] Both literally and metaphorically, sleep is the norm; spiritual awakeness is the abnormal state.[26]

Lessing has noted elsewhere that under the influence of mescaline (in her single experience with the drug) she experienced "both giving birth and being given birth to. Who was the mother, who was the baby? I was both but neither"—surely a resonant image of the creative artist giving birth to her own self. (Lessing emphasizes, however, that drugs are not the most valuable path into the mind; with discipline and patience, "if you can train yourself to concentrate you can travel great distances."[27]) Stanislav Grof, working with psycholytic (psychedelic) drug-induced experiences and extrapolating from the psychoanalytic concept of "birth trauma," has proposed that the universal intrauterine state and the subsequent stages of labor and delivery form biological paradigms for the ecstatic and stressful extremes of psychic experiences at successive levels of consciousness; these may manifest themselves in certain aspects of both drug-induced and psychotic experiences.[28]

Those same extremes of unity and separation permeate the consciousness of the protagonist of Lessing's novel. Each framing of the journey repeats certain patterns in Watkins's split personality, as Lessing illustrates through a variety of contexts the same emotional truths of her protagonist's situation. That the inner journey is itself both a reflection of and an effort to heal the division is the central assumption of the novel. As R. D. Laing has remarked, the "cracked mind of the schizophrenic may *let in* light which does not enter the intact minds of many sane people whose minds are closed."[29] The narrator of *Briefing for a Descent into Hell* describes the mental hospitals that house the "millions who have cracked, making cracks where the light could shine through at last . . ." (p. 154).

Like Laing, whose ideology Lessing shares more explicitly in this novel than in any of her other works (despite her own consistent disclaimers),[30] the author emphasizes that "mental illness" —manifested as unconventional behavior or abnormal consciousness—is a cultural label that permits the potential for vision or even self-healing to be drugged and nullified by the very institutions that ostensibly promote recovery. The medical model of psychic disequilibrium prevents doctors (and others) from accepting the possibility that, in Anton Boisen's words,

> certain types of mental disorder are not in themselves evils but problem-solving experiences. They are attempts at reorganization in which the entire personality, to its bottommost depths, is aroused and its forces marshaled to meet the danger of personal failure and isolation. . . . The acute disturbances . . . arise out of awareness of danger. The sufferer is facing what for him are the great and abiding issues of life and death and of his own relationship to the universe.
> . . . In some cases the charge of pathology as applied to religious experience is due simply to the failure to recognize that such phenomena as hallucinations spring from the tapping of the deeper levels of the mental life, and that as such they are not necessarily symptomatic of mental disorder but may be creative and constructive. But in a large number of cases the association of the mystical and the pathological is due to the fact that a fundamental reorientation is a necessary stage in the development of the individual.[31]

If the first major section of *Briefing for a Descent into Hell* shows the "light shining through" the cracked mind of the protagonist, the remainder of the novel provides a partial explanation for the crack. As in *The Golden Notebook*, the scrambling of chronology is essential to the novel's meaning. Lessing provides the immediate subjective experience of Watkins's abnormal consciousness first, and only subsequently furnishes its context by showing the data of his outer world that have been translated into the particular images of his journey. The literal link between the divided layers of his being is Watkins's photographic memory (a capacity later reported by one of his colleagues). The narrative organization thus expresses two kinds of knowledge: the "information" of the external world of social interaction, and its imaginative transformations at the unconscious levels of the protagonist's psyche. Their juxtaposition both invites and expresses the implicit questions of the novel: which mode is the "real" one? And, is their synthesis possible within contemporary social and political contexts?

Once Watkins's social identity is established, by means of a photograph found in his recovered wallet, the doctors attempt to reconstruct his former identity for him. Watkins, however, categorically rejects the role and name assigned to him by his former intimates, having found his true center in the modality of psychic space he has recently circumnavigated. Concurrently, the testimonies from his wife, mistress, colleagues, and acquaintances to the doctors contribute a picture of the social persona that Watkins has vacated, and one that contrasts sharply with the illuminated Everyman of the first part of the novel. The commentaries of his familiars emphasize the ways in which Watkins—to *their* perceptions—was always somehow different, abnormal. Impervious to basic social conventions and feelings, he was "the original eccentric oddball" (p. 223) who did not even "pay lip service to ordinary feelings" (p. 227), according to his colleague Jeremy Thorne. His disillusioned former mistress, Constance Mayne, found him "above every human emotion" (p. 232). His wife, Felicity, who might be expected to know him best, seems to know him least, though she does volunteer the fact that he "always sleeps much less than most people" (p. 172). Conversely, Rosemary Baines, a bare acquaintance from one of his lecture audiences, had been so struck by his ideas and his presence that she had written an extraordinary letter, which forms a major section of the narrative (almost to the extent of straining narrative realism), to share with him her ideas on education and other matters.

Though he had initially dismissed Rosemary Baines's remarkable effort at communication, one learns subsequently that Watkins had met with her and her archaeologist friend, Frederick Larson, the night before the onset of his amnesia. Many of the ideas detailed in her letter reappear in altered form as images and events in the inner space journey that he subsequently undergoes (already narrated earlier in the novel). Rosemary discusses the problem of education—the process of indoctrinating children into social norms and thus anaesthetizing their inborn capacity for perceiving wholeness. She describes the psychic wavelength that Watkins's lecture on the topic had struck within her: the feeling of "beings briefly, on a different, high, vibrating current, of the familiar becoming transparent" (p. 183). Her reflections clearly parallel the experience Watkins himself lives out at the climax of his inner journey, which in turn alludes to the elevated awareness of the Sufi mystic.

Moreover, Rosemary Baines reiterates her friend Frederick Larson's archaeological speculations on the forms of life of earlier civilizations. Observations on the roofing materials of archaic houses and the implicit ethnocentric bias of archaeology resonate with Watkins's discovery of the idyllic city with roofless houses; Rosemary's long discussion of Larson's (and others') mid-life crises, precipitated by the questioning of basic assumptions about one's profession and identity, resonates with Watkins's own breakdown. Like Larson, Watkins has suffered from a stammer that is symptomatic of his inner turmoil; like Larson, Watkins is also a student of ancient civilizations, but his intellectual mastery of the heritage of Western thought has failed to develop in him any insight into the larger relationship between the collective past and his personal history. His mind journey of the first part of the novel thus acquires further meaning as a reflection of aspects of the self he has not assimilated into his mundane conscious personality. Ironically, his psychic travels make existentially real his identification with classical mythic figures and motifs from his intellectual discipline.

Though that journey is interrupted by the doctors' efforts to restore him to his pre-amnesiac identity, it is resumed in another form in response to the more sensitive Doctor Y's suggestion that Watkins recall his wartime experiences. Stylistically, this section is one of the novel's most effective passages—almost a set-piece that can be appreciated separately as the representation of an emotionally powerful experience. The sense of immediacy and detail is all the more heightened by the reader's subsequent discovery that it is a pure fantasy—neither "realistic" nor, from the perspective of Watkins's literal past life, "true." His war buddy Miles Bovey, whose death is described in the account, later confirms not only that he is still alive but that Watkins had never seen action in Yugoslavia, the location of his "recollection." Instead, these events are closer to Bovey's own war experience.

Watkins describes a number of events in a political matrix that resonate with those already encountered within a cosmic setting as patterns of his emotional reality: a briefing (this time a military one) followed by a descent (a parachute drop into Yugoslavia), and the experience of belonging to a larger collective whole (participation in the partisan Resistance). Communism is expressed in a pure, ideal form, wherein "an individual could only be important insofar as he or she was a pledge for the future . . ." (p. 258). The experience of self-transcendence manifests itself through not divine but earthly harmony and union, in a love relationship with a partisan named Konstantina (an idealized fantasy of Watkins's former real-life mistress, Constance).

Again his (and the author's) nostalgia for Paradise surfaces, as he envisions "the world as it was before man filled and fouled it. . . . Those vast mountains, in which we moved like the first people on earth. . . . It was as if every one of us had lived so, once upon a time, at another time, in a country like this, with sharp sweet-smelling air and giant uncut trees, among people descended from a natural royalty, those to whom harmfulness and hate were alien . . ." (pp. 256–58). Characteristically, the antithetical shadow emerges. In a variation of the birth-in-death spasm of a rat-dog in Watkins's earlier journey, Konstantina is fatally gored by a threatened doe about to give birth. The cycle of birth and death is the paradigm for the antinomies of human experience; only in the imaginative mythic and spiritual dimensions are they reconciled.[32]

But the more realistic necessity remains of reconciling the divided personality in the social context. In the final movement of *Briefing for a Descent into Hell*, Lessing poses the task one more time. Watkins is by then tenuously balanced midway between the two extremes of his being: the vivid experience of wholeness in its several formulations, and the urgings of his contemporaries to resume his former social identity. He is convinced that he must "remember" something that is crucial to his psychic survival, but what he must remember—the reality of unity—is antithetical to what the doctors urge him to remember—the split identity he has vacated. For a time he preserves his suspension between the two, sharing his intermediate state with a young patient named Violet Stoke. To her he describes the discrepancy in his condition as he and the doctors perceive it: "'They say I lost my memory because

I feel guilty. . . . I think I feel guilty because I lost my memory'"
(p. 287). Violet's status as a girl who does not want to grow up
emphasizes the ambiguity of Watkins's condition.

In this context, one theory of schizophrenia suggests that the
condition is the individual's response to "paradox intolerance,"
particularly as embodied in the antithetical emotions of love and
aggression. Because of the pressure of those conflicting experiences, he seeks a "personal paradise": "a hypothetical life situation where each person can creatively express himself openly,
directly, and honestly, and come to fulfillment without double-
binds, games, hidden agendas, and complexes. . . . [T]he person
who ends up with the appellation 'schizophrenic' is in some way
more imbued with the need to find that paradise for himself, that
is, he not only needs to, but has to. Such an archetype is more
central to his being. . . ."[33] Mircea Eliade describes the ambivalence inherent in the desire for paradise within the sacred context,
noting that "on the one side, man is haunted by the desire to
escape from his particular situation and regain a transpersonal
mode of life; on the other, he is paralyzed by the fear of losing
his 'identity' and 'forgetting' himself."[34] Man must leave Eden in
order to grow—but he may spend the rest of his life trying to return to it. The nostalgia for wholeness is his oldest memory, for
unity is located, symbolically, at both the beginning and the end of
consciousness.

Watkins submits to shock treatment in the hope that it may help
him to remember the truth that hovers like a shadow on the edge
of his awareness. His final insight before the shock treatment is
his explanation to Violet of the phenomenon of timing at work in
the level of human evolution and change:

> "It's desperately urgent that I should remember, I do know that.
> It's all timing, you see. . . . There are lots of things in our ordinary
> life that are—shadows. Like coincidences, or dreaming, the kinds of
> things that are an angle to ordinary life. . . . The important thing is
> this—to remember that some things reach out to us from that level
> of living, to here . . . all these things, they have a meaning, they are
> reflections from that other part of ourselves, and that part of our-
> selves knows things we don't know. . . . [W]hat I have to remember
> has to do with time running out." (Pp. 301–2)

193

As Neumann has observed, in mythology the sense of other-worldly knowledge that must be remembered "is usually projected into a knowledge acquired before birth or after death. . . . Man's task in the world is to remember with his conscious mind what was knowledge before the advent of consciousness."[35]

In Watkins's long explanation to Violet, Lessing distills a number of the ideas that appear in various forms throughout the novel. In fact, their recapitulation in this segment comes precariously close to didactic excess, given the more inventive shapings of the same ideas earlier in the novel. The "message" intrudes uncomfortably upon the narrative design, and belies the occasional tension in Lessing's work between aesthetic and ideological concerns.

Despite Watkins's various illuminations, the ultimate prognosis is negative; time runs out for him as medical science pre-empts his personal struggle to remember wholeness. The shock treatment works with rather than against the split in his personality, and the amnesia of his earlier life merely reverses itself and becomes an amnesia of his inner journey. Watkins leaves the hospital, presumably fully recovered but in fact as split as before. His wife and friends confirm the Watkins they had known before his breakdown. The tragedy of his medical "cure" is that he has recovered his former identity only to lose, once again, the meaning of his journey.

However, in this novel Lessing suggests that the fault lies not with his choices but with the establishment itself, for its endorsement of that very state of separateness and inner division as the norm. R. D. Laing has enjoined, "Can we not see that *this voyage* [into the self] *is not what we need to be cured of but that it is itself a natural way of healing our own appalling state of alienation called normality?*"[36] Lessing somewhat more pessimistically implies that in society as it is presently constituted, abnormal consciousness is a mixed blessing, for the self cannot exist without reference to a world. If Watkins reflects the schizophrenia of contemporary life, the cure is no better than the disease. Ultimately failing to overcome his self-division, he hovers in the perilous straits between inner illumination and the external manifestations often identified as psychosis, with no certainty as to which is "real," since the definition of reality is established by consensus. By the latter standard, the effort to relinquish the personal ego in order to embrace transcendence is a pathological one. What distinguishes between the schizophrenic and the mystic or enlightened individual, as Lessing has already suggested, is partly the capacity of unique personality to harmonize its own dissonant elements and partly the judgment of the orthodox establishment that labels it.

John Vernon has postulated that Western tradition is fundamentally "schizophrenic" in its very conceptualization of what is "real." The intrinsic dualism of logical thought shapes perception at such a basic level that not only are the patterns discerned in experience split into opposing categories (real/unreal, sane/insane, and so on), but these splits in turn create the further dichotomies in the perception of separation between the self and the world.[37] Accordingly, the politicization of madness leads to the logical paradoxes of either the sanity of insanity, in the form of a retreat into a privately meaningful but ultimately solipsistic awareness, or the insanity of sanity, in the form of capitulation to the division endemic in contemporary life. Both are "schizophrenic," for "each mode of being, the real and the fantastic, the sane and the insane, excludes the other, and each is intolerable because of that exclusion."[38]

Lessing's increasing use of paradox, symbolic imagery, and nonlogical frames of reference indicates her attempt to formulate an imaginative way around that logical contradiction. Though the reduction in scope, diversity of characters and events, and density of language (in contrast to the earlier major novels) result in a more schematic work of fiction with occasional stylistic lapses, *Briefing for a Descent into Hell* as a whole is an innovative and effective fusion of form with idea. The suspension between realism and fantasy retains both the metaphysical and formal ambiguity of the whole—a narrative strategy that allies the author with others for whom the "open" ending is the only way to express the uncertainties inherent in the subjective or confessional mode. One thinks of Dostoevsky's divided antihero in *Notes from Underground*, as well as of more contemporary fictions by John Barth, Anthony Burgess, William Golding, Kurt Vonnegut, Thomas Pynchon, and others who have departed from strict representational narrative, adapting conventions from fable, romance, and speculative fiction in order to render "glimmers of a reality hidden from us by our present set of preconceptions."[39] The ambiguous tension between realism and myth, between division and unity, remains the central dynamic of Lessing's fiction. As insistently as her protagonists seek forms of consciousness that can accommodate contradiction and embrace the moment of transcendence, Lessing seeks fictional resolutions of the antinomies erected by the mind itself.

NOTES

1. Lynn Sukenick hypothesizes that, though "*Briefing* may feature a man's consciousness simply as a preference of imagination [one] suspects . . . that a man was chosen in order to give madness its fullest due and its deepest persuasion: the fact that women are more often considered irrational would give a conventional taint to a disordered female and rob madness of the novel authority it possesses in *Briefing*." She adds that in this novel and the preceding one, "sexuality and gender begin to fade into a transcendent condition and are greatly reduced in stature under pressure of a higher androgynous knowledge." See "Feeling and Reason in Doris Lessing's Fiction," in *Doris Lessing: Critical Essays*, ed. Annis Pratt and L. S. Dembo (Madison: University of Wisconsin Press, 1974), p. 116.

2. From letter from Doris Lessing to Roberta Rubenstein dated 28 Mar. 1977. See Lessing's further comments on madness and on psychoanalysis from the same letter on pp. 80 and 110–11, n. 14, above, and compare with her Stony Brook interview, quoted on pp. 147–48 above.

3. Lessing, *Briefing for a Descent into Hell* (New York: Alfred A. Knopf, 1971), frontispiece (this statement does not appear in the paperback edition of the novel). Subsequent page references will be indicated in the text.

4. Northrop Frye, *The Secular Scripture* (Cambridge, Mass., and London: Harvard University Press, 1976), p. 102.

5. That journey is described in R. D. Laing's *The Politics of Experience and The Bird of Paradise* (1967; rpt. Middlesex, England: Penguin Books, 1970), pp. 120–37. Elsewhere I have identified a number of parallels between Charles and Jesse Watkins's journeys. See Roberta Rubenstein, "Briefing on Inner Space: Doris Lessing and R. D. Laing," *Psychoanalytic Review* 63, no. 1 (1976), 83–93. Marion Vlastos discusses similar, and additional, parallels in her comprehensive analysis of the correspondences between Lessing's and Laing's views of madness and the psychotic experience, in "Doris Lessing and R. D. Laing: Psychopolitics and Prophecy," *PMLA* 91, no. 2 (1976), 245–58.

6. Laing, *Politics of Experience*, p. 104.

7. Without directly acknowledging the origin or degree of her own familiarity with Laing's work, Lessing has identified him as "a peg" upon which intellectuals have hung their need for "a key authority figure who will then act as a law giver. Laing became that figure." From Lessing's lecture at the New School for Social Research, quoted by Nancy Shields Hardin in "Doris Lessing and the Sufi Way," in *Doris Lessing*, ed. Pratt and Dembo, pp. 154–55.

Moreover, in personal correspondence to me—in response to my suggestion of the strong parallels between her novel and Laing's work—Lessing wrote, "I had not taken Laing as my starting point. I had not read the piece in question by him, or the book *Politics of Experience*.

"My book was written out of my own thoughts, not other people's.

". . . It seems almost impossible for people to grasp that people can write from their own experience.

"As for the name Watkins, being used: I took the name out of the telephone book, which is my usual practice . . . [because of British libel laws]. I always use the commonest name I can find. . . ." From Letter to Roberta Rubenstein dated 17 Nov. 1972.

8. Campbell, "Mythology and Schizophrenia," in *Myths to Live By* (New York: Viking, 1972), pp. 202–3.

9. Frye, *Secular Scripture*, p. 58.

10. Nasrollah S. Fatemi, "A Message and Method of Love, Harmony, and Brotherhood," in *Sufi Studies: East and West*, ed. L. F. Rushbrook Williams (New York: E. P. Dutton, 1973), p. 59.

11. A particularly striking documentation and synthesis of these several approaches, in which states of altered consciousness are induced with the psycholytic drug LSD, are given in the study by Stanislav Grof, M.D., *Realms of the Human Unconscious* (New York: Viking, 1975). Robert E. L. Masters and Jean Houston, *The Varieties of Psychedelic Experience* (New York: Holt, Rinehart and Winston, 1966), and John White, ed., *The Highest State of Consciousness*, 2nd ed. (New York: Doubleday, 1972), bring together a wide cross-section of information on the same broad topic.

12. In an excellent analysis of the themes and patterns of the novel, Robert S. Ryf has similarly described the circle motif as both a structural and a thematic organization within the work. See "Beyond Ideology: Doris Lessing's Mature Vision," *Modern Fiction Studies* 16, no. 3 (1975), 193–204.

13. Rumi, *Couplets of Inner Meaning: Tales from the Masnavi*, trans. A. J. Arberry (London: Murray, 1961), cited by William Foster in "Sufi Studies Today," in *The Elephant in the Dark*, ed. Leonard Lewin (1972; rpt. New York: E. P. Dutton, 1976), p. 127.

Erich Neumann has described the imagery of the parallel courses of the evolution of consciousness in psychodynamic terms: "The fact that the dawn of consciousness and the creation of the world are parallel processes which throw up the same symbolism indicates that the world actually 'exists' only to the degree that it is cognized by an ego. A differentiated world is the reflection of a self-differentiating consciousness." See *The Origins and History of Consciousness*, trans. R. F. C. Hull, Bollingen Series XLII (Princeton, N.J.: Princeton University Press, 1954), p. 329.

14. See Mircea Eliade, *Patterns in Comparative Religion*, trans. Rosemary Sheed (1958; rpt. New York: New American Library, 1963), pp. 157–60.

15. Marie-Louise von Franz, "The Process of Individuation," in C. G. Jung et al., *Man and His Symbols* (1964; rpt. New York: Dell, 1970), p. 221. See also p. 112, n. 33.

16. Cited in Idries Shah, *The Sufis* (1964; rpt. New York: Doubleday, 1971), pp. 122–23.

17. Frye, *Secular Scripture*, pp. 129, 140.

18. Underhill, *Mysticism* (1910; rpt. New York: E. P. Dutton, 1930), p. 195.

19. Shah, *The Sufis*, p. 142.

20. Quoted in Hardin, "Doris Lessing and the Sufi Way," p. 148.

21. Ibid., p. 153.

22. In his incisive analysis of the structure of science fiction, Robert Scholes suggests that "all future projection is obviously model-making, poiesis not mimesis. And freed of the problem of correspondence or noncorrespondence with some present actuality or some previously experienced past . . . the imagination can function without self-deception as to its means and ends. Projections can be held tightly to a line of greatest probability, extrapolating from perceptions of current reality according to current notions of what is probable. But it is also possible to project more freely, discarding as many current notions as possible, or accepting as likely things that now seem unlikely." See *Structural Fabulation* (Notre Dame and London: University of Notre Dame Press, 1975), p. 18.

23. In his survey of a variety of occult systems of belief, Colin Wilson observes that many esoteric religious traditions presume an element of amnesia, implying that "life is basically some kind of game, whose pre-condition is that the players should suffer from amnesia, and then cope as best they can with the series of choices presented over three-quarters of a century. . . . The founder of scientology, L. Ron Hubbard, teaches that men are gods who invented the world as a game, into which they 'descended,' and then became victims of their own amnesia, so they became trapped in their game." See *The Occult* (1971; rpt. New York: Random House, 1973), p. 102.

24. Shah, *The Sufis*, p. 440.

25. In the context of psychopathology, R. D. Laing points out that "good" babies may become "good" schizophrenics, since the attributes that parents may value as "good" (passivity, conformity to parents' convenience, absence of demanding or assertive behavior) may actually prefigure existential deadness and lack of autonomy in later development. See *The Divided Self* (1960; rpt. Middlesex, England: Penguin Books, 1965), pp. 182–88.

26. The same reversal of meaning of sleep and waking is prominent in certain esoteric traditions. The Russian mystic Gurdjieff (whose teachings derive from Sufism) emphasized that man is typically asleep; only diligent "self-remembering" elevates consciousness to a true waking state. See Kenneth Walker, *A Study of Gurdjieff's Teaching* (1957; rpt. London: Jonathan Cape, 1965), pp. 35 and following.

27. "Doris Lessing at Stony Brook: An Interview by Jonah Raskin" (1969), in *A Small Personal Voice*, ed. Paul Schlueter (New York: Alfred A. Knopf, 1974), pp. 58, 66.

28. Grof, *Realms of the Human Unconscious*, pp. 102–7.

29. Laing, *The Divided Self*, p. 27.

30. In correspondence to me, Doris Lessing wrote, "If I sounded cross about [the Laing matter] [see earlier letter, quoted in n. 7 above] it was because I've had Laing too much—not that I don't admire him for his battles with the British Establishment, which as we all know, is as stuffy a medical citadel as any anywhere.

"It has been my experience again and again—and also that of other writers—that you have only to write something and what you write starts coming true in all kinds of direct and indirect ways. It is as if you bring something towards you if you imagine it and then write it. My new novel [*The Summer before the Dark*], coming out in spring, isn't even in print, and already it starts, the coincidences and the correspondences." From Letter to Roberta Rubenstein dated 31 Dec. 1972.

More recently, Lessing has reiterated, "My view of Laing is that at an appropriate time in Britain, he challenged certain extreme rigidities in psychiatry with alternative viewpoints, and made other attitudes than the official ones possible. That is what he did. No more and no less.

"There was a certain atmosphere abroad in the late fifties and sixties—I mean, of course, unofficially—to do with mental illness. Laing was only part of a much wider movement." From Letter to Roberta Rubenstein dated 28 Mar. 1977.

31. Boisen, *The Exploration of the Inner World* (New York: Harper and Brothers, 1936 [1962]), pp. 59–60, 82.

32. As Frye observes, "Romance . . . begins an upward journey toward man's recovery of what he projects as sacred myth. At the bottom of the mythological universe is a death and a rebirth process which cares nothing for the individual; at the top is the individual's regained identity. At the bottom is a memory which can only be returned to, a closed circle of recurrence; at the top is the recreation of memory." See *Secular Scripture*, p. 183.

33. Arthur Burton, "The Alchemy of Schizophrenia," in Burton et al., *Schizophrenia as a Lifestyle* (New York: Springer Publishing Co., 1974), pp. 65–66.

34. Eliade, *Mephistopheles and the Androgyne: Studies in Religious Myth and Symbol*, trans. J. M. Cohen (New York: Sheed and Ward, 1965), p. 123.

35. Neumann, *Origins*, pp. 23, 24.

36. Laing, *Politics of Experience*, p. 136, emphasis in original.

37. Vernon, *The Garden and the Map: Schizophrenia in Twentieth-Century Literature and Culture* (Urbana: University of Illinois Press, 1973), pp. ix–xi and 3–28.

38. Ibid., p. xi.

39. Scholes, *Structural Fabulation*, p. 18.

8

The Summer before the Dark

Though *Briefing for a Descent into Hell* concludes, temporarily at least, the author's central preoccupation with schizophrenia as a metaphor for the radical self-divisions of contemporary life, Lessing's concern with the potentialities and forms of consciousness in its progress toward wholeness continues to occupy the central place in her fiction. Her next novel extends the exploration of psychic geography through the now characteristic motivation of her female characters to break free of the life-roles and values they had earlier chosen when these prove inadequate for further inner growth.

The bridge between *Briefing for a Descent into Hell* and *The Summer before the Dark* is the novella entitled "The Temptation of Jack Orkney," which was published chronologically between them.[1] The main character, Jack Orkney, like Charles Watkins, is a professional man (an ex-journalist) who finds himself undergoing a change in consciousness. Temporarily adrift between careers and confronted with his father's imminent death and his wife's and children's increasing independence, he recognizes that he has been in a state of depression for some time. His father's death becomes a catalyst for Orkney's discovery of his own fear of dying and his deeper spiritual drift—the "temptation" of inertia. Unlike Watkins, however, Orkney does not suffer from an acute psychic split. Instead, he finds himself in the middle of a kind of stock-taking of his past which ultimately leads him into his inner self along a less precipitous route. From fear of the dreams that he begins to remember in which he dies with his father, he gradually comes to "hear" the messages from his unconscious self as a gift, a guide to further growth.

In his gentle initiation into the resources of the underside of consciousness he had never known before, Orkney prefigures Lessing's next protagonist, Kate Brown. The process of psychic integration as the author now envisions it requires and is facilitated not by a radical self-division but by a state of receptivity. Age itself carries with it certain advances in readiness which may meld the divisions within the self in a less traumatic manner than through crises like those experienced by Lessing's earlier characters. It is almost as if the more shattering confrontations within the psyche resulting from fragmentation and mental trauma (Mary Turner, Anna Wulf, Thomas Stern, Lynda Coldridge, Charles Watkins) or from ambitious forays into the psychic depths (Martha Quest) have subsided into a more natural state of alert anticipation. Still, Lessing mourns (through Orkney) the necessity for this process to have to be repeated anew by each individual. The aspect of abnormal consciousness originally manifested in Lessing's characters through madness and acute inner schism gives way to what is more recognizable as "normal" consciousness— though far from ordinary in its untypically high degree of sensitivity, synthesis, and integration.

Jung identifies the unfolding of the potentialities of the consciousness in the second half of life as analogous to the course of the sun—which "after having lavished its light upon the world . . . withdraws its rays in order to illumine itself."[2] It is this pattern that shapes the central movement in Lessing's later fiction, not only in the failed attempt of Charles Watkins to recover his real center of being (and in the more tentatively successful attempt of Jack Orkney) but in the extended psychic journey of Kate Brown in the novel significantly entitled *The Summer before the Dark*.

Like both Charles Watkins and Jack Orkey, Kate Brown is middle-aged and, at the novel's outset, unaware that she is on the verge of a shift in her life preoccupations and identity. The quarter of a century she has invested in the care and well-being of her family—a successful neurologist husband and four children currently in various stages of late adolescence—has shaped her personality along the easily identified roles of supportive wife and nurturing mother. In fact, they have so completely defined her that the "summer before the dark" is her first opportunity to separate herself from her family and to confront the self that exists beneath those roles. Unlike the Martha Quest of *The Four-Gated City* at the same age, Kate Brown has never deliberated over who or what she is, once the initial choice of marriage propelled her into its inevitable string of consequences. It is almost as if Lessing had returned to reconsider the young Martha Quest before she had broken out of those roles as wife and mother, projecting her life and imagining the state of consciousness and identity she would have twenty years later. As in those early volumes of *Children of Violence*, the protagonist of *The Summer before the Dark* has been shaped by biological and societal forces; much of the novel concerns her gradual recognition of the degree to which they have determined her character. The author's implication, even more pronounced in the later novels, is that the nuclear family is an unviable social form that competes with, rather than promotes, the growth of the inner self.

In *The Summer before the Dark* the dual focus that runs throughout Lessing's work assumes yet another form, comparable to the inner/outer or romantic/realistic narrative lines of *Briefing for a Descent into Hell*. Rather than emphasizing the irreconcilability of these two modes of experience, however, this novel describes their gradual alignment and convergence. Less self-divided than Charles Watkins, Kate Brown still traverses both a geographical and psychological circle during the course of the novel, a journey generated by the changes taking place in the biological cycle of her being. What happens on the surface in her experience of her own aging is refracted in her deeper self until (unlike Watkins) she gradually synthesizes them. The dark side of the personality at this stage is not the self-hater or the "inner enemy," as it is for Lessing's younger protagonists, but the changing biological self as it affects and reflects consciousness.

The first sentence of *The Summer before the Dark*—"A woman stood on her back step, arms folded, waiting"—becomes a clue to the protagonist's psychic state.[3] Though this opening description is amended to include the fact that Kate Brown is waiting for the kettle to boil, the rest of the novel reveals that it is her state of psychological anticipation that shapes the novel's meaning. For three years, since a family confrontation in which her youngest son (then sixteen) had accused her of smothering him, Kate has felt the gnawing sense that she must reflect on her domestic life. But she resists that impulse; only when external events propel her into a new situation does she slowly confront its necessity. Lessing dispatches the plot rather quickly to convey her protagonist to that point: Kate's husband is about to depart for the United States for a summer lecturing commitment, her four children have made diverse travel arrangements, and Kate herself is persuaded to take on a temporary job as a simultaneous translator as a favor to one of her husband's friends. Ironically, what has been most characteristic of her life, her "passivity, adaptability to others" (p. 22), sweeps her into a series of choices through which she acknowledges those elements of her personality and gains more control over her own identity.

Kate's journey begins with her new job translating Portuguese into English at an international conference on coffee in London. The first sign of change is her outer appearance, as she refurbishes her hair and clothing to reflect the new professional role she has assumed. For the first time she is conscious that her real self is an invisible core, while her public self is actually a fluid mask or image (like the Jungian persona) that can be almost arbitrarily manipulated to create a variety of "identities." The narrator's observations on the public female roles—such as that of the airline stewardess who is employed partly as an anonymous "love supplier" (p. 61)—are especially trenchant.

At the same time Kate discovers that her expertise as a translator is only part of her success in the new job; her employer begs her to stay because she fulfills an equally important, though unconscious, need as an organizer, a "tribal mother" (p. 51). The overt role she plays is analogous to her actual external appearance; underneath, analogous to her true self, are the covert needs she satisfies because she is "unable to switch herself out of the role of provider of invisible manna, consolation, warmth, 'sympathy'" (p. 52). That role of the maternal figure is a central and ambivalent one throughout Lessing's fiction, representing as it does the focus for often irreconcilable alternatives between biology and ideology, freedom and responsibility. Those conflicts are most thoroughly examined in Martha Quest's deep antipathy toward her own mother, her own early rejection of the maternal role herself, and her later resumption of it as surrogate mother in the Coldridge household. By that latter stage Martha is far more conscious of her own deeper self, and is able to live out the demands of the nurturing role with a strong sense of the "true" Martha Quest beneath it.

The same conflict is dramatized in Anna Wulf's split between the demands of mother and mistress and her unconscious and inappropriate assumption of the former role in her relationships with men. The destructive mother pattern is also implicit in the sterile childlessness of Mary Turner, who infantilizes first her husband and then Moses (*The Grass Is Singing*); in Julia Barr's efforts at mothering (and dominating) Jan Brod before she retreats to a safe and conventional marriage (*Retreat to Innocence*); even in Charles Watkins's desertion of his family obligations during his mid-life crisis (*Briefing for a Descent into Hell*). By contrast, Lessing's few sympathetic male characters—Jan Brod, Thomas Stern, Mark Coldridge, Francis Coldridge—are nurturers. In *The Summer before the Dark* Kate Brown's task for the summer becomes the delineation of an inner self that is not identical with the maternal role she has lived for so long. Her job, in providing a temporary rearrangement of her external circumstances, enables her to see herself from a fresh perspective.

The only one of Lessing's novels with cued chapter titles, this novel is divided into five sections: "At Home," "Global Food," "The Holiday," "The Hotel," and "Maureen's Flat." As in several of the preceding works, rooms and locations are analogues of psychic configurations. One of Kate's first discomforts in accepting the temporary job is her family's casual dispatch of the house for the summer. "The point was, she was feeling dismissed, belittled, because the problem of the house was being considered so unimportant" (p. 22). As the center of its activities, Kate is most closely identified with the house and unconsciously feels its unimportance as her own. Her concern with it assumes a deeper meaning in view of the intervening rooms she occupies before she returns to it, transformed, at the end of the summer.

Once separated from her home and family, Kate's awareness of her inner situation begins to surface, in the hotel room where she stays while working for the conference: "In her room, before going to sleep, she looked at its neatness, its indifference to her, and thought that yes, this was much better than her large family house . . . full, crammed, jostling with objects every one of which had associations, histories, belonged to this person or that, mattered, were important. This small box of a room, that had in it a bed, a chair, a chest of drawers, a mirror—yes, this is what she would choose, if she could choose . . ." (p. 34). Kate still feels that she does *not* choose where she "lives," though already she has begun the process of simplification symbolized by the new room.[4] Temporarily relieved of the responsibility of her large household, she can direct her psychic energy toward stripping away the clutter of her past, the elements of her self that are outworn and no longer viable.

That process is developed in *The Summer before the Dark* through the form of the extended interior journey—by now the central narrative event in Lessing's fiction—conveyed through a series of dreams on a recurring theme. Throughout Lessing's work dreams function prominently as a narrative device for presenting condensed images of psychological and thematic issues, particularly as they work themselves into the protagonists' awareness. In this novel they occupy the crucial symbolic level of the narrative, providing a running commentary on the more literal events of Kate's experience. Though Kate feels she has "always been on good terms with her dreams, had always been alert to learn from them" (p. 142), the dreams of this summer take on a special significance. They are "her business for this time in her life" (p. 143), as crucial, she later comes to realize, as the social plane of her life. The dreams recast and eventually overtake her external itinerary, as she moves (circularly) from her country home to London, to Turkey, to Spain, and north again to London and then home. As the narrative, and Kate's self-reflection, progress, she realizes that the dream was "feeding off my daytime life" (p. 230), providing a way for her to examine and ultimately reconcile her inner self with the life script in which she is imbedded.

Significantly, her first dream takes place immediately after she imagines her more appropriate room. Like those that follow, this dream concerns Kate's involvement with a dying seal struggling to get back to water. At various times the seal languishes near death, and it grows progressively heavier, but Kate never doubts that it is her "responsibility"; her only doubt is whether she is traveling in the right direction with it. Metaphorically, the seal is her own inner self, dying from lack of sustenance—landlocked like the younger Martha Quest.

On the external or literal plane of events, Kate goes to Turkey to function in the same capacity as she had at the London convention, as translator and "organizer" at another international conference. The subject of this meeting is food, an ironic one in view of Kate's own psychic starvation. Moreover, her job parallels her private task: to translate and organize what is happening to her through the language of what is happening within her. Though she indulges herself in the benefits of her position, both financial and intangible, she knows in another part of herself that what she should do is return to London and find a room where she can reflect on things alone. Eventually she does just that; the intervening weeks of her summer journey ultimately lead her to the same location in herself, for they accelerate a process that is already inevitable.

Once the novelty of her new professional status wears off, she gives more attention to her own past, including the recent three years since the domestic crisis that had so jarred her. In refusing to face the implications of her family's increasing independence, she has clung to an outdated role that no longer sustains her. Slowly she acknowledges that "the picture or image of herself as the warm centre of the family, the source of invisible emanations like a queen termite, was two or three years out of date. (Was there something wrong with her memory perhaps? It was seeming more and more as if she had several sets of memory, each contradicting the others.) The truth was that she had been starved for two years, three, more—at any rate, since the children had grown up" (p. 59). At the same time her dream of the seal demands that she focus on the aspect of herself she has allowed to lie fallow: her responsibility for the self that exists beneath her relationships with other people.

Though in her seal dream Kate must travel north toward cold and darkness, her external itinerary takes her south from Turkey to Spain with a young man named Jeffrey Merton. Their liaison is almost a parody of an older woman's fling with an attractive younger man, for it transmogrifies rapidly from a sexual to a nurturing relationship when Jeffrey develops a fever and Kate reverts to her familiar role of protective maternal figure. She sees her tendency toward excessive adaptability more clearly with Jeffrey than she has been able to discover in her more habitual family relationships, recognizing it for the first time not as a virtue but as "a form of dementia" (p. 103) in which her own needs are subordinated to those of others. Like Martha Quest, who discovers that certain life stages are in fact archetypal roles that one assumes, grows through, and ultimately discards, Kate Brown identifies the constraints to her own growth imposed by her facile acceptance of her roles as a wife and mother.

At the same time, she questions the issue of sexuality, refracted both in her relationship with Jeffrey and in her friendship with her neighbor Mary Finchley, who appears frequently in her daydreams. She wonders "what Mary meant to her, what she was standing for" (p. 104). Later Kate decides that it is Mary's indifference to social norms of behavior and her lack of guilt in engaging in casual marital infidelities—violations of the roles Kate enacts so scrupulously—that focus both her envy and her anxiety. Though traveling with a younger man may appear to others as a sexual fling, for Kate its real significance lies in the opportunity it gives her to reflect on her own sexuality.

> For it was seeming to her more and more (because of this sexuality, something displaced, like an organ lifted out of her body and laid by her side to look at, like a deformed child without function or future or purpose) as if she were just coming around from a spell of madness that had lasted all the years since that point in early adolescence when her nature had demanded she must get herself a man (she had put it romantically then of course) until recently, when the drug had begun to wear off. All those years were now seeming a betrayal of what she really was. While her body, her needs, her emotions—all of herself—had been turning like a sunflower after one man, all that time she had been holding in her

hands something else, the something precious, offering it in vain to her husband, to her children, to everyone she knew—but it had never been taken, had not been noticed. But this thing she had offered, without knowing she was doing it, which had been ignored by herself and by everyone else, was what was real in her. (P. 140)

The seal dream provides a running counterpoint to these recognitions, and emphasizes the degree to which they are first formulated on a deeper psychic stratum and then integrated into Kate's conscious awareness. While watching over Jeffrey, she dreams of taking the seal to an abandoned house which she must prepare for the winter. Her lover, "a tall fair young man with blue eyes," is in the house and desires her, but she rejects his entreaties, apologizing that she "must take the seal to the sea first" (p. 113). In finding her new bearings in the stage of middle age, with its implicit advance toward death, she must attend to her spirit before she can indulge her body. The *rite de passage* in which Kate Brown is engaged is the shedding of desire or, at least, the harmonizing of the material and spiritual aspects of her being.

This pressure makes any sexual relationship with Jeffrey Merton impossible. In fact, in many ways he functions in the narrative as the external projection of her psychic dilemma. Like the seal, he is weak, dehydrated (by fever), and dependent on her nurturance as they travel northward. Lessing makes the displacement explicit in several places. Once, after urging Jeffrey to drink quantities of water, Kate collapses in fatigue; concurrently, in her dream the "inner tutor" presents the heavy seal, "still damp from the water she had put on it" at the wooden bath house (p. 133).

Jeffrey's illness allows Kate to view not only the reorientation of her sexuality (part of her burden) but her own psychic crisis more clearly. She suspects that his illness is partly a "spiritual crisis" (p. 132) generated by an inner conflict (in his case, whether to be a lawyer or a vagabond) comparable to her own: a form of opting out" (p. 125) of the contrary pulls of responsibility and freedom, or social role and inner integrity. Consistent with the particular imagery of this novel, in which physical processes are manifestations of psychological changes and vice versa, inner conflict is expressed through physical rather than mental breakdown: "There is a temperature or a cold or a lowering of vitality that merits a doctor's visit and some days in bed, but the point is the days in bed. Why, [Kate] used the evasion herself, quite consciously, when life got too much of a good thing. It is a state of affairs like winter for the earth: it feels as if all heat has retreated inwards, the fire is deeply hidden under rock, the sun is too far away" (p. 126). One recalls Martha Quest's occasional fevers and periods of torpor, which are in fact physiological expressions of psychological turmoil.

Kate's defense of illness as an occasionally necessary form of escape foreshadows her own temporary retreat; as she ministers to Jeffrey's fever the advancing chill in herself becomes alarmingly oppressive. In Spain she anxiously observes women who appear physically aged who are probably no older than she. The sun is so dazzling that she prefers dusk or moonlight, when it is both cooler and darker, and when her consciousness can flow more easily from daydream into dream and back again. Her direction in the seal dreams is always north, toward darkness and cold. When the chill of her dreams produces snow, Kate senses that she must reach the sea soon or both she and the animal will die. Her travels inland with Jeffrey are both literally and symbolically taking her in the wrong direction—away from the sea, and from herself. Thus, abandoning Jeffrey in Spain, she symbolically sheds her nurturer role and returns (north) to England to experience her own illness without distraction.

Consistent with the imagery through which Lessing has signaled various psychic configurations in her protagonists' consciousness, Kate takes a room in a London hotel like the one she had temporarily occupied earlier in the summer, "the size of the smallest bedroom in her home" (p. 152). Now relieved not only of the family house she has figuratively carried around for years but also of her "tribal mother" role, Kate has simplified herself sufficiently for the inner retreat she had been resisting for months.

As she enters her own private room completely, the perspective of abnormal consciousness takes over. Her illness lasts for several weeks, during which the seal dream becomes the foreground of her reality and the progress of her physical devitalization its hazy background. The dream is populated by some of the same now admittedly mythical figures she has encountered before, including the fair young king. The latter's attention, followed by what Kate experiences as his rejection of her for other (younger) women, gives form to her anxieties about losing her sexual attractiveness

as a corollary of the process of aging and of shedding her outworn personas. This segment of the dream also expresses her emotional dependence on her husband, and her fear of his possible
infidelity.

The inner landscape becomes even more severe, reflecting the
urgency of Kate's task; the seal, temporarily neglected, hovers
near death, and she must resume her northward trek. Her appearance mirrors the rigors of her journey, as she strips off the physical
and psychological trappings of her mother-wife image and (for
the remainder of the novel) tries on other images that will express
her evolving self more authentically. She loses weight, and the gray
of her hair roots creeps through the red tint. Her outer appearance
is thus a physical manifestation of that inner process of change.
As Lessing has explained elsewhere, an attractive young woman
"finds it very hard to separate what she really is from her appearance. Because you only begin to discover the difference between what you really are, your real self, and your appearance
when you get a bit older which is the most fascinating experience
. . . . It's one of the most valuable experiences I personally ever
had. A whole dimension of life suddenly slides away and you realize
that what in fact you've been using to get attention has been
what you look like."[5]

Thus physically changed, Kate returns for a covert visit to her
house, curious to see it "when tenanted by other people. It would
be like looking in at her own life" (p. 162). Not only does her
friend Mary Finchley not recognize Kate (to her annoyance and
then delight), but she finds herself strangely detached from the
house "in which she had lived for nearly a quarter of a century"
(p. 163)—a long way from her identification with it at the beginning of the summer.

Back in London, Kate attends a theatrical performance of Turgenev's *A Month in the Country*, during which her altered mental
state comes closest to the form of abnormal consciousness dramatized in Lessing's earlier fiction. The play, which Kate had chosen
at random in order to "see people dressed up in personalities not
their own" (p. 168), initially recalls her own circumstances, for
"the household of Natalia Petrovna was very like her own" (p.
170). More obliquely, the play itself concerns an older married
woman's ambivalent flirtation with a younger man as a diversion

from the incipient stagnation of her own life. The exaggerated situation of the theater itself—actors playing roles as other people —amplifies Kate's own psychic turmoil. She behaves eccentrically, talking back to the actors on the stage in irritation at the self-deceptions they enact both as actors playing roles and as the particular *dramatis personae* whose identities are being projected.

Significantly, Lessing's own narrative position, like that of her protagonist, is one of ironic distance and detachment from what she describes. Whereas the most subjective passages describing abnormal consciousness in the earlier novels sustain the illusion of unmediated direct experience, passages in this novel observe, rather than render, the perceptions themselves. The very moderation of perspective occasionally vitiates the impact of events described by the narrator, for the ironic tone produces a kind of emotional flatness, reducing the sense of intensity or immediacy one comes to expect in Lessing's fiction.

Even in her somewhat dissociated state, Kate realizes that her behavior appears "mad" to the audience, which has come to the theater prepared to suspend disbelief and cooperate in the theatrical illusion. She has enough objectivity about her mental state to realize that "once normality had set in" (p. 176), she would again be able to appreciate the convention of theater without such distortions. But the altered focus nevertheless brings new insights to consciousness. She concludes that role-playing—a phenomenon of everyday life thrown into high relief on stage—is the real form of madness, a ritualized pretense in which the audience is also implicated. Her perception of the people around her as varieties of animals who wear and eat other animals and who attempt to disguise their own animal natures, echoes a dream image in which Kate struggles to rescue her seal from an arena of wild beasts. Her effort to understand her physical being becomes not just a sexual redefinition but one involving her entire corporeal reality. Her own physical nature is part of the animal self that she must accommodate, including the fact that the body ages and eventually dies. The disguises must be shed in order to confront directly the reality they conceal.

The final movement in Kate's journey takes place in still another room, this time in a chilly basement flat that faces north: her external room amplifies even more explicitly the state of her own psyche. "The room was small, and had in it a narrow bed and a cupboard. It was many degrees colder than the front of the flat, which was on the south. This room had a chill on it that connected with the cold that lay permanently around Kate's stomach" (p. 183). Her roommate is a young girl named Maureen, whose preference for baby food expresses her ambivalence about growing up to assume the adult role of a married woman; she is the "before" to Kate Brown's "after," also symbolizing (like Violet Stoke for Charles Watkins) the inner child Kate must leave behind. That aspect of her relationship to Maureen gains further significance in light of the reflections Kate makes (at the beginning of the novel) concerning the way crucial life experiences are often simplified in cliché expressions:

> for towards the crucial experiences custom allots certain attitudes, and they are pretty stereotyped. *Ah yes, first love! . . . Growing up is bound to be painful! . . . My first child, you know . . . But I was in love! . . . Marriage is a compromise. . . . I am not as young as I once was. . . .* You have to deduce a person's real feelings about a thing by a smile she does not know is on her face, by the way bitterness tightens muscles at a mouth's corner, or the way air is allowed to flow from the lungs after: *I wouldn't like to be a child again!* (P. 3)

The last location before Kate's return to her own family is a replay and examination of the meaning of these critical transitions themselves within the script that a woman assumes in choosing the role "wife-mother."

Kate recognizes that moving into a rented room where no one knows her is "the first time in her life that she had been alone and outside a cocoon of comfort and protection, the support of other people's recognition of what she had chosen to present" (p. 190). She takes that opportunity to experiment with the range of roles open to her outside of such expectations. Together she and Maureen explore the disparity between appearances or created images and reality, by trying on different identities for one another; they extend this serious "game" by parading different styles of clothing and bearing in front of others to gauge the effect of such external cues. At the same time Kate grapples with her relationship with Maureen in the effort to discover a form of communication that does not rely on her own habitual maternal role.

One of the truths she comes to see about herself through Maureen is the discrepancy between her adult intelligence and her small child's feelings. In serving as the center for her family's emotional life for so many years, she has lost contact with her own emotional center of being. However, this is a harsh and somewhat false dichotomy of the life alternatives Kate has chosen, as she concedes herself. Throughout the novel Lessing has portrayed Kate's marriage as an essentially successful and happy one; the tension issues not from her particular marriage but from the limitations imposed by the institution itself. Never a defender of the existing shape of conventional marriage and family patterns, Lessing critiques the often irreconcilable contradictions between the demands of the social and private spheres of experience; in her divided universe, one aspect is often gained at the expense of the other. Kate's difficult task, like that of most of Lessing's major characters, is to bring these into some sort of equilibrium or synthesis—a goal complicated by the fact that all self-examination is limited by the shifting relationships between past and present time. As Kate phrases it, "We spend our lives assessing, balancing, weighing what we think we feel . . . it's all nonsense. Long after an experience which has been experienced as this or that kind of thought, emotion, and judged at the time accordingly—well, it is seen quite differently" (p. 256). Kate herself allows for the fact that her self-judgment at this point in her life does not nullify what has gone before; its purpose is to find a balance between self-image and self, between body and psyche, and between private and societal expectations. Her reassessment of the past is a variation of Lessing's concern with its elusiveness, and of the necessity to integrate one's previous experiences into present consciousness.

Kate almost accedes to the habitual role of "tribal mother organizer" when she learns that her family is returning early, the tenants have left her house, and the household must be put to order. But Maureen's difficulties in choosing whether, and whom, to marry provide a context for Kate's reflections about her own domestic situation. In the face of Maureen's decision *not* to marry one of several suitors who offer her all of the trappings of a conventional marriage, Kate gains strength to resist the pull of habitual duty herself, and lets her family reclaim the house without her as stage-manager.

While thus putting her inner house in order, Kate feels the seal dream slipping away, though she knows she has not completed her task; "in her sleep she felt like someone a couple of yards from the centre of the maze, but no matter how she turned and tried, she could not reach it" (p. 195). Though her journey is decidedly less mystical than Martha Quest's, the image of the center or circle again conceptualizes the elusive goal of inner unity. Kate tries to revive the dream journey by relating the entire sequence to Maureen, first as if telling a fairy tale to a child and then—as Lessing makes explicit the congruence between the mythic and personal planes of the narrative—as her own story. Concurrently, in the dream the snow becomes sharp cutting ice which wounds her and the seal, and she wonders if the darkening landscape reflects something negative in her immediate circumstances.

Though Kate repudiates more and more of her past self-image, acknowledging that she "must have been mad" (p. 232) to disguise her physical aging, the dream still expresses negation, darkness, and pain. As she recalls moments from her own past for Maureen, more realizations seep in, including her discovery that Mary Finchley's achievement of freedom depends upon a total absence of guilt, the "invisible chains" (p. 249) that condition most behavior. Such freedom faces two directions, however, for the more difficult challenge is not to escape responsibility altogether but to create a lifestyle that can accommodate it. To Maureen, Kate observes, "'There are times you know when there's a sort of switch in the way I look at things—everything, my whole life since I was a girl—and I seem to myself like a raving lunatic. Love, and duty, and being in love and not being in love, and loving, and behaving well and you should and you shouldn't ask and you ought and you oughtn't. It's a disease'" (p. 252).

The shedding of what Kate comes to identify as the cages of desire and duty erected in the interest of social intercourse triggers the conclusion of her inner journey. Two more sequences of the dream cycle bring it to its resolution. First the air grows lighter and Kate finds a cherry tree blooming in the snow—symbolizing the regeneration that has taken place beneath the layer of cold and torpor in her own psyche (comparable to the psychic changes that emerge out of Martha Quest's "dormant" periods). In the final dream she finds herself walking no longer in snow but in green grass; spring is in full flower, and she reaches the sea filled with hope. She gently delivers the seal into the water and acknowledges that she has completed her task. Simultaneously she sees that "the sun was in front of her, not behind, not far far behind, under the curve of the earth, which was where it had been so long" (p. 267). Though the sun, her inner light, is restored, another light has been extinguished: "The light that is the desire to please had gone out" (p. 269).

Kate searches for a way to communicate her abandonment of her earlier accommodating personality to the family she is about to rejoin. The solution which will gather together the "little bits" of herself that are "distributed among [her] family" (p. 271) is in her physical appearance, for its corresponding alteration proclaims the redefined Kate Brown. What is symbolized is not so much her literal independence of her family—for she does not abandon her husband and children—but the more subtle integrity of the private self within the social framework. Maureen makes an almost ritual endorsement of Kate's visual statement with one of her own: she cuts off her long silken hair and fashions it into a "figure like a harvest doll" (p. 271) which she wears on her wrist at the party she gives that night. The novel concludes with Kate's unnoticed departure from Maureen's party to her home.

The Summer before the Dark thus ends not in winter darkness but in the symbolic sacrifices of autumn; Kate's assimilation of the dark side of her self, her inner life, makes it possible for her to face the inevitable darkness of older age and, eventually, death. However, while concerned with the exploration of the self and the totality of consciousness, as are its predecessors, this work approaches those concerns from a different angle of vision, one that reflects somewhat different central issues. Through her previous characters Lessing has explored various aspects of the unconventional consciousness; in each case the underlying meaning is in the relationship between mind and world, or in the disjunction between mind and body. In *The Summer before the Dark* the focus is the restoration of the relationship between mind and body, with a greater emphasis on the changes generated by the body itself. Thus the catalyst for inner discovery is not mental but physical illness. Kate Brown is subject to the very visceral discomforts of her fever; she vomits, sweats, faints, and even adds to her vocabulary the slang obscenities that refer to body functions. Moreover, she must face her changing sexuality as both a physical and a psychological alteration in her total self-image.

The physical dimension of the evolving self thus shapes the central images of the novel, as Kate's psychic transformation manifests itself in corporeal form: loss of weight; graying, frizzy hair; baggy clothes; and the more arbitrary signals of body adornment that create images for others. The dream sequence that parallels these changes is decidedly physical in its symbolism. The seal is heavy; it is wounded by ice splinters and the rocky land over which it has moved; it is helplessly crippled outside of water, its own natural element. Moreover, the psychic landscape through which Kate and the animal travel is anchored in nature and the physical world: Kate observes the temperature, the angle and degree of light or darkness, the position and direction of the sun, the seasonal variations, the need for water. If Martha Quest's consciousness evolves into the "lighter," more rarefied psychic states symbolized by air and fire, Kate Brown's evolution is firmly rooted in the elements of earth and water. Her journey culminates with the symbolic return of spring and fecundity to the barren landscape, and in the delivery of the seal to the sea.

All of these images in both the dream narrative and the surface narrative that parallels it reflect the dimension of the self that Kate Brown explores. It is as if biology overtakes psychology as the catalyst for self-discovery. Changes in consciousness concern not so much the potentially infinite possibilities of the mind as the very finite processes of the body, subject to physical limits and bounded by the certitudes of desire and mortality. As Lessing has remarked, the process of aging is "a biological thing. It's totally and absolutely impersonal. It has nothing to do with you. It really is a most salutary and fascinating experience to go through, shedding it all. Growing old is really extraordinarily interesting." [6]

Though the imagery and symbolism of *The Summer before the Dark* thus evoke the theme of change from another perspective, the novel extends and is continuous with the central "growing, point" of Lessing's concerns, dealing as it does with the transformations of consciousness as well as the relationships between perception and experience, self and others, self and self-image or persona. The interior landscape of Kate's dream is not projected outward onto the external world as an extension of consciousness; rather, it becomes the inward language of her own condition. Her insights thus come less from projections than from images readily identified as messages from her own unconscious self. Psychic realities are translated—by Kate, the simultaneous translator—into physical expressions of her total identity.

Psychologically, both the realistic and symbolic lines of the narrative suggest an affirmative revaluation of the nurturing capacity: the seal is reunited with its life element, Kate chooses to be reunited with her family. Her implied return is an important expression of her new and deeper self-definition, and an acceptance of the limits of freedom: a room has meaning only in relation to the larger structure of which it is a part. Thus to be disappointed in Kate's decision to return to the same status quo that she had vacated earlier is to misunderstand the significance of her experience and of that return. The process of inner change has resulted in an essential accommodation between the realistic demands of social responsibility (as well as the biologically inevitable process of aging) and the private romantic desire for wholeness and absence of guilt.

Kate's travels thus conclude with a less radical self-division and a more meaningful reconciliation with her world than that of the preceding novel's protagonist, Charles Watkins. Though Kate's intended visual "statement" to her family may not succeed in altering its dynamics, the change within Kate herself is the primary value of her journey. Like Anna Wulf, she reconnects herself to the same social structures that had initially prompted her self-estrangement (the circular design that shapes Lessing's fictional universe). That resolution is the path out of the dangerous solipsism and near romanticization of madness in *Briefing for a Descent into Hell*.

While the psychological validity of Kate's self-discovery and reorientation in *The Summer before the Dark* is convincing enough within the context of the integration of the private personality, the formal aspect of the work is ultimately less satisfying. Though

217

this novel is not the first of Lessing's works in which earlier pre-occupations reappear in new ways—the examination and challenge of conventional roles, the interior journey with its dream analogues—in this novel those patterns occasionally create a sense of self-imitation. One of Lessing's consistent strengths is her ability to document the actual current social history of the times as she observes them, through a strong sense of detail, event, psychological insight, dialogue, and the felt texture of social experience. These are surely present in the literal level of Kate Brown's gradual metamorphosis. Yet the persuasiveness of the private, inner dimension of those same experiences comes to depend upon the effectiveness of the symbolic imagery.

While realism or mimesis assumes the authority of the literal social context of experience, developed along a linear dimension, romance assumes the authority of the metaphorical or mythic aspects of experience, understood as part of a cyclic and archetypal process. The tension between them is an important element of Lessing's narrative design. In *The Summer before the Dark* these two dimensions of the narrative are not totally integrated. As in some of the early novels the tone occasionally wanders between earnestness and irony; we are not always certain in which sense the overtly stylized mythic images of the dream sequence are to be understood. The elements of fable and dream that have been used elsewhere with striking effect are here sometimes too transparent or schematic as vehicles of the central theme to sustain an imaginative equilibrium between the two narrative layers. Thus, as the working out of a particular idea, the artistry of the novel is less successful than its psychological truth. The temporary diminution of conception and intensity (accurately translated into Kate Brown's own psychic enervation) ultimately leads the author forward, in her next novel, to a fresher and more vital formulation of her visionary angle of perception.

NOTES

1. The collection of short stories in which this novella appears (*The Temptation of Jack Orkney and Other Stories* [New York: Alfred A. Knopf, 1972]) also includes "Report on the Threatened City," which used a more traditional science fiction framework to express some of the same concerns developed in the previous novels, including the indifference of the collective to the likelihood

of catastrophe. In it Lessing also exploits the ironic tone to describe human beings from an unemotional "alien" and cosmic point of view in which their limited vision is thrown into high relief.

2. Jung, *Modern Man in Search of a Soul*, trans. W. S. Dell and Cary F. Baynes (1933; rpt. New York: Harcourt, Brace, and World, n.d.), p. 109.

3. Lessing, *The Summer before the Dark* (New York: Alfred A. Knopf, 1973), p. 3. Subsequent page references will be indicated in the text.

4. Lessing's short story "To Room Nineteen," written ten years earlier, adumbrates the theme of a woman who periodically leaves her husband and four children to retreat to an impersonal hotel room by herself. Her self-alienation begins slowly but culminates more negatively than Kate Brown's, in the literal self-annihilation of suicide. See "To Room Nineteen," in *A Man and Two Women* (New York: Simon and Schuster, 1963).

5. Quoted by Josephine Henden, "Doris Lessing: The Phoenix 'Midst Her Fires," *Harper's Magazine* (June 1973), p. 85.

6. Ibid.

9

The Memoirs of a Survivor

Given Lessing's cyclical fictional universe, in which certain patterns inevitably recur in the structure of her novels as well as in the natural, political, social, and psychological processes they depict, one expects to find in her most recent novel some of the same issues and patterns that have become the central preoccupations of her work. What is refreshing is to find them envisioned in a new form that reveals the variety of possibilities inherent in her mythopoeic vision of reality. Lessing has called *The Memoirs of a Survivor* "an attempt at autobiography" [1]—a comment that should be taken more literarily than literally, it would appear. The novel is a kind of artistic history of the development of consciousness in her characters as well as in their creator.

As Doris Lessing herself has grown older, she has created protagonists who represent maturing people, and the access to the nonordinary consciousness becomes increasingly a function of time and readiness rather than traumatic personal upheaval. The "task" of increasing the knowledge of the self remains central, and is conceived as both a physical inevitability and a psychological goal. Whereas *The Summer before the Dark* focuses on the biological and inward dimensions of the process of maturation, *The Memoirs of a Survivor* shows the further effort to place that growth within the larger social matrix once again. And, as in the Appendix to *The Four-Gated City*, the extrapolation from present realities into an imagined future enables Lessing to frame both a judgment of and a prescription for the alternatives of the future.

220

The setting of the novel is London, in a fantasied time that follows the present Age of Affluence, when societal and technological order has virtually disintegrated. Near anarchy reigns (though a bureaucratic class, dedicated to maintaining itself, exists); most people have migrated from the city, and none have returned to recommend that alternative; goods and services are available only intermittently or illegally, encouraging the practice of various forms of barter and contraband. Vague illnesses and diseases (reminiscent of those suffered by the Coldridges and their acquaintances in the pre-catastrophe England of *The Four-Gated City*) proliferate; young marauders, wandering the streets in animal-like packs, keep fear alive. The "enemy" thus surfaces again in the young generation of city-dwellers in *The Memoirs of a Survivor*, as the process of breaking down occurs yet again in the macrocosm.

The narrator, one of the shrinking number of residents still living in the heart of chaos, attempts to recount her personal experience of this time in which what she calls the bizarre and the ordinary coexisted. The "ordinary" is the utterly splintered social order which shapes the business of living; the "bizarre" is another dimension she discovers just beyond her livingroom walls: a world of rooms and changing scenes, entered partly by accident, partly by concentration. One recalls Martha Quest's discovery that the door into the world of altered consciousness "had been standing here, ready for her to walk in any time she wished" (*The Four-Gated City*, p. 468). In *The Memoirs of a Survivor* the narrator makes a similar discovery, acknowledging that

> the consciousness of that other life, developing there so close to me, hidden from me, was a slow thing, coming precisely into the category of understanding we describe in the word "realise," with its connotation of a gradual opening into comprehension. Such an opening, a growing, may be an affair of weeks, months, years. And of course one can "know" something, and not "know" it. (One can also know something and then forget it!) Looking back, I can say definitely that the growth of that other life or form of being behind that wall had been at the back of my mind for a long time before I *realised* what it was I had been listening to, listening for.[2]

The analogue of rooms becomes the shaping metaphor of the entire novel, taking the metaphoric form of the three-tiered geography developed in *The Four-Gated City*: room, flat (or house), and city, corresponding to intrapsychic, interpersonal, and public dimensions of experience.

While in *The Four-Gated City* Martha Quest and Lynda Coldridge work to break through the psychic walls that restrict them, the narrator of *The Memoirs of a Survivor* penetrates them quite easily and spontaneously as she concentrates on her white living room wall.[3] Its paint barely covers a wallpaper scene of birds and trees, suggesting the thin veneer of civilization that conceals the organic pattern beneath it. Such an implication is in fact heightened during the course of the narrative—humanity becomes less distinguishable from its animal relatives and the animals conversely become representatives of values worth defending—as the veneer dissolves and human civilization self-destructs.

That the rooms the narrator enters beyond her wall are part of a psychological rather than a physical location is obvious from the outset, for she notes that what is literally on the other side is the hall corridor of her building. Interestingly, in terms of Lessing's earlier symbolism, this protagonist (hereafter referred to as the Narrator) does not "descend" into the basement-unconscious. Instead she lives in a flat "on the ground floor, at earth-level" (p. 5), and finds the other world adjacent to her ordinary one with only the margin of wall separating them. Symbolically, the unconscious is no longer so deeply hidden "below" consciousness, as it is for Charles Watkins, who only has access to it when he "forgets" his ordinary life. The dual schema remains, but with horizontal rather than vertical coordinates.

Once the Narrator becomes aware of the other world, the relative importance of her ordinary reality diminishes.

> All this time my ordinary life was the foreground, the lit area—if I can put it like that—of a mystery that was taking place, had been going on for a long time, "somewhere else." I was feeling more and more that my ordinary daytime life was irrelevant . . . as if the centre of gravity of my life had moved, balances had shifted somewhere, and I was beginning to believe—uncomfortably, still—that what went on behind the wall might be every bit as important as my ordinary life in that neat and comfortable, if shabby, flat. (P. 11)

If, as Lessing has suggested, the novel is a "kind of autobiography," this passage may allude to the manner in which the author's own focus gradually shifted from the exterior to the interior dimension of experience, reflected in her fiction by the evolution from the realistic to the symbolic mode, from socialism to mysticism, and by the increasing presence of the Sufi view of psychic evolution. The Narrator recognizes her state of readiness for such a shift in her reality orientation, as if she had been waiting for a fertile egg—an obvious symbol of gestation or birth—to hatch. She experiences "the most vivid expectancy, a longing: this place held what I needed, knew was there, had been waiting for—oh, yes, all my life, all my life" (p. 13).

Her initial visit beyond the wall discloses vacant rooms that appear in need of repair; subsequent visits reveal dilapidated and vaguely familiar furnishings and objects, in different degrees of disorder. Symbolically, the Narrator is called to a neglected or dormant area of her self. Her willing submission to such a call is so strong that once she discovers the realm beyond the wall, she expects and even hopes that she will soon be leaving the deteriorating city that exists outside the actual walls of her flat.

This preference of the Narrator's for the inner reality amplifies the introverted solipsistic tendency already incipient in several of the immediately preceding novels. However, as always, a countervailing psychic force emerges to restore balance between the two dimensions. Just when the numinous private realm opens up as a seductive exit from external chaos, the Narrator is distracted from it by the arrival at her flat of a young girl named Emily Cartwright. The child is left for her to take care of, with only the explanation by the man who leaves her, "'She's your responsibility'" (p. 15).

Symbolically, the Narrator's state of psychological pregnancy (the egg) produces a child. According to Jung, the appearance of the child archetype in individual psychic development is an anticipation of the synthesis of conscious and unconscious elements within the personality, as well as a symbol of healing, of wholeness, of opposites mediated.[4] The child also personifies the Narrator's social conscience. While Kate Brown's "responsibility" is to follow the call of her inner instinctive life, embodied by the wounded seal, the Narrator's is, as it were, to balance that inner voice with the necessary attention to the outer life, embodied by Emily. Moreover, the tension once again is between freedom and duty. The Narrator confesses, "I longed simply to walk through the wall and never come back. But this would be irresponsible; it would mean turning my back on my responsibilities" (pp. 23–24).

The Narrator's task is not simply to turn her back on a fragmenting outer reality to indulge exclusively in the exploration of her inner landscape, but to reconcile the complementary dimensions of private and social experience, and to find a positive form for them within her own consciousness in order to survive. As she recognizes, looking back (and the entire narrative is retrospective, though presented in the immediacy of present experience): "It is as if two ways of life, two worlds, lay side by side and closely connected. But then, one life excluded the other, and I did not expect the two worlds ever to link up. I had not thought at all of their being able to do so, and I would have said this was not possible" (p. 25). Once these complementary dimensions of experience have been established at the narrative level, both worlds evolve and ramify, until they re-merge at the end. The Narrator recounts the history of their gradual alignment and convergence.

The inner world is further developed along several matrices, reflecting the dialectical tendency of the psyche to split into opposites, as well as the fact that consciousness can transcend space and time. The wall of the Narrator's flat provides the thin barrier (or bridge) between the two modalities of reality. While these metaphoric correspondences connect the "spatial" layers of the fictional world of the novel, the temporal dimension is personified through Emily, who arrives as a child of about twelve and rapidly matures through "chrysalis after chrysalis" (p. 59), becoming psychologically if not chronologically a middle-aged woman by the novel's ending. The Narrator's relationship with her recalls Martha Quest's with the younger generation of Coldridges: as a surrogate mother or guardian, she watches the stages of childhood and adolescence adapted to the social conventions of the next generation, but marked by the constant underlying pattern of human maturation. She almost feels herself "not to exist, in my own right. I was a continuation, for her, of parents, or a parent, a guardian, foster-parents" (p. 27). Moreover, Emily also embodies the dimension of fixed time, the past; her new guardian is depressed by her from the day of her arrival partly because she reminds the Narrator so insistently of her own younger self. Emily is thus the nexus of several different dimensions of the symbolic world created in the narrative. Through her the Narrator observes the rapid breakdown taking place in the outer world, faces her involvement in it, and at the same time examines the overlapping temporal layers of her own inner world.

Emily's function as a mediator among different regions of consciousness takes other forms as well. Shortly after her arrival Emily and the Narrator share a vision of the "golden age"—another reformulation of the nostalgia for Eden or unity that recurs throughout Lessing's fiction, from the image of Martha Quest's city to the several paradisial settings in Charles Watkins's mental wanderings. In *The Memoirs of a Survivor* it is envisioned as a "farm, our future, hers and mine, like a fable where we would walk hand in hand, together. And then 'life' would begin, life as it ought to be, as it had been promised—by whom? When? Where?—to everybody on this earth" (p. 34). Significantly, Emily's few belongings (besides her endearing dog/cat Hugo) include a Bible, a book of animal photographs, and several science fiction paperbacks—all metaphorical signposts in Lessing's alternative reality.

Whereas before the child's arrival the world beyond the wall had possessed a quality of potentiality and expectation for the Narrator, following Emily's appearance it bifurcates further into two distinctly different regions: an impersonal, active level, embodying choice, potentiality, or the future; and a personal and passive level, expressing the encapsulated memories that Emily herself reactivates in the Narrator's consciousness. Rooms that had been empty before are despoiled and disordered, as if they had absorbed the attributes of the societal disintegration taking place outside the Narrator's flat, albeit transposed into another key. While those rooms involve her active participation, the other rooms are immutable, fixed in their negativity. Their atmosphere communicates oppressive tension, guilt, sterility, and entrapment, and her only role in them is as a helpless observer. The contrasting sets of rooms conceptualize complementary aspects of consciousness:

> One, the "personal," was instantly to be recognized by the air that was its prison, by the emotions that were its creatures. The impersonal scenes might bring discouragement or problems that had to be solved—like the rehabilitation of walls or furniture, cleaning,

> putting order into chaos—but in that realm there was a lightness, a freedom, a feeling . . . of the possibility of alternative action. . . . But to enter the "personal" was to enter a prison, where nothing could happen but what one saw happening, where the air was tight and limited, and, above all where time was a strict unalterable law. . . . (Pp. 41–42)

The controlling metaphor of the novel is the spatialization of time: chronology translated into geography. In the "personal" area the Narrator witnesses a series of scenes from infancy and childhood that dramatize the impotence produced by emotions withheld or fabricated. The baby or young child in these tableaux is usually Emily, although once it is Emily's own mother and another time her infant brother, as equally unhappy young children. Symbolically, these are the fixed points of the Narrator's own childhood; as she remarks, Emily's condition "was as close to me as my own memories" (p. 47). The visits are painful precisely because they are impervious to change and because they recreate the emotional claustrophobia of the past. The sense of cocoon-like enclosure that dominates the "personal" world recalls Lessing's own experience, under mescaline, of being/bearing a baby that "had been born many times before, and the mere idea of 'having to go through it all over again' (a phrase the baby kept using) exhausted it in advance." [5]

In contrast to the fixed and permanent quality associated with the "personal" area, the Narrator later identifies the "impersonal" aspect of her explorations as evocative of "anarchy, of change, of impermanence" (p. 66). These complementary regions also correspond to the contents of different areas of the unconscious. According to Jung, the personal unconscious contains not only repressed past experiences but unactualized potentialities of the personality; still beneath those is the transpersonal collective unconscious. While the Narrator is powerless to "correct" Emily's childhood imprisonment (the past), she is challenged by the opportunity open to her to alter or give order to the uninhabited rooms (the dormant future potentialities of the self) and eventually to reach the layer of the collective memory.

Emily's symbolic role is expressed in yet another way. Soon after she appears, the Narrator notes her habit of observing and commenting on people outside the window of the flat: "She simply could not let anyone pass without swallowing them, and regurgitating them covered in her slime: the clever child, the one who could not be deceived, who could not have anything put over on her . . ." (p. 30). The child's perception that the outside world is threatening and must be neutralized in this manner is merely the exaggeration of an attitude the Narrator recognizes in everyone, in herself. (That perspective is in fact characteristic of most of Lessing's protagonists, from Mary Turner on.) Later Emily is described during a stage of compulsive eating, in which "her mouth was always in movement, chewing, tasting, absorbed in itself, so that she seemed all mouth, and everything else in her was subordinated to that; it seemed as if even the intake of words through her eyes was another form of eating, and her daydreaming a consumption of material, which was bloating her as much as her food" (p. 53). In thus consuming, digesting, and transforming experience, Emily embodies not only the stages of incorporation in the life of every human infant, in which the mouth and what it takes into itself are the central experiences, but also, more figuratively, the critical and transforming functions of ego consciousness. The metaphor itself recalls Martha Quest's "swallowing whole" of her experiences (*Martha Quest*, p. 194) and her much slower digestion of their meanings.

Emily eventually reverses herself, changing from consumer to consumed as she falls in love with Gerald, one of the leaders of the roving gangs outside the flat, and struggles to be accepted as part of the group. Gerald is an insubstantial figure in the novel, seen primarily as a kind of power center for the amorphous groupings of the street population that "had relinquished individuality . . . individual judgement and responsibility . . ." (p. 34). Like Mark Coldridge in *The Four-Gated City*, he embodies the conventional outwardly directed masculine intelligence, whose mode of relationship to his world is one of imposing order on external events. Gerald is also the cause of Emily's masochistic subjection by passion for a young man whose energies are directed not at the interpersonal but at the collective level of experience.

Moreover, the history of Emily's unsatisfactory relationship with Gerald recapitulates the disillusionments of erotic love that resonate throughout Lessing's fiction, in every female protagonist from Mary Turner to Kate Brown. "Like the jaded women of our dead civilisation, she knew love like a fever, to be suffered, to be lived through: 'falling in love' was an illness to be endured, a trap which might lead her to betray her own nature, her good sense, and her real purposes. It was not a door to anything but itself: not a key to living. It was a state, a condition, sufficient unto itself, almost independent of its object" (p. 197). In Lessing's fiction love between men and women proves too susceptible to destruction by mutual dependencies, passion, deception (and self-deception), and egotistical self-interest to serve as a true conduit to the growth of the larger self—though it may provide the catalyst for such growth. The repudiation of the male-female relationship, and of sexuality, reinforces Lessing's turning away from both the public or social world and the body in favor of a reality that is paradoxically private but less personal—the incorporeal dimension of experience in which the individual self and the collective merge. Consistently in her fiction sexuality and the family are exposed as bondages that the individual must break through to achieve a freedom that is initially social and ultimately psychological and spiritual.

The index of the emotional pain and futility of Emily's struggle for a place in Gerald's crowded life is Hugo, the girl's faithful dog/cat. Hugo's emblematic role in the novel is rather different from that of the animal figures in Lessing's previous fiction. The Narrator finds herself "trying to come to terms with [Hugo] and understand the right he assumed to be there in my life . . ." (p. 62). No longer suggestive of the distrusted sexual instinct, he is more positive, though still anomalous: a union of "opposites" suggestive of the androgynous figures of mythology. Hugo also embodies the precious link with the larger continuum of sentient life in a rapidly splintering social order. Like the bear in Faulkner's story of the same name, he ultimately becomes the embodiment of "fidelity, humility, endurance" (p. 62). When the outer world deteriorates further and the prohibition against eating domesticated pets disappears along with other civilized restraints, defending Hugo ironically becomes one of the remaining affirmations of humanness.

Concurrent with the events concerning Emily, Hugo, and Gerald, the Narrator is engaged in her prior task of "working" on the rooms beyond her wall. Her efforts at mending the damage are discouraging, however, for each time she returns to resume that task, other rooms need to be redone all over again. Suggestively, the evolving consciousness, in its effort to retain new self-discoveries, inevitably repeats the cycle of recovering and then forgetting the knowledge housed in its own deeper layers—the leitmotif of Lessing's Sufi-inflected later fiction.

Images of wholeness, archetypal structures awaiting realization, and psychic integration that increasingly populate this inner realm reveal their Jungian basis most explicitly in the "centering" activity in which the Narrator participates. She finds herself in a hexagonal (mandala-shaped) room which, unlike the others, is occupied. In it is a carpet containing "a design, an intricate one, but the colours had an imminent existence, a potential, no more" (p. 78). The occupants of the room are engaged in fitting multicolored pieces of cloth into the carpet design, thereby bringing its pattern to life. The Narrator joins in this activity which, though it resembles a game, is quite serious and is marked by an attitude of cooperation rather than competition. "I, too, sought for fragments of materials that could bring life to the carpet, and did in fact find one. . . . I realised that everywhere around, in all the other rooms, were people who would in their turn drift in here, see this central activity, find their matching piece" (p. 79). Though the room vanishes as the others have done when she leaves them, the Narrator knows "it had not disappeared, and the work in it continued, must continue, would go on always" (p. 79). Symbolically, the process of self-realization—the Sufi "work"—remains the dynamic necessity of the growing personality, whether conscious or not.

As Jung has pointed out in clarifying the nature of archetypes in the psyche, "The archetype is essentially an unconscious content that is altered by becoming conscious and by being perceived, and it takes its colour from the individual consciousness in which it happens to appear. . . . A primordial image is determined as to its content only when it has become conscious and is therefore filled out with the material of conscious experience."[6] Further, the ego is "the center of the field of consciousness," subordinated to the "Self"—the larger hypothetical construct representing the sum total of the actual and potential dimensions of the personality—

like a part to the whole.[7] In *The Memoirs of a Survivor* Emily is a personification of the ego, while the Narrator, who both includes and is more than Emily in her exploration of the "personal" and "impersonal" dimensions of being, is analogous to the Self. Emily's growth follows the biological pattern, "the achievement of the top of the curve of her existence as an animal, then a falling away towards death" (p. 93); the Narrator's growth traces a psychological and spiritual trajectory that transcends physical catabolism and embraces Emily's life pattern within it. As Emily pursues the finite, the Narrator pursues the infinite. The two forms of experience that have been present from the beginning of Lessing's fiction—the linear or historical and the cyclical or mythic—thus resonate both literally and symbolically between the two central figures of this novel.

Lessing's adaptation of suggestively Jungian emblems within a mystical landscape is interesting in view of her earlier fictionalized observations about the process of self-realization. In *The Golden Notebook* Anna Wulf discusses individuation with her (Jungian) analyst, Mother Sugar, remarking,

> "So far what it has meant to me is this: that the individual recognises one part after another of his earlier life as an aspect of the general human experience. When he can say: What I did then, what I felt then, is only the reflection of that great archetypal dream, or epic story, or stage in history, then he is free, because he has separated himself from the experience, or fitted it like a piece of mosaic into a very old pattern, and by the act of setting it into place, is free of the individual pain of it." (*The Golden Notebook*, p. 403)

In fact, Anna challenges this assumption, wanting instead to separate the unique from the universal in her own self.[8] By contrast, the older Narrator of *The Memoirs of a Survivor*, significantly nameless, seeks to fit her unique self back into that symbolic unity contained in and summed up by the larger pattern of psychic growth. While Lessing's younger characters strive toward particularization and discovery of their individuality, her older characters seek reunion with that which is general and universal in their human experience.

From her current psychological and philosophical perspective, which embraces the Sufi view, Lessing has written of Jung, "I think Jung's views are good as far as they go, but he took them from Eastern philosophers who go much further. Ibn El Arabi and El Ghazzali, in the [M]iddle [A]ges, had more developed ideas about the 'unconscious,' collective or otherwise, than Jung, among others. He was a limited man. But useful as far as he went. Both Jung and Freud were useful as far as they went."9 Though she disclaims Jung's influence, Lessing's fiction reflects her exposure to his theoretical assumptions that, at the very least, are congruent with those of the Sufi tradition that have been more recently absorbed into her work. *The Memoirs of a Survivor* expresses the pattern of self-realization, extended and enlarged to frame a concept of self-transcendence: consciousness is in a continual state of evolution, progressively actualizing or discovering more of the contents of both personal and transpersonal memory. Tracing a dialectical route, it moves along the "growing point" toward a more comprehensive and, for the exceptionally sensitive consciousness, cosmic perception of reality. The Sufi wisdom identifies that process as one of acquiring the appropriate organs of perception to facilitate the mystical commingling of the personal with the universal. The Indian novelist R. K. Narayan describes the cosmic vision that would transcend our more conventional linear perspective:

> The full view of a personality would extend from the infant curled up in the womb and before it, and beyond it, and ahead of it, into infinity. Our normal view is limited to a physical perception in a condition restricted in time, like the flashing of a torchlight on a spot, the rest of the area being in darkness. If one could have a total view of oneself and others, one would see all in their full stature, through all the stages of evolution and growth, ranging from childhood to old age, in this life, the next one, and the previous ones.10

At the culminating stage in the process of psychic growth, the two dimensions—biological and spiritual, or ego and Self—converge. In this novel that convergence draws together several levels of the narrative, since Emily has appeared almost from the beginning in both the interior and exterior worlds that the Narrator inhabits. The interpenetration of the fixed past and the unrealized future (the historic and mythic dimensions of time) accelerates in the second half of the novel, as the Narrator senses that "it was time to step from one life into another. . . . I was being taken, was being led, was being shown . . ." (p. 100). The hunger she has always felt (the psychic or spiritual yearning present in most of Lessing's protagonists, particularly beginning with Anna Wulf) "was being assuaged" (p. 100).

What she is in fact ready for is the termination of one form of life and the beginning of another. As she examines that anticipation through Emily, she recognizes that "what I was really waiting for (just as, somewhere inside herself, *she* must be) was the moment she would step off this merry-go-round, this escalator carrying her from the dark into the dark. Step off it entirely. . . . And then?" (ellipsis in original, p. 93). In mythic terms the Narrator wants to leave the recurring cycle which is the shape of human life. The "merry-go-round" and the "escalator" metaphorically express the intersecting circular and linear patterns that structure Lessing's fiction.

As the Narrator penetrates further into the inner realm, she moves beyond the rooms altogether; ceilings disappear and the walls become insubstantial, transparent, giving way to an increasingly organic world of forests and gardens. She senses the benign numinous Presence that she has felt beginning with her first visit to the inner region. One is reminded, once again, of the recurring motif of Eden—the nostalgic dream of wholeness and harmony generated out of the dreamer's subordination of the private self to some larger unity. The Narrator finds herself in a place with

> room after room all open to the leaves and the sky . . . with no boundaries or end that I could find, much larger than I had ever understood. Long ago, when it had stood up thick and strong, a protection from the forest and from the weather, how very many must have lived here, multitudes, yet all had been subdued to the one Presence who was the air they breathed—though they did not know it—was the Whole they were minuscule parts of. . . . (P. 99)

While this aspect of the collective memory is utopian and infinite, the collective body on the external and present level of the narrative is chaotic: to move through the streets outside the Narrator's flat was "like a foray into enemy territory, or into the past of the human race" (p. 104). The "enemy" or shadow invariably rises to counteract the progress toward unity. In contrast to the Narrator's idyllic garden beyond her wall, Emily's commune garden fails because the children, incapable of understanding the principle of shared labor for the common good, cannot or will not follow her simple instructions. Emily and Gerald can offer them no more than "the old arguments that life is more comfortable for a community if the members keep the place clean, share work, respect each other's individuality. And the children had survived without such thoughts ever having come near them" (p. 176).

In these observations one discerns the echo of Lessing's own disillusionment with the Leftist ideal. The gap between the ideal and the practice of socialism proves too great to be bridged; the only constructive pattern for collective harmony that replaces it is the mythic ideal of the "golden age." That motif is itself a depoliticized form of the Marxist philosophy: both are utopian and eschatological at base.[11]

The Narrator tries to console Emily with the observation that it has always been this way: every human being is socialized into a structure of behavior and belief carrying with it constraints and repressions. In struggling to escape such conditioning once it is identified, each generation also rejects the wisdom achieved by its predecessors and is thus doomed to repeat the same errors. The democratization of the family is as destructive of wholeness as are the rigidities of the traditional family structure with its conditioning from childhood, for "they" (the enemy) inevitably materialize to oppose "us." The stray children of the street packs and the "unassimilable" (p. 118) Ryans symbolize the irreducible principle of anarchy present at the deeper layers of the collective and individual psyche.

If *The Memoirs of a Survivor* is autobiography (and the Narrator reminds the reader, "This is a history, after all, and I hope a truthful one" [p. 108]), this is Lessing's most pessimistic pronouncement so far. There seems to be no way to truly begin "from scratch" that would not carry with it the seed of its own destruction, given the inherent predisposition of both macrocosm and microcosm toward self-division. The central psychic task of the Narrator is the marshaling of the imaginative energy to counteract despair with an inner vision of wholeness, without which external reality cannot be survived at all. Yet, to the extent that any "reality" is partly an interpretation perceived and conceived by consciousness itself, anarchy and solipsism emerge as the dangerous and always-threatening extremes of Lessing's fictional universe.

The Narrator's visit to Emily's "other home" (p. 139) (her communal house with Gerald) connects the public Emily to the Emily of the rooms beyond the wall and of the flat. As in the three-tiered universe of *The Four-Gated City*, the room, the house, and the city correspond to intrapsychic, interpersonal, and public dimensions of being. In this novel they additionally symbolize the three temporal states. The past invades the Narrator's present life as she hears the helpless sobbing of a child beyond the wall. Her unsuccessful attempts to rescue it by getting physically through the barrier recall Lynda Coldridge's futile offensive on the walls of her basement flat. Just as the past cannot be "corrected" but only viewed from different perspectives as it is progressively assimilated into present consciousness and reinterpreted at different stages of self-knowledge, so the inner realm cannot be stormed by a deliberate act of will.

Disorder is increasingly refracted in both the world beyond the Narrator's wall and the one outside her flat, conceptualizing the psychic dissonance in the Narrator's shifting consciousness as well as in the macrocosm. But as external breakdown becomes ubiquitous, the Narrator discovers further inner regions of order and generativity to counteract outer chaos and division. In another variation of the inner garden (Lessing's allusion, perhaps, to *The Secret Garden* of the Sufi sage Mahmoud Shabistari), the Narrator observes "the food the earth was making, which would keep the next winter safe for us, for the world's people. Gardens beneath gardens, gardens above gardens: the food-giving surfaces of the earth doubled, trebled, endless—the plenty of it, the richness, the generosity . . ." (p. 158).

Significantly, the underworld imaged in this novel is not hell, nor is it a paradise repeatedly destroyed by its opposite, as in Charles Watkins's bifurcated consciousness in *Briefing for a Descent into Hell*. Rather, it is a generative place, and the Narrator's access to it reflects her growth of consciousness beyond the self-divisions of Lessing's preceding characters. In narrative terms these developments resemble motifs in the tradition of pastoral romance, wherein "the closer the romance comes to a world of original identity [wholeness], the more clearly something of the symbolism of the garden of Eden reappears, with the social setting reduced to the love of individual men and women within an order of nature which has been reconciled to humanity." [12] Though the Narrator's earlier sense of possibility shrinks to a feeling of inevitability, she manages with effort to hold on to both realms—"though it was hard to maintain a knowledge of that other world, with its scents and running waters and its many plants, while I sat here in this dull shabby daytime room. . . . Intimations of that life, or lives, became more powerful and frequent in 'ordinary' life, as if that place were feeding and sustaining us, and wished us to know it" (p. 159).

At the intersection of past and future, experience becomes literally topsy-turvy. The top floor of the Narrator's building houses domestic animals; the packs of orphan children who menace the streets live, significantly, in abandoned tunnels of the underground, becoming more animal-like in their behavior. [13] The paradoxical geography—a metaphorical expression of the fact that space and time are relative concepts when perceived from the nonlogical dimension of consciousness—signals the approaching synthesis of opposites. The Narrator longs to escape from the burden of civilization, "simply to close up my home and go" (p. 164). She even suspects that her visit to the street culture "was a sign of an inner intention to leave which I knew nothing about yet" (pp. 161–62). Psychologically, she desires dissolution of the self as the only escape from collective chaos, but "responsibility" (Emily/ego) holds her to the phenomenal world.

Indicative of the mystical dimension that the Narrator approaches, one of her visits to the inner realm is a movement through fire. Accompanied by Hugo, who is "necessary to the events" (p. 183), she enters the visionary world through firelight, and witnesses an incongruous scene whose key images are sexual. It is her last visit to the "personal" realm, and in it Emily appears distorted into a debased sexual object, almost like the biblical Whore of Babylon with her provocative mannerisms and scarlet dress. As the Narrator watches, Emily turns into a doll and shrinks (before her mother) in "a flash of red smoke, like a morality tale of the flesh and the devil" (p. 185). Once again, the destructive mother figure assumes her characteristic role of domination and annihilation of her daughter's threatening sexuality. From the more suggestively mystical perspective, the Narrator, witnessing that final confrontation, passes through the purifying flame that consumes passion.

By contrast, Emily's situation in the outer world is one of dishevelment. Her house and garden in further shambles, she lives in a nest of animal furs in one room of Gerald's house. However, the animal state, like Hugo himself, is an ironic metaphor. Emily's lair-like room is one of the rare places where pure air can be had, the basic elements of survival having been contaminated in the macrocosm. "The elements we swim in, move in, of which we are formed and re-formed, continuously, perpetually, re-created and renewed . . . for how long had we to distrust them, evade them, treat them as possible enemies?" (ellipsis in original, pp. 188–89). The contamination of the life elements themselves, so often essential metaphors in Lessing's fiction, and the purity of the animal lair emphasize the extraordinary reversals of the phenomenal world.

On the literal level of the narrative nearly everybody has fled the city, migrating to uncertain destinations, intent on "surviving at all costs" (p. 192). Ironically, Emily, Gerald, and the Narrator are better off than before, with purified air and water, food, and heat more available as the competition for them decreases. When anarchy overwhelms civilized behavior so completely that Gerald is attacked by the young children of his own pack, he finally abandons his attempt to organize the group into collective action for survival, and joins the Narrator, Emily, and Hugo in their vigil of waiting for an unknown deliverance or an end. The Narrator doubts the value of migrating, since there is no prospect of better alternatives elsewhere. As Martha Quest had acknowledged earlier in Lessing's fiction, the only answers are those beneath one's own nose. The common task becomes the protection of Hugo from marauders—the remaining activity through which the survivors can still subordinate self-interest and affirm a common humanity that is more valuable than bare survival for its own sake.

After an interminable wait through a winter reminiscent of Kate Brown's dark, cold journey to the sea, deliverance does come. In the final pages of the novel the two worlds that have been approaching each other both literally and symbolically finally mesh. The culminating event is effected not by an act of will but by patient waiting and readiness—the "timing" Charles Watkins had dimly understood. The Narrator's various personas (Emily, Gerald, Hugo), psychological dimensions (inner and outer), and states of being in time (past, present, future) are incorporated into one last expansion of consciousness that Lessing dramatizes symbolically. Like Charles Watkins's transmutation into a lighter, finer substance as a result of his absorption by the Crystal, the figures of the Narrator's universe are "absorbed" by the benign Presence intimated earlier in her explorations. Emily is "transmuted, and in another key," as is Hugo, who "fitted her new self" (p. 213). At the last moment Gerald joins them, bringing his flock of wayward children with him, and all are led by "One who went ahead showing them the way out of this collapsed little world into another order of world altogether" (p. 213).

As the elements of the Narrator's two realities merge, the dimension beyond the wall fuses with the dimension of this side of it, and the wall itself disappears; symbolically, the boundary between inner and outer dissolves at the moment of spiritual gnosis. Ernst Cassirer has described the "dynamic which belongs to the essence of every true spiritual form of expression," in which "the rigid limit between 'inside' and 'outside,' the 'subjective' and the 'objective,' does not subsist as such but begins, as it were, to grow fluid. The inward and outward do not stand side by side, each as a separate province; each, rather, is reflected in the other, and only in this reciprocal reflection does each disclose its own meaning." [14] The ending of The Memoirs of a Survivor is a rendering into language and image of the essentially ineffable experience of transcendence—the state of elevated consciousness characteristic of the mystical experience, whether conceived as union with the deity, dissolution of ego boundaries, satori, enlightenment, illumination, or apotheosis: "a self-transforming perception of one's total union with the infinite [in which] one's socially conditioned sense of 'me' is shattered and swept away by a new definition of the self, the 'I.' In that redefinition of the self, I equals all mankind, all life, and the universe. The usual ego boundaries break down, and the ego passes beyond the limits of the body." [15]

Moreover, the symbol of wholeness, the One (the numinous Presence felt by the Narrator as a quality of her experience beyond the wall) is female, suggesting a number of resonating meanings. [16]

237

That entity suggests the archetypal Great Mother figure who, in her benign aspect, both produces and reclaims her progeny, the human family. Psychologically, the image also suggests the unitary state of undifferentiated consciousness that precedes psychic separation from the mother or characterizes symbiosis with her. In the centering paradigm of individuation, the Self is often conceptualized symbolically as divinity;[17] the female "One" of *The Memoirs of a Survivor* thus suggests the apotheosis of the Self within the female Narrator of the novel. The Sufi scholar Nasrollah S. Fatemi says of the achievement of transcendence, "Man is complete when he has gained gnosis, but gnosis is also the primal element; so it is the beginning and the end, the first and the last, and thus the mystic circle is perfect."[18]

Even given these possible glosses, the conclusion of *The Memoirs of a Survivor* is the most obscure of any of the endings of Lessing's novels. Metaphorically, the final goal of the enlightened consciousness is the dissolution of the barriers that segregate experience into compartments—ego from self, self from world, rational from nonrational, past from future—to synthesize all such antinomies at a higher level of consciousness. Yet language is incapable of rendering that state exactly, since, at the level of discourse, paradox and contradiction can be expressed but not resolved. As Anna Wulf discovers in the course of freeing herself as a whole person, "the real experience can't be described" (*The Golden Notebook*, p. 542). Increasingly in Lessing's fiction the rational and verbal modality is subordinated to the nonrational and mythic one in which paradox and logical contradictions are permissible. Narratively, the two dimensions explored in *The Memoirs of a Survivor*—the events that take place beyond the outer wall and those that take place beyond the inner wall of the Narrator's flat—are disclosed as interpenetrable. Both are metaphorical framings of reality, and the concluding image of the novel, the dissolution of all walls, is their synthesis.

What makes that ending to the novel formally paradoxical but ultimately more aesthetically satisfying than the conclusions of the two novels that precede it is that the Narrator both participates in and observes the experience of transcendence. The elements of her gnosis are the elements of her own self, projected into other characters within the fictional world she occupies. Yet she is the "survivor" who narrates her experience in retrospect for the reader—in effect, translating the ineffable back into language, as nearly as possible. Like Anna Wulf, who by the end of *The Golden Notebook* is revealed as the narrator of even the most apparently "omniscient" sections of the novel (*Free Women*), the Narrator of *The Memoirs of a Survivor* detaches herself from the narrative in which she is the central character, circling back upon her experience to retell it in the form of a memoir which is the novel itself.

Thus, like *The Golden Notebook*, *The Memoirs of a Survivor* is the "autobiography" of one central character. As the Narrator seeks her piece to fit into the symbolic carpet representing the "work" that always goes on, her own qualities are distributed among the other characters as personas of her psychic past and the future. She is to Emily as Anna Wulf is to Ella: each, the invention of Doris Lessing, "invents" her own alter ego as the vehicle of the fiction within the fiction. Robert Alter, who uses the term "self-conscious" for such novels, further posits that the writer who projects history forward in time into an apocalyptic future is

readily drawn to a contemplation of how the mind, working through literary tradition, projects images of a Promised End, and how the mind can also set up against the void images of order and perfection in the here-and-now. This tendency at its most extreme can result in sheer escapism, but it is not necessarily escapist, for many writers have been able to concentrate on an assessment of their own imaginative resources for coping with reality without fleeing reality.[19]

Furthermore, the Narrator's memoir is also the anatomy of the abnormal consciousness as it evolves in the course of Doris Lessing's novels—a kind of collective biography of the author's fictional creations. Thus Emily, besides being a representative of aspects of the Narrator in this novel, is a suggestive condensation of a number of Lessing's other central characters, from young Martha Quest and Julia Barr to Anna Wulf and the later Martha Quest. The Narrator's transparent quality makes her function more as a symbolic lens through which the reader observes the various renderings of chaos and its alternatives, rather than as a realistic character like Martha Quest or even Anna Wulf. That quality is consistent with her gradual self-transcendence as she divests herself of personal qualities and becomes identified with the communal experiences she describes. Her insubstantiality may also be understood as the shedding of the ego in preparation for entry into the world beyond the wall—the death of the personal entity in either the physical or metaphysical sense. The apparent alternative to the descent into anarchy at the collective level is the progressive spiritualization of perceived experiences: if the macrocosm cannot be altered, the individual consciousness survives by constructing a private vision, effecting an alteration in its relationship to and perception of the phenomenal world. As Jung has phrased it psychologically, "We stand between two worlds, or between two totally different psychological systems of perception; between perception of external sensory stimuli and perception of the unconscious. The picture we have of the outer world makes us understand everything as the effect of physical and physiological forces; the picture of the inner world shows everything as the effect of spiritual agencies." [20]

Jung has also pointed out that the process of individuation is never actually completed, since life—and consciousness—is a process. Lessing, going beyond the psychological framework to embrace the mystical orientation more explicitly, conceives the temporary reconciliation within that ongoing process as spiritual gnosis. Since the states she attempts to conceptualize are increasingly inexpressible, she relies more directly on a mythopoeic framework in which "'the phenomenal is the Bridge to the Real.'" [21] *The Memoirs of a Survivor* is, finally, another breakthrough in Lessing's charting of the forms of consciousness: the oblique rendering of the mystical path of self-transcendence.

At the same time, this most recent of Lessing's eleven novels communicates the multifarious nature of the artistic consciousness itself. The author's return to the center of her own vision—the recapitulation of themes, images, and characters in new forms, as well as the apotheosis of the Narrator by the end of the novel—almost gives the impression of a finale to her canon. One wonders where Lessing can go from here. But, just as her fictional persona explores a new area of the psychic geography, shapes an image of wholeness out of chaos and despair, and "returns" to tell of it, so one expects that Doris Lessing will continue to bring her artistic imagination to bear upon transforming capacities of image, language, and fiction.

NOTES

1. Lessing, *The Memoirs of a Survivor* (New York: Alfred A. Knopf, 1974), dust jacket.

2. Ibid., p. 7, emphasis in original. All subsequent page references will be indicated in the text.

3. Recall Lessing's comment that "if you can train yourself to concentrate you can travel great distances." See "Doris Lessing at Stony Brook: An Interview by Jonah Raskin," in *A Small Personal Voice*, ed. Paul Schlueter (New York: Alfred A. Knopf, 1974), p. 66.

4. As Jung states further, the "child" symbolizes the "pre-conscious and the post-conscious nature of man. His pre-conscious nature is the unconscious state of earliest childhood; his post-conscious nature is an anticipation by analogy of life after death. In this idea the all-embracing nature of psychic wholeness is expressed. Wholeness is never comprised within the compass of the conscious mind—it includes the indefinite and indefinable extent of the unconscious as well. Wholeness is therefore, empirically speaking [,] of immeasurable extent, older and younger than consciousness and enfolding it in time and space." See Jung and C. Kerenyi, *Essays on a Science of Mythology*, trans. R. F. C. Hull, Bollingen Series XXII, 1949; rpt. in *Psyche and Symbol*, ed. Violet S. de Laszlo (New York: Doubleday, 1958), pp. 127–28, 144.

5. "Interview with Doris Lessing by Roy Newquist" (1964), in *A Small Personal Voice*, ed. Schlueter, pp. 59–60.

6. Jung, *The Archetypes and the Collective Unconscious*, 2nd ed. vol. 9 of *The Collected Works*, trans. R. F. C. Hull, Bollingen Series XX (Princeton, N.J.: Princeton University Press, 1968), pp. 5, 79.

7. Jung, *Aion*, vol. 9 of *The Collected Works*, trans. R. F. C. Hull, Bollingen Series XX (New York: Pantheon Books, 1959), pp. 3, 5.

8. See Lessing's specific comments on the process of individuation on pp. 110–11, n. 14.

9. Letter from Doris Lessing to Roberta Rubenstein dated 28 Mar. 1977.

10. Narayan, *My Days* (New York: Viking Press, 1974), p. 148.

11. In crediting the revolutionary aspect of romance, Northrop Frye suggests that the ideal is reached "through a progressive bursting of closed circles, first of social mythology, whether frivolous or serious, then of nature, and finally of the comic-providential universe of Christianity and other religions, including Marxism, which contains them both." See *The Secular Scripture* (Cambridge, Mass., and London: Harvard University Press, 1976), p. 173. See also Chapter III above.

12. Frye, *Secular Scripture*, p. 149. Later he adds that the vision of a "pastoral, paradisal, and radically simplified form of life obviously takes on a new kind of urgency in an age of pollution and energy crisis" and—as a kind of

wish-fulfillment given literary form—accounts for the revitalization of romance elements in contemporary fiction (p. 179).

13. One is reminded of the total breakdown of the societal structure and values described by Colin Turnbull in his study of the Ik tribe of eastern Africa, in *The Mountain People* (New York: Simon and Schuster, 1972).

14. Cassirer, *The Philosophy of Symbolic Forms*, vol. 2: *Mythical Thought*, trans. Ralph Manheim (New Haven, Conn.: Yale University Press, 1955), p. 99.

15. John White, ed., *The Highest State of Consciousness* (New York: Doubleday, 1972), p. vii.

16. Mircea Eliade has proposed that a religious symbol reveals a multitude of related meanings, creating a "perspective in which diverse realities can be fitted together or even integrated into a 'system.'" Further, perhaps the most central function of a religious symbol is "its capacity for expressing paradoxical situations or certain patterns of ultimate reality that can be expressed in no other way." See *Mephistopheles and the Androgyne: Studies in Religious Myth and Symbol*, trans. J. M. Cohen (New York: Sheed and Ward, 1965), pp. 203, 205.

17. Jung, *Aion*, pp. 36–37.

18. Fatemi, "A Message and Method of Love, Harmony, and Brotherhood," in *Sufi Studies: East and West*, ed. L. F. Rushbrook Williams (New York: E. P. Dutton, 1973), p. 62.

19. Alter, *Partial Magic: The Novel as a Self-Conscious Genre* (Berkeley and Los Angeles: University of California Press, 1975), p. 149.

20. Jung, *Civilization in Transition*, vol. 10 of *The Collected Works*, trans. R. F. C. Hull, Bollingen Series XX (New York: Pantheon Books, 1964), pp. 17–18.

21. Lessing, "The Ones Who Know," *Times Literary Supplement*, 30 Apr. 1976, p. 514.

Closing

If the beginning is in the end—to remain faithful to the myth-opoeic view—this analysis of Doris Lessing's novels should close its own circle; now is the moment to return to the premises and assumptions with which this study began and to examine their implications. My intention has been to show that, regardless of the varied forms in which it is conveyed, the center of Lessing's fictional universe is the perceiving mind as it translates the phenomenal world through its own experience—a process which makes reality a subjective interpretation and simultaneously seeks an objective or even absolute point upon which to anchor it. Lessing's primary orientation as a writer is thus less an aesthetic than an ideological one. It is not gracefulness of style but a steadily high level of intellectual energy and the provocative framing of ideas, embodied through deeply felt characters experiencing both typical and unconventional life situations, that invigorate her fiction. Her continuing incorporation of a broad spectrum of social concerns ranging from Leftist politics to racial issues, female roles, sexuality, esoteric tradition, science fiction extrapolations, mid-life crises, the various insanities of contemporary life for which madness itself is the most expressive analogy, and a number of others, may obscure the fact that all of these are meaningful within the larger metaphysical coherence of her vision.

The novels grouped in the first section, "Breaking Down, Breaking Out," concern young women who struggle for self-definition within their perceived social matrix. For each woman that self-discovery or failure is generated by a number of experiences, the most central of which are relationships with men whose expectations and beliefs shape her initial break from her family and upbringing. The response to that break is the key to the further direction or constriction of growth of the self, as each young woman confronts herself through the men who "create" her. While the

245

narrator of each work is aware of the presence of the forces that culminate in either temporary liberation or breakdown, the protagonists are not, and part of their breaking out is the process of identifying—or fleeing—them.

With the publication of *The Golden Notebook*, the impasses of form as well as of consciousness itself assume new and richer conceptualizations. The attempt of each of the fictional protagonists to break out of external or institutional frameworks—family, marriage, the color bar, sexual stereotypes, sexual identity, political dogmas, literary conventions—becomes, in addition, an effort to understand the world as a function of the perceiver's own consciousness. Instead of being created by others, she struggles to create herself. Being a "free woman" takes on further dimensions of meaning as the protagonist shares the insights previously dispensed by the more omniscient narrator. Subjectivity and relativity of perspective replace objectivity and omniscience as the orientations of the fictional world contained by each of Lessing's major novels that dramatize such breakthroughs of consciousness.

Moreover, both the linear and circular patterns that animate them evolve from simple to complex, becoming more multilayered during the course of her pursuit of a comprehensive vision of reality. Increasingly the novels themselves become formal analogues, patterns of the experiences they describe, as Lessing mythologizes the realities of her central characters. Beginning with *The Golden Notebook*, her novelistic goal seems to be to transcend the linear restrictions of the narrative form altogether, to strain for an almost nonverbal means through which to resolve the psychological and aesthetic tensions created between the historical and mythic paradigms of experience.

Though not all of Lessing's subsequent novels are experimental in form, they carry forward the initial conceptual breakthrough formulated in *The Golden Notebook*. Martha Quest would not have become what she does become by the final volume of *Children of Violence* if Lessing had not detoured to write *The Golden Notebook* midway through the series. The author's own tangents from the five-volume *Bildungsroman* thus reveal important aspects of the artistic process itself, as well as the unfolding consciousness depicted through it. In considering the novels in the order in which they were published, I have not intended to obscure the manifold differences among either the unique characters or the individual works. Yet, since the differences are more apparent, my aim has been to suggest their underlying similarities, for in those one finds the coherence of Doris Lessing's fictional world.

As the protagonists of the novels discussed in the final section of this study explore further dimensions of their psychic lives, consciousness elaborates its efforts to achieve wholeness by transcending its own divisions. The author reformulates earlier ideas from different perspectives, framing alternative possibilities as the mind continues to break down the enclosures of its own isolation. Lessing's most recent novels culminate in personal or societal apocalypse, or at least propose as the alternative to chaos and despair an interior journey that attempts to annihilate the boundaries separating two dimensions of reality. As the protagonists of her novels retreat from outer chaos to a vision of inner order, the external world becomes progressively psychologized, mythologized, and even spiritualized and is thus occasionally attenuated in relation to the inner, sometimes isolated world of the fictional perceiver. The frequency of images of enclosure, and the description of rooms or houses as metaphors for configurations of consciousness, emphasize that particular sense of the self as circumscribed, even while it attempts to enlarge the enclosure itself.[1] At the same time, the aesthetic or structural enclosures of the novels become first more comprehensive and then more condensed in their design. As the author focuses more centrally on the possibilities within the nonrational dimension, the novels begin to reflect conventions of the romantic literary tradition: the symbolic level amplifies the meaning of the empirical events described through formal realism, displaced into archetypal or mythic motifs.

The ultimate goal of the interior journey is an escape from "outer" chaos, a visionary exit from the persuasively described societal breakdown that the protagonist observes, and an attempt to project a new form of order. Lessing's appropriation of the conventions of fantasy and speculative fiction establishes another of her innovative adaptations of the narrative form. In this context, she joins a literary tradition that includes the fiction of one of her acknowledged mentors, H. G. Wells,[2] as well as works by Jonathan Swift, Samuel Butler, Aldous Huxley, and, more recently, William Golding, John Barth, Anthony Burgess, Thomas Pynchon, Kurt Vonnegut, and a number of other writers who have used the framework of speculative, apocalyptic, or utopian fiction to pose serious social and moral issues. Speaking about her own more recent work, one feels, Lessing emphasizes in an essay written in appreciation of Vonnegut that the fantasies of speculative or science fiction writers may in fact couch the author's anguish about where we are now, and express his moral commitment through fictionally projected consequences or alternatives. She proposes that Vonnegut has been facilely misrepresented as a practitioner of science fiction, whereas instead he "has made nonsense of the little categories, the unnatural divisions into 'real' literature and the rest. . . . Vonnegut is one of the writers who map our landscapes for us, who give names to the places we know best."[3]

It is perhaps the shift from the deterministic realism of the early works toward highly symbolic expression that has startled Lessing's readers, and that may initially appear discontinuous with her early novels. As her fiction becomes increasingly metaphysical and mythopoeic, the rendering of the relationship between self and world becomes more complex and nondiscursive; symbol, analogy, image, paradox, and fantasy replace traditional narrative realism as vehicles for converting intuitive knowledge into aesthetic form. The density of detail of the earlier novels gives way to more schematic, fable-like narratives. If, as some readers and critics might argue, there is an occasional diminution of artistic energy in the later fiction, it is because, one suspects, the author's energy has been diverted elsewhere—into further explorations of consciousness. Lessing's challenge remains that of finding appropriate verbal and formal equivalents through which to communicate those states. In the process of articulating a progressively interior and less verbally accessible vision, she occasionally fails to satisfy that aesthetic claim. In the more recent novels one senses a certain redundancy in the themes and variations, an occasionally too visible seam connecting inner and outer, surface and depth, of the parallel narrative lines. Readers may even acknowledge from time to time the feeling articulated by Martha Quest in the final volume of *Children of Violence*, that they have "been here before."

If it almost seems that Lessing has chosen perfection of the vision rather than perfection of the work (to paraphrase Yeats), then we are pressed to choose between the spirit and the letter of her fiction, and to recall the author's own expressed dissatisfaction with the conventional novel form as a vehicle for her particular vision. In her artistic credo, verbalized early in her career (in 1957) —before either her experiments with the novel form or her gradual evolution from rationalism and atheism to nonlogical modes of perception and belief—Lessing asserted that "the act of getting a story or a novel published is an act of communication, an attempt to impose one's personality and beliefs on other people. If a writer accepts this responsibility, he must see himself, to use the socialist phrase, as an architect of the soul. . . . But if one is going to be an architect, one must have a vision to build towards, and that vision must spring from the nature of the world we live in."[4]

What has altered is not Lessing's commitment to the moral act of writing but her vision of the nature of the world we live in. As a result, her more recent novels leave strict realism behind in the effort to "use the future . . . as a probe into the truth of the present."[5] The synthesis of conventions from both realistic and romantic traditions is itself a major narrative strategy with sources as far back as Cervantes. Lessing's particular originality lies not only in her varied formulations of interior architectures of the soul but in their expression as narrative architectures that continue to express the realistic details of our collective social condition.

That the new dispensation in her work is a transcendent one is clear; to identify the last stage in this evolution of consciousness toward internal coherence as a religious or sacred one requires further explanation. William James captures the meaning intended here of religion in its broadest sense as "the belief that there is an unseen order, and that our supreme good lies in harmoniously adjusting ourselves thereto."[6] Even in orthodox belief systems the religious impulse is, as Hans-Joachim Schoeps observes,

> the striving for a lost unity. Religion always proceeds from an existential dichotomy between man and the world, between man and God or the gods. Man longs for unity, longs to overcome the dichotomy; wholeness rather than division seems to him necessary for living. But—and this is the crucial element—he can never achieve in reality the unity he seeks. Thus the essence of religion may be seen as springing from contradiction, at the focus and source of which stands the dichotomy of life itself.[7]

Lessing's fiction discloses the variety of ways in which consciousness reflects that basic dichotomy as well as the urge to overcome it. In reviewing her own perception toward a more explicitly religious comprehension and orientation, Lessing acknowledges that crucial shift.

> I cannot describe a,b,c, how I moved from a rationalist position to a different one, though surely that is gone into fairly thoroughly in what I have written? . . . Then [during the time of her involvement with Jungian analysis] I was only interested in secular religions—politics, communism, and now my interest has extended to the familiar religions. . . . I now see all the symbols of the various religions as interchangeable—a religion being as it were a dialect among many of a central language, where ideas, symbols, etc. can be no other than the same, since human beings are basically the same. . . .[8]

The central tension between rational and nonrational modes of perception dominates Lessing's work from its beginning; the constant, and the point of temporary equilibrium, is the experience of dissolution of categories or boundaries of consciousness. The abnormal or extraordinary consciousness that typifies Lessing's major characters manifests the extremes of psychic division or fusion that occur in states of both mental breakdown and self-transcendence (and—though infrequently in her fiction—erotic union). The forces of social disintegration and the need for an escape from their encroaching destructiveness begin with *The Grass Is Singing*; inner breakdown makes sense only in the context of the way the outer world is perceived. The distance from Mary Turner to the Narrator in *The Memoirs of a Survivor*, however, shows the degree to which the psychological elements and the narrative formulation of the route out of chaos have altered. For both women the threat is the chaotic fragmentation of the outer world; the task is the necessity of finding a way around, or through, or beyond, or back from that chaos; and the results—madness in the former, gnosis in the latter—represent the antithetical potentialities of consciousness.

Between the two novels Lessing has explored the multivalent, shifting patterns of relationship between fact and truth, self and world, sanity and madness, body and mind, private and communal realities, as her characters seek ways to reconcile the Cartesian split of the logical mind itself. The insistent dialectic is both the pattern of consciousness and the form of its expression in the fictional realities that Lessing's characters inhabit and create. Her novels chart the gradual conversion of the abnormal consciousness from passive to active, from negative to positive, from recorder of a reality initially perceived as outside the self to creator of a reality ultimately construed as a function of the mind as it transcends the labels of "subjective" or "objective." In this evolution, dissolution of categories itself ultimately modulates from a depersonalized psychotic vision to a transpersonal mystical one; reality becomes a creation of the mind rather than the converse.

That route to the enlarged center of consciousness is not a straight line, however, but a diverse succession of circumambulations given fictional form, as each of Doris Lessing's protagonists searches for or extends further the circumference of the circle of which she (or he) is the center, either by hard-won advances in self-knowledge or (for the reader) by the manner in which failure occurs. The positive and negative poles oscillate from that center at each level of Lessing's fictional world: from the individual, whose internal schisms are mended in moments of transforming fusion; to the interpersonal, with its complementary relationships and rhythms; to the collective, in which the chaos of contemporary life is counteracted by the idealized city or garden. The novels thus pose a series of antinomies that begin in the phenomenal world and grow more psychological and ultimately more metaphysical as Lessing penetrates further into their implications. Formally, that progression is expressed as an evolution from mimesis to poiesis, as the motifs of myth, fable, and fantasy assume greater prominence in the narrative design. Only the past is fixed, and those of Lessing's characters who are able to extricate themselves from its entrapments by digesting its meaning and thus disarming their inner enemies are free to create their own futures. Consciousness is conceived as both generator and mediator of opposing tensions—susceptible to fragmentation but capable of converting that very process into a higher integration of the personality.

While her later works dramatize the quest for the point of inner unity, they also imply the urgent necessity felt by her characters to dissolve the boundaries between mind and body, mind and world: to overcome the subjectivity of the self in order to experience an absolute reality or truth. The psychological end point of that search is the fusion of the "I" with the "we." The implicit or explicit urge for selflessness in Lessing's protagonists raises several possibilities of interpretation: in a political context, it suggests the altruism of the dedicated and committed individual who subordinates self-interest and identifies himself with the group to the extent that its goals are his own. Psychologically, it suggests the nostalgia for the primary experience of wholeness and unity or, more pathologically, the denial of the self and the desire for symbiotic union or even annihilation.[9] Metaphysically, it suggests the urge toward the universal consciousness.[10] Even mysticism begins with "a quest for the 'primordial state,' since this state means human perfection which is the only basis for the spiritual ascent."[11] Mystical gnosis is the positive form in which consciousness achieves the resolution of inner dissonance. In a literary context, that moment typifies the vision of wholeness and original identity embodied in the narrative traditions of myth and romance.

Yet regardless of the frame of reference, the achievement of a unitive vision is necessarily temporary. Since life is process, the basic contradictions of human experience cannot be permanently dissolved through the altered perception. Furthermore, the price of admission into the timeless state carries with it certain dangers of its own: responsibility to the private self without a corollary sense of connection to the social macrocosm would result, finally, in an autistic or solipsistic state. Lessing's later protagonists may appear dangerously close to that condition. Esther Harding has observed, however, that while a preoccupation with the subjective inner life may seem to be totally narcissistic, "if the individual makes a clear differentiation between the personal self, the autos or the ego, and this centre of nonpersonal compelling power, the activity is certainly not auto-erotic but reflects a concern with a super-ordinated value of the utmost significance for the development of the psyche and therefore also for mankind."[12] Expressed in literary terms, that impetus is the verbal recreation of myth as the creative dimension of human consciousness, both private and collective.

The larger ambiguity of Lessing's fiction—beyond the fictional resolutions themselves which approach paradox—stems from the fact that union and dissolution are similar states, psychologically if not spiritually; their distinction lies in affect more than effect. The mature Martha Quest of *The Four-Gated City* and the Narrator of *The Memoirs of a Survivor* embody the knowledge that in states of elevated consciousness the personal and the universal become identical; but so do they in the unconscious experiences of the deeply divided Charles Watkins. The individual must still find a satisfactory equilibrium between the inner and outer worlds; though the "work" on the self must not be neglected, neither must it overwhelm the essential connection to the outer world, to the macrocosm. Either, in the absence of the corrective balance of its counterpart, creates stasis, inertia, death. Thus, though Doris Lessing's view of the collective condition and her passion for the absolute converge in her latest works, the vision of wholeness remains equivocal. The gnosis of the Narrator of *The Memoirs of a Survivor* is the expression of the perennial pattern of the return to the beginning—that utopian ideal located at both the inception and conclusion of consciousness. Lessing's fiction formulates the realization that such unity is an apprehension of the same divided world we know from another perspective.

If the most mysterious and intangible development within the personality is the transformation of the self, the equally mysterious tangible form of that process is the transformation of experience into art. At various points in her fictional canon thus far, one might identify the author's novelistic affinities in a variety of ways. Lessing herself regards her "formal and respectable influences" as "the Russians, particularly Tolstoy. Then Dostoievsky, Turgenev, Chekov. I read and re-read Proust. *The Scarlet and the Black* and others of Stendhal. Thoreau—a lot. Thomas Hardy, D. H. Lawrence, Virginia Woolf, Meredith. Olive Schreiner. H. G. Wells: a great deal." Perhaps equally instructively, Lessing adds,

> I do think that when writers list their formal and respectable influences, like the above, they tend to ignore what went before. Most writers have read a lot as children. What did they read? Not always the best and the highest! I have sometimes wondered what it did to me: I read good things, like the *Three Royal Monkeys* (de la Mare), over and over again—I did tend to read and re-read things I liked; and Dickens, and odd bits of Scott, and the romantic poets. But

253

> what of *Anne of Green Gables* and *What Katy Did* and *Little Women* and *Jock of the Bushveld* (a marvellous book) and *Biffel a Trek Ox* (also marvellous, floods of tears), and, and, and. . . .

Lessing also refers to the influence on her imagination of fascinating human interest stories and "letters to the editor" in countless obscure newspapers like

> the Rhodesia Herald, a great school for comedians, like all letters in small local papers. (If the Herald will forgive me.) Mother of Ten. Old Rhodesian. Old Pioneer. and so forth. And what of that bedrock of tales that underlies every family, repeating on and on throughout your childhood: father and mother create their lives, for the benefit of the youth. In my case: the First World War, interminably. The country boyhood of my father. The London girlhood of my mother, all musical evenings and frugality and parks and churches and visits between cousins.
>
> After all, what is *War and Peace* compared to the thousand-times repeated tale of "How my leg was shot off by a shell, luckily for me just before Paschendaele, otherwise I wouldn't be here to tell the tale, because all my Company copped it in that one." [13]

These personal anecdotes notwithstanding, in her philosophical seriousness and concern with metaphysical questions, embedded in narratives that sometimes resemble the "loose and baggy monsters" that Henry James so deplored, Lessing belongs with some of her own mentors in the realist tradition, including Tolstoy, Balzac, Stendhal, Mann. Her fascination with the dialectic of consciousness and the spiritual dimension it discloses allies her even more deeply with Dostoevsky. Her thorough observations of the social and material forces that shape character, along with her interest (at least in her pre-1970s fiction) in the sexual politics of male-female relationships, recall her expressed affinities with Lawrence.

In granting her characters narrative credibility to the extent that they must and do take up their identities within a social context (except for Mary Turner and the later Martha Quest, who die), Doris Lessing is a realist. But in her vision of the ideal—whether formulated as city or garden, a world more harmonious and unified than the phenomenal one that is our collective condition— Lessing has evolved to a more explicitly romantic stance. In the latter context, one recognizes her membership in a literary tradition that validates the artist's exploration of his (her) own inner life—a willed or unwilled encounter with intuitive and nonrational dimensions of experience—as a representative one. Within that context one also finds the exaltation of subjectivity, individual freedom, and the powers of the imagination; the desire to discover and represent through art the essential harmony of the cosmos; the oracular role of the writer; and the inclusion of the anagogic as a legitimate dimension of the literary work.[14] The balancing of this perspective with the view of the rational intelligence as the necessary vehicle for mediating and integrating such knowledge accounts for the most consistent and interesting tensions within Lessing's work, both thematically and formally.

Certainly her detailed recreation of the nuances of female consciousness guarantees her central position in a tradition of women writers extending backward to Austen, the Brontes, Eliot, Chopin, Richardson, Schreiner, Woolf, and, more currently, Drabble, Atwood, and others. Within that group she has added important new facets to the model of the female hero who, in her pursuit of autonomy, identifies, challenges, and transcends the psychological and economic dependencies she has inherited from culturally determined sex-roles. Through both orthodox and innovative images, Lessing has framed the questions that face women in their uniquely female and more inclusively human destinies.

Among her twentieth-century contemporaries, Lessing might also be placed among those novelists who have dramatized the various processes of consciousness in more experimental forms, including (in addition to Woolf and Richardson) Kafka, Joyce, Proust, and Faulkner—though her formal narrative strategies simultaneously invite other comparisons. The narrative geometry of *The Golden Notebook* relates her form-breaking work to such postmodern experimenters in the genre as Robbe-Grillet, whose "anti-novels" circle back upon themselves and make "wordless statements" in their very subversion of the traditional novel conventions. Robbe-Grillet's technique stresses that "objectivity," whether construed as a narrative or a psychological convention, produces a supreme subjectivity when pushed to its inevitable limits. (Stylistically, his works are of course quite unlike Lessing's, for while his aim is to reduce the connotative surfaces of language, Lessing's style exploits the very multiplicity of meanings embedded

255

in perception, perspective, memory, and self-canceling frames of reference.) Gide's *The Counterfeiters*, Huxley's *Point Counterpoint*, Fowles's *The French Lieutenant's Woman*, Sartre's *Nausea*, and other works come to mind as fictions that, like *The Golden Notebook*, self-consciously challenge traditional novelistic conventions and narrative assumptions. And, as mentioned earlier, Lessing's most recent fiction allies her with the fabulists and apocalyptic visionaries in the tradition of H. G. Wells.

Since Doris Lessing's novelistic canon is so broad—spanning traditional as well as experimental forms, with the permutations of *Bildungsroman*, psychological and speculative fiction, and mythic fables—I hesitate to locate her too facilely or exclusively in any particular tributary of the novel's protean course. Moreover, such efforts at categorization work uncomfortably against the very use of such arbitrary delineations that, in all forms, Lessing herself has so consistently challenged; more seriously, they dislocate the coherence of her own special vision. If the primary locus of the novel as a form is to give fictional shape to human enterprises, even the more unconventional or private ones, then Lessing's fiction is surely at the growing point of that tradition. (It is beyond the scope of this study to engage in the tired debate over whether or not the novel as a form is dead.) In creating verbal models of experience that analogically mirror the interior landscapes they conceptualize, Lessing has continued to move with the cutting edge of innovative fiction. At the same time, in continuing to adapt the novel form as a serious moral vehicle, she is engaged at the vital center of its tradition.

Lessing's longer fiction bodies forth a vision which, while admittedly not always aesthetically flawless, is always provocative, impassioned, morally serious, and ideologically courageous. Ultimately, what she has to communicate takes precedence over the way in which she communicates it, for which reason her admirers willingly forgive her stylistic lapses while her detractors object to her artlessness. Her efforts to break through not only the intellectual blinders to perception and knowledge, and conventional assumptions concerning the nature of reality itself, but also the limitations of verbal expression, should assure her stature as one of the major, unique, and visionary writers of our time.

As Proust wrote in *A La Recherche du Temps Perdu*, any reading of a book is in fact a reading of oneself; the novel enables us to see things that we might never have perceived without the book to bring them into focus and awareness for us. Through intuitive insights about the nature of experience, rendered into the language of ordinary discourse, Doris Lessing will, one hopes, continue to give narrative shape to the progress of the extraordinary consciousness imaginatively breaking through yet other forms of its own containment.

NOTES

1. Elaine Showalter has suggested the prominence of room and house images in novels by British women—including the "red room" of Jane Eyre's subjugation at the Reeds' house, and the series of houses that symbolize stages of Jane's psychic maturation, as well as the "room of one's own" that becomes emblematic of enclosure within the private consciousness (and ultimately death) in the novels of Virginia Woolf. See *A Literature of Their Own: British Women Novelists from Bronte to Lessing* (Princeton, N.J.: Princeton University Press, 1977).

2. See text of Lessing's letter to Roberta Rubenstein on p. 253.

3. Lessing, "Vonnegut's Responsibility," in *A Small Personal Voice*, ed. Paul Schlueter (New York: Alfred A. Knopf, 1974), p. 142.

4. "The Small Personal Voice," in *A Small Personal Voice*, ed. Schlueter, p. 7.

5. Robert Scholes, *Structural Fabulation* (Notre Dame and London: University of Notre Dame Press, 1975), p. 24.

6. James, *The Varieties of Religious Experience* (1902; rpt. New York and London: Longmans, Green, 1929), p. 53.

7. Schoeps, *The Religions of Mankind* (New York: Doubleday, 1966), p. 10.

8. Letter from Doris Lessing to Roberta Rubenstein dated 28 Mar. 1977.

9. A strictly psychoanalytic reading of Lessing's fiction would no doubt develop the evidence of regressive fantasies characteristic of an unresolved mother-complex—in the frequent images of an idealized unity and the equally frequent pressures of the personality toward escape, retreat, and dissolution into a larger whole. The interior journey, dreams of fusion, and other images can be seen in this context as expressions of symbiosis fantasies or, less pathologically, as forms of "regression in the service of the ego." The behaviors identified as passivity, dependency, and masochism are consistent with the mother-complex. Such a reading would be comprehensible in terms of Lessing's protagonists, in their varied and ambivalent experiences as mothers or (particularly Martha Quest) in their troubled relationships to their own mothers, and in the mental states to which such tensions give rise. However, to describe these elements of Lessing's work through that particular neurotic pattern would still fail to illuminate the meaning of the integrative resolutions that her fiction renders. See Sigmund Freud, "The Psychology of Women," in *New Introductory Lectures on Psychoanalysis*, trans. W. J. H. Sprott (New York: W. W. Norton, 1933), pp. 153–85.

In the Jungian model the complex of images concerned with dissolution and unity suggests variations of the archetypal Great Mother in her ambivalently benign and threatening aspects. The nostalgia for paradise is, psychodynamically considered, an image of desired return to the good mother, while madness is the threat of annihilation under the sway of her terrible aspect. See Jung, *The Archetypes and the Collective Unconscious*, 2nd ed., trans. R. F. C. Hull, vol. 9 of *The Collected Works*, Bollingen Series XX (Princeton, N.J.: Princeton University Press, 1968), esp. pp. 39–101.

10. Hegel's ideal of the universal consciousness and Kant's concept of the transcendental ego can be instructively applied to Lessing's implicit metaphysics.

11. Martin Lings, *What Is Sufism?* (Berkeley and Los Angeles: University of California Press, 1975), p. 56.

12. Harding, *Psychic Energy: Its Source and Its Transformation*, Bollingen Series X (1948; rpt. New York: Random House, 1963), pp. 24–25.

13. Letter from Doris Lessing to Roberta Rubenstein dated 11 Jan. 1977.

14. Michael Magie defines Lessing's romanticism in negative terms, judging her intellectual position, as expressed in the fiction, inadequate. Her recent work reveals, in his view, an increasing abdication of a rational and philosophically comprehensible position for one that is quasi-religious and sentimental. See "Doris Lessing and Romanticism," *College English* 38, no. 6 (Feb. 1977), 531–52.

Bibliography

Works by Doris Lessing

Novels (in order of publication)

The Grass Is Singing. 1950; rpt. New York: Crowell, 1975.

Martha Quest. [*Children of Violence*, vol. 1.] 1952; rpt. New York: Simon and Schuster, 1964.

A Proper Marriage. [*Children of Violence*, vol. 2.] 1954; rpt. New York: Simon and Schuster, 1964.

Retreat to Innocence. 1956; rpt. New York: Prometheus, 1959.

A Ripple from the Storm. [*Children of Violence*, vol. 3.] 1958; rpt. New York: Simon and Schuster, 1966.

The Golden Notebook. London: Michael Joseph, 1962; rpt. with Preface, 1972.

Landlocked. [*Children of Violence*, vol. 4.] 1965; rpt. New York: Simon and Schuster, 1966.

The Four-Gated City. [*Children of Violence*, vol. 5.] New York: Alfred A. Knopf, 1969.

Briefing for a Descent into Hell. New York: Alfred A. Knopf, 1971.

The Summer before the Dark. New York: Alfred A. Knopf, 1973.

The Memoirs of a Survivor. New York: Alfred A. Knopf, 1974.

Short Stories, Essays, and Plays Cited (in order of publication)

"The Eye of God in Paradise." In *The Habit of Loving*. New York: Ballantine Books, 1957. Pp. 193–254.

Play with a Tiger: A Play in Three Acts. London: Michael Joseph, 1962.

"To Room Nineteen." In *A Man and Two Women*. New York: Simon and Schuster, 1963. Pp. 278–316.

"Report on the Threatened City" and "The Temptation of Jack Orkney." In *The Temptation of Jack Orkney and Other Stories*. New York: Alfred A. Knopf, 1972. Pp. 79–116 and 231–308.

"What Looks Like an Egg and Is an Egg?" *New York Times Book Review*, 7 May 1972, pp. 6 and 41–42.

"An Ancient Way to a New Freedom." In *The Elephant in the Dark*. Ed. Leonard Lewin. 1972; rpt. New York: E. P. Dutton, 1976. Pp. 73–81.

A Small Personal Voice: Essays, Reviews, Interviews. Ed. Paul Schlueter. New York: Alfred A. Knopf, 1974.

"A Revolution." *New York Times*, 22 Aug. 1975, p. 31.

"The Ones Who Know." *Times Literary Supplement*, 30 Apr. 1976, p. 514.

Letters from Doris Lessing to Roberta Rubenstein dated 17 Nov. 1972, 31 Dec. 1972, 11 Jan. 1977, 28 Mar. 1977.

Works Cited Concerning Doris Lessing

Barnouw, Dagmar. "Disorderly Company: From *The Golden Notebook* to *The Four-Gated City*." In *Doris Lessing: Critical Essays*. Ed. Annis Pratt and L. S. Dembo. Madison: University of Wisconsin Press, 1974. Pp. 74–97.

Bolling, Douglass. "Structure and Theme in *Briefing for a Descent into Hell*." In *Doris Lessing: Critical Essays*. Ed. Annis Pratt and L. S. Dembo. Madison: University of Wisconsin Press, 1974. Pp. 133–47.

Brewster, Dorothy. *Doris Lessing*. New York: Twayne Publishers, 1965.

Carey, John. "Art and Reality in *The Golden Notebook*." In *Doris Lessing: Critical Essays*. Ed. Annis Pratt and L. S. Dembo. Madison: University of Wisconsin Press, 1974. Pp. 20–39.

Ellman, Mary. *Thinking about Women*. New York: Harcourt Brace Jovanovich, 1968.

Hardin, Nancy Shields. "Doris Lessing and the Sufi Way." In *Doris Lessing: Critical Essays*. Ed. Annis Pratt and L. S. Dembo. Madison: University of Wisconsin Press, 1974. Pp. 148–64.

Henden, Josephine. "Doris Lessing: The Phoenix 'Midst Her Fires." *Harper's Magazine* (June 1973), pp. 83–86.

Howe, Florence. "A Conversation with Doris Lessing" (1966). In *Doris Lessing: Critical Essays*. Ed. Annis Pratt and L. S. Dembo. Madison: University of Wisconsin Press, 1974. Pp. 1–19.

———. "Doris Lessing's Free Women." *Nation* 200 (11 Jan. 1965), 34–37.

Kaplan, Sydney Janet. *Feminine Consciousness in the Modern British*

Novel. Urbana: University of Illinois Press, 1975.

Karl, F. R. "Doris Lessing in the Sixties: The New Anatomy of Melancholy." *Contemporary Literature* 13 (Winter 1972), 15–33.

Magie, Michael. "Doris Lessing and Romanticism." *College English* 38, no. 6 (Feb. 1977), 531–52.

Morgan, Ellen. "Alienation of the Woman Writer in *The Golden Notebook*." In *Doris Lessing: Critical Essays*. Ed. Annis Pratt and L. S. Dembo. Madison: University of Wisconsin Press, 1974. Pp. 54–63.

Porter, Nancy. "Silenced History—*Children of Violence* and *The Golden Notebook*." *World Literature Written in English* 12, no. 2 (Nov. 1973), 161–79.

Pratt, Annis. "The Contrary Structure of Doris Lessing's *The Golden Notebook*." *World Literature Written in English* 12, no. 2 (Nov. 1973), 150–60.

———, and L. S. Dembo, eds. *Doris Lessing: Critical Essays*. Madison: University of Wisconsin Press, 1974.

Rubenstein, Roberta. "Briefing on Inner Space: Doris Lessing and R. D. Laing." *Psychoanalytic Review* 63, no. 1 (Spring 1976), 83–93.

———. "Doris Lessing's *The Golden Notebook*: The Meaning of Its Shape." *American Imago* 32, no. 1 (Spring 1975), 40–58.

Ryf, Robert S. "Beyond Ideology: Doris Lessing's Mature Vision." *Modern Fiction Studies* 16, no. 3 (Summer 1975), 193–204.

Schlueter, Paul. *The Novels of Doris Lessing*. Carbondale: Southern Illinois University Press, 1973.

Seligman, Dee. "The Sufi Quest." *World Literature Written in English* 12, no. 2 (Nov. 1973), 190–204.

Showalter, Elaine. *A Literature of Their Own: British Women Novelists from Bronte to Lessing*. Princeton, N.J.: Princeton University Press, 1977.

Singleton, Mary Ann. *The City and the Veld: The Fiction of Doris Lessing*. Lewisburg, Pa.: Bucknell University Press, 1977.

Spacks, Patricia Meyer. *The Female Imagination*. New York: Alfred A. Knopf, 1975.

Spilka, Mark. "Lessing and Lawrence: The Battle of the Sexes." *Contemporary Literature* 16, no. 2 (1975), 218–40.

Sukenick, Lynn. "Feeling and Reason in Doris Lessing's Fiction." In *Doris Lessing: Critical Essays*. Ed. Annis Pratt and L. S. Dembo. Madison: University of Wisconsin Press, 1974. Pp. 98–118.

Vlastos, Marion. "Doris Lessing and R. D. Laing: Psychopolitics and Prophecy." *PMLA* 91, no. 2 (Mar. 1976), 245–58.

Zak, Michele Wender. "*The Grass Is Singing*: A Little Novel about the Emotions." In *Doris Lessing: Critical Essays*. Ed. Annis Pratt and

L. S. Dembo. Madison: University of Wisconsin Press, 1974. Pp. 64–73.

Other Works Cited

Alter, Robert. *Partial Magic: The Novel as a Self-Conscious Genre.* Berkeley and Los Angeles: University of California Press, 1975.

Arguelles, José and Miriam. *Mandala.* Berkeley and London: Shambhala, 1972.

Becker, Ernest. *The Denial of Death.* New York: Free Press, 1973.

Boisen, Anton. *The Exploration of the Inner World: A Study of Mental Disorder and Religious Experience.* New York: Harper and Brothers, 1936.

Brenner, Charles. *An Elementary Textbook of Psychoanalysis.* Rev. ed. New York: International Universities Press, 1973.

Brown, N. O. *Life against Death.* Middletown, Conn.: Wesleyan University Press, 1959.

Bucke, Richard M. *Cosmic Consciousness: A Study in the Evolution of the Human Mind.* 1901; rpt. New York: E. P. Dutton, 1969.

Burton, Arthur, Juan J. Lopez-Ibor, and Werner Mendel. *Schizophrenia as a Life Style.* New York: Spring Publishing Co., 1974.

Campbell, Joseph. *The Hero with a Thousand Faces.* 2nd ed. Bollingen Series XVII. Princeton, N.J.: Princeton University Press, 1968.

———. "Mythology and Schizophrenia." In *Myths to Live By.* New York: Viking, 1972. Pp. 201–32.

Cassirer, Ernst. *Language and Myth.* Trans. Susanne K. Langer. New York: Dover, 1946.

———. *The Philosophy of Symbolic Forms.* Trans. Ralph Manheim. Vol. 2: *Mythical Thought,* and vol. 3: *The Phenomenology of Knowledge.* New Haven, Conn.: Yale University Press, 1955 and 1957.

De Beauvoir, Simone. *The Second Sex.* Trans. and ed. H. M. Parshley. New York: Alfred A. Knopf, 1953.

Eliade, Mircea. *Mephistopheles and the Androgyne: Studies in Religious Myth and Symbol.* Trans. J. M. Cohen. New York: Sheed and Ward, 1965.

———. *The Myth of the Eternal Return, or, Cosmos and History.* Trans. Willard R. Trask. Bollingen Series XLVI. 1954; rpt. Princeton, N.J.: Princeton University Press, 1971.

———. *Patterns in Comparative Religion.* Trans. Rosemary Sheed. 1958; rpt. New York: New American Library, 1963.

————. *The Sacred and the Profane: The Nature of Religion.* Trans. Willard R. Trask. New York: Harcourt, Brace, and World, 1969.

Erikson, Erik. "Womanhood and the Inner Space." In *Identity: Youth and Crisis.* New York: W. W. Norton, 1968. Pp. 261–94.

Fatemi, Nasrollah S. "A Message and Method of Love, Harmony, and Brotherhood." In *Sufi Studies: East and West.* Ed. L. F. Rushbrook Williams. New York: E. P. Dutton, 1973. Pp. 46–73.

Foster, William. "Sufi Studies Today." In *The Elephant in the Dark.* Ed. Leonard Lewin. 1972; rpt. New York: E. P. Dutton, 1976. Pp. 123–36.

Freud, Sigmund. *Civilization and Its Discontents.* Vol. 21 (1927–31) of *The Complete Psychological Works of Sigmund Freud.* Trans. and ed. James Strachey. London: Hogarth Press and the Institute of Psychoanalysis, 1961. Pp. 59–145.

————. "The Psychology of Women." In *New Introductory Lectures on Psychoanalysis.* Trans. W. J. H. Sprott. New York: W. W. Norton, 1933. Pp. 153–85.

Frye, Northrop. *The Secular Scripture: A Study of the Structure of Romance.* Cambridge, Mass., and London: Harvard University Press, 1976.

Grof, Stanislav. *Realms of the Human Unconscious.* New York: Viking, 1975.

Harding, M. Esther. *Psychic Energy: Its Source and Its Transformation.* Bollingen Series X. 1948; rpt. New York: Random House, 1963.

Hegel, George Wilhelm Friedrich. *Hegel's Philosophy of Mind,* Part III of *Encyclopedia of the Philosophical Sciences,* 1830, trans. William Wallace. Together with the *Zusätze* in Boumann's Text, 1845, trans. A. V. Miller. Oxford: Clarendon Press, 1971.

Houston, Jean. "Myth, Consciousness, and Psychic Research." In Edgar D. Mitchell, *Psychic Exploration: A Challenge for Science.* Ed. John White. New York: G. P. Putnam's Sons, 1974. Pp. 578–96.

Hyppolite, Jean. *Genesis and Structure of Hegel's Phenomenology of Spirit.* Trans. Samuel Cherniak and John Heckman. Evanston, Ill.: Northwestern University Press, 1974.

James, William. *The Varieties of Religious Experience: A Study in Human Nature.* 1902; rpt. New York and London: Longmans, Green, 1929.

Jung, Carl G. *Aion: Researches into the Phenomenology of the Self.* Trans. R. F. C. Hull. Vol. 9 of *The Collected Works of C. G. Jung.* Bollingen Series XX. New York: Pantheon Books, 1959.

————. *The Archetypes and the Collective Unconscious.* 2nd ed. Trans.

R. F. C. Hull. Vol. 9 of *The Collected Works of C. G. Jung*. Bollingen Series XX. Princeton, N.J.: Princeton University Press, 1968.

————. *Civilization in Transition*. Trans. R. F. C. Hull. Vol. 10 of *The Collected Works of C. G. Jung*. Bollingen Series XX. New York: Pantheon Books, 1964.

————. *Modern Man in Search of a Soul*. Trans. W. S. Dell and Cary F. Baynes. 1933; rpt. New York: Harcourt, Brace, and World, n.d.

————. *The Psychogenesis of Mental Disease*. Trans. R. F. C. Hull. Vol. 3 of *The Collected Works of C. G. Jung*. Bollingen Series XX. Princeton, N.J.: Princeton University Press, 1960.

————. *Psychological Types*. Trans. R. F. C. Hull. Vol. 6 of *The Collected Works of C. G. Jung*. Bollingen Series XX. New York: Pantheon Books, 1959.

————. *Two Essays on Analytical Psychology*. Trans. R. F. C. Hull. Vol. 7 of *The Collected Works of C. G. Jung*. Bollingen Series XX. New York: Pantheon Books, 1953.

————, and C. Kerenyi. *Essays on a Science of Mythology*. Trans. R. F. C. Hull. Bollingen Series XXII. 1949; rpt. in *Psyche and Symbol*, ed. Violet S. de Laszlo. New York: Doubleday, 1958.

————, et al., eds. *Man and His Symbols*. 1964; rpt. New York: Dell, 1970.

Laing, R. D. *The Divided Self: An Existential Study in Sanity and Madness*. 1960; rpt. Middlesex, England: Penguin Books, 1965.

————. *The Politics of Experience and The Bird of Paradise*. 1967; rpt. Middlesex, England: Penguin Books, 1970.

————, and A. Esterson. *Sanity, Madness, and the Family: Families of Schizophrenics*. 1964; rpt. Middlesex, England: Penguin Books, 1970.

Lings, Martin. *What Is Sufism?* Berkeley and Los Angeles: University of California Press, 1975.

Maslow, Abraham. *Toward a Psychology of Being*. 2nd ed. New York: Van Nostrand Reinhold, 1968.

Masters, Robert E. L., and Jean Houston. *The Varieties of Psychedelic Experience*. New York: Holt, Rinehart and Winston, 1966.

Maupin, Edward. "On Meditation." In *Altered States of Consciousness*. Ed. Charles T. Tart. 2nd ed. New York: Doubleday, 1972. Pp. 181–90.

Mitchell, Edgar D. *Psychic Exploration: A Challenge for Science*. Ed. John White. New York: G. P. Putnam's Sons, 1974.

Mure, G. R. C. *The Philosophy of Hegel*. London: Oxford University Press, 1965.

Narayan, R. K. *My Days*. New York: Viking Press, 1974.

Neumann, Erich. *The Origins and History of Consciousness*. Trans. R. F. C. Hull. Bollingen Series XLII. 1954; rpt. Princeton, N.J.: Princeton University Press, 1969.

Ornstein, Robert E. *The Psychology of Consciousness*. San Francisco: W. H. Freeman, 1972.

Rich, Adrienne. "Jane Eyre: The Temptations of a Motherless Woman." *Ms.* 2, no. 4 (Oct. 1973), 68–72, 98, 106–7.

Rogers, Robert. *The Double in Literature*. Detroit: Wayne State University Press, 1970.

Rumi, Jalaluddin. *Couplets of Inner Meaning: Tales from the Masnavi*. Trans. A. J. Arberry. London: Murray, 1961.

Schoeps, Hans-Joachim. *The Religions of Mankind*. New York: Doubleday, 1966.

Scholes, Robert. *Structural Fabulation: An Essay on Fiction of the Future*. Notre Dame and London: University of Notre Dame Press, 1975.

Shah, Idries. *The Sufis*. 1964; rpt. New York: Doubleday, 1971.

Tart, Charles T. "Out of the Body Experiences." In Edgar D. Mitchell, *Psychic Exploration: A Challenge to Science*. Ed. John White. New York: G. P. Putnam's Sons, 1974. Pp. 349–73.

————, ed. *Altered States of Consciousness*. 2nd ed. New York: Doubleday, 1972.

Turnbull, Colin S. *The Mountain People*. New York: Simon and Schuster, 1972.

Tymms, Ralph. *Doubles in Literary Psychology*. Cambridge: Bowes and Bowes, 1949.

Underhill, Evelyn. *Mysticism: A Study in the Nature and Development of Man's Spiritual Consciousness*. 1910; rpt. New York: E. P. Dutton, 1930.

Van Eeden, Frederick. "A Study of Dreams." In *Altered States of Consciousness*. Ed. Charles T. Tart. 2nd ed. New York: Doubleday, 1972. Pp. 147–60.

Vernon, John. *The Garden and the Map: Schizophrenia in Twentieth-Century Literature and Culture*. Urbana: University of Illinois Press, 1973.

Walker, Kenneth. *A Study of Gurdjieff's Teaching*. 1957; rpt. London: Jonathan Cape, 1965.

————. "The Supraconscious State." In *The Highest State of Consciousness*. Ed. John White. New York: Doubleday, 1972. Pp. 14–16.

Wapnick, Kenneth. "Mysticism and Schizophrenia." In *The Highest*

State of Consciousness. Ed. John White. New York: Doubleday, 1972. Pp. 153–74.

White, John, ed. *The Highest State of Consciousness*. New York: Doubleday, 1972.

Williams, L. F. Rushbrook, ed. *Sufi Studies: East and West*. New York: E. P. Dutton, 1973.

Wilson, Colin. *The Occult: A History*. 1971; rpt. New York: Random House, 1973.

Index

Africa, 17, 21, 25, 31, 33, 46, 74, 78, 88, 132, 153, 159, 165. *See also* Zambesia

Alter, Robert, 110n., 239

Anima, 23, 81–82. *See also* Jung, Carl

Animus, 23, 81–82, 91. *See also* Jung, Carl

Archetype, 23, 59, 88, 135, 153, 157, 164, 180, 182, 193, 207, 218, 223, 229, 238. *See also* Jung, Carl

Attar, Fariduddin, 183

Atwood, Margaret, 255

Austen, Jane, 255

Balzac, Honoré de, 11, 254

Barnouw, Dagmar, 168n.

Barr, Julia (character in *Retreat to Innocence*), 50–56, 57, 58, 63, 71, 113, 117, 176, 204, 239

Barth, John, 195, 248

Becker, Ernest, 83

Boisen, Anton, 189

Breakdown, 17, 27, 30, 31, 58, 71, 80, 84, 86, 87, 88, 89–92, 94, 95, 96–99, 104, 107, 108–9, 113, 117, 118. *See also* Consciousness

Breakthrough, 99, 106, 109, 146–47, 175, 176, 178, 240, 246, 250, 256. *See also* Consciousness

Brenner, Charles, 32

Brewster, Dorothy, 13n.

Briefing for a Descent into Hell, 4, 13, 17, 88, 140, 175–99, 200, 202, 204, 217, 234

Brod, Jan (character in *Retreat to Innocence*), 50–56, 57, 60, 63, 113, 204

Brontes, Charlotte and Emily, 255

Brown, Kate (character in *The Summer before the Dark*), 17, 88, 201–18, 227, 236

Brown, Norman O., 9

Bucke, Richard, 47n.

Burgess, Anthony, 195, 248

Butler, Samuel, 247

Campbell, Joseph, 179

Carey, John, 112n.

Carson, Rachel, 128, 177

Cassirer, Ernst, 87, 105, 237

Chekhov, Anton, 11, 253

Children of Violence, 4, 12, 13, 33, 34, 36, 38, 39, 41, 45, 47, 49, 55, 56, 65, 71, 72, 89, 113, 125, 127, 31, 137, 162, 164, 166, 167–68, 176, 202, 246

Chopin, Kate, 255

Coldridge, Lynda (character in *The Four-Gated City*), 17, 129, 135–36, 138, 140, 143, 146, 147, 148, 150, 151, 152, 154, 156, 157, 158, 159, 161–63, 165, 176, 201, 222

Coldridge, Mark (character in *The Four-Gated City*), 129, 133, 135, 136, 137, 139, 142, 143, 145, 146, 150, 151, 152, 153–56, 159, 161, 164, 165, 204, 227

Collective unconscious, 152–53, 156,

166–67, 184, 226, 233. *See also* Jung, Carl

Communism/Communist party, 49, 53–54, 56, 57–58, 73, 78, 86, 114, 192

Consciousness: abnormal, 9, 10, 17, 24–25, 26–30, 39, 51–52, 55, 60, 71, 82, 85, 89, 95, 96, 99, 103, 118, 132, 146, 151, 155, 156, 158–60, 166, 175–76, 188, 189, 190, 194, 201, 209, 210–11, 251; altered states of, 10, 59, 85, 93, 180, 221, 238; breaking the form of, 11, 73, 106, 108, 255; field, 85, 94, 153; visionary, 39–40, 120, 144, 147, 153, 185, 247, 256. *See also* Breakdown; Breakthrough; Madness; Mental illness; Mystical illumination

de Beauvoir, Simone, 47, 63

de la Mare, Walter, 253

Dialectic, 9, 18, 30–31, 50, 57, 64, 66n., 82, 86, 92, 109, 120, 153, 157, 166, 224, 231, 251

Dickens, Charles, 253

Dostoevsky, Fyodor, 5, 11, 25, 195, 253, 254

Drabble, Margaret, 255

Dreams, 21, 22, 24, 25, 86, 87, 88, 89, 95–96, 97, 99, 100, 115, 134, 144, 145, 147, 205, 206, 207, 214, 216, 218

Eliade, Mircea, 56, 169n., 193, 197n., 242n.

Eliot, George, 255

Eliot, T. S., 32n.

Ellman, Mary, 34

Erikson, Erik, 66n.

Fatemi, Nasrolleh S., 122, 166, 238

Faulkner, William, 103, 228, 255

The Four-Gated City, 6, 12, 17, 38, 52, 59, 125–71, 175, 177, 181, 186, 202, 220, 221, 222, 227, 253

Four-gated city (image), 37–38, 45, 56, 127, 135, 137, 139, 164, 165, 181, 225

Fowles, John, 256

Freud, Sigmund, 22, 23, 36, 47n., 56, 170n., 231, 257n.

Frye, Northrop, 126, 169–70n., 171n., 179, 199n., 241n., 241–42n.

Gide, André, 110n., 256

The Golden Notebook, 4, 6, 11, 12, 13, 17, 26, 55, 56, 65, 71–112, 114, 115, 117, 126, 127, 129, 130, 137, 150, 152, 162, 175, 176, 185, 189, 230, 239, 246, 255, 256

Golding, William, 195, 248

The Grass Is Singing, 4, 12, 17–28, 33, 34, 46, 80, 102, 115, 176, 204, 238, 250

Green, Saul (character in *The Golden Notebook*), 77, 89–92, 94, 95, 97, 98, 99, 100, 101, 102, 103, 104, 105, 117, 129, 137, 142

Grof, Stanislav, 188, 197n.

Hardin, Nancy Shields, 124n.

Harding, M. Esther, 88, 112n., 252

Hardy, Thomas, 253

Hegel, George Wilhelm Friedrich, 9, 48n., 56, 57, 112n., 126, 169n., 258

Henden, Josephine, 219n.

Hesse, Anton (character in *A Ripple from the Storm*), 59–64, 114, 115, 118

Houston, Jean, 160, 197n.

Howe, Florence, 3

Huxley, Aldous, 110n., 247, 256

Individuation, 23, 111n., 165, 230, 240. *See also* Jung, Carl

James, Henry, 254

James, William, 10, 47n., 95, 112n., 249

Joyce, James, 102, 103, 255

Jung, Carl, 9, 22–24, 30–31, 45, 56, 58, 59, 76, 80, 81–82, 84–85, 107, 126, 127, 137, 144, 146, 148–49, 150, 170n., 201, 203, 223, 226, 229, 230–31, 240, 241n., 257. *See also* Anima; Animus; Archetype; Collective unconscious; Individuation; Persona; Self; Shadow

Kafka, Franz, 255
Kant, Immanuel, 258n.
Kaplan, Sydney Janet, 47n., 170n.
Karl, F. R., 47n., 168n.
Kierkegaard, Soren, 13

Laing, R. D., 28–29, 59–60, 96,
    111n., 144, 179, 188, 194, 196–97n.,
    198n.
Landlocked, 12, 17, 63, 88, 113–24,
    136, 137, 152, 165, 176
Lawrence, D. H., 124n., 253, 254
Lessing, Doris: biographical informa-
    tion on, 4; feminist, 5–6, 255;
    novels of: *see* individual listings by
    title and major characters; on aging,
    210, 216; on consciousness, 11, 23,
    108, 156, 184, 188, 250; on con-
    ventional novel form, 72; on
    dreams, 145; on Freud, 23, 231; on
    individuation, 110–11n.; on Jung,
    85, 110–11n., 150, 230–31; on
    Laing, 196–97n., 198–99n.; on
    leftist politics, 66n.; on madness and
    mental illness, 80, 147–48, 177; on
    science fiction, 160; on Sufism,
    121–23, 169n., 231; on writing, 5,
    73, 131, 149, 249; other works by:
    "The Eye of God in Paradise"
    (story), 110n.; *Play with a Tiger*
    (play), 100; "Report on the
    Threatened City" (story), 218n.;
    "The Temptation of Jack Orkney"
    (story), 199–200; "To Room Nine-
    teen" (story), 219n.

Madness, 17, 26, 30, 31, 71, 81, 92, 97,
    103, 104, 120, 123, 129, 133, 138,
    139, 144, 146–47, 151, 152, 157,
    158–59, 162, 166, 176, 177, 185,
    195, 201, 211, 214, 217, 250. *See
    also* Breakdown; Consciousness;
    Mental illness
Magie, Michael, 258n.
Mann, Thomas, 254
Martha Quest, 12, 33–41, 45, 46, 73,
    123, 148, 227
Marx, Karl, 9, 56, 57, 66n.
Marxism, 56, 64, 66n., 87, 141, 233

Maslow, Abraham, 47n.
Masters, Robert E. L., 197n.
The Memoirs of a Survivor, 13, 17,
    220–42, 253
Mental illness, 26, 80, 141, 144, 189.
    See also Breakdown; Consciousness;
    Madness
Meredith, George, 253
Mitchell, Edgar D., 85
Morgan, Ellen, 110n.
Mure, G. R. C., 112n.
Musil, Robert, 128, 168n.
Mystical illumination, 39–41, 56,
    94–95, 109, 117, 130, 135, 153, 158,
    167, 176, 180, 183, 186, 191, 195,
    235–36, 237, 240. *See also* Mysti-
    cism; Sufism; Underhill, Evelyn
Mysticism, 40, 94–95, 180, 183, 186,
    191, 195, 223, 252. *See also* Mysti-
    cal illumination; Sufism; Underhill,
    Evelyn
Myth/mythic, 6, 7, 8, 53, 56, 87, 88,
    89, 107, 109, 114, 126, 127, 134, 135,
    149, 160, 164, 165, 167, 176, 177,
    179, 183, 191, 192, 194, 196, 209,
    214, 218, 228, 230, 231, 238, 240,
    245, 246, 247, 248, 251

Narayan, R. K., 231
Narrator (character in *The Memoirs of
    a Survivor*), 17, 221–41, 250, 253
Neumann, Erich, 59, 127, 138–39,
    155, 166, 170n., 194, 197n.
Nietzsche, Friedrich, 36

O'Hara, John, 120

Persona, 137, 148–49, 190, 203, 210,
    217, 237, 239, 240. *See also* Jung,
    Carl
Porter, Nancy, 124n.
Pratt, Annis, 110n.
A Proper Marriage, 12, 35, 42–48, 49,
    73
Proust, Marcel, 253, 255, 256
Pynchon, Thomas, 195, 248

Quest, Martha (character in *Children
    of Violence*), 5, 17, 33–47, 52, 54,

57–65, 71, 72, 78, 88, 91, 92, 94, 101, 113–23, 125–68, 176, 187, 201, 202, 204, 206, 207, 208, 214, 215, 216, 221, 222, 224, 227, 236, 239, 246, 248, 253, 254
Quest, May (character in *Children of Violence*), 35, 44, 140, 142–43

Retreat to Innocence, 4, 12, 49–56, 57, 58, 60, 64, 65, 71, 89, 113, 176, 204
Rich, Adrienne, 169n.
Richardson, Dorothy, 255
A Ripple from the Storm, 12, 49, 57–66, 72, 78, 113
Robbe-Grillet, Alain, 27, 255
Rogers, Robert, 110n.
Romantic tradition, 13, 126, 129, 154, 178, 182, 186, 195, 199n., 218, 234–35, 247, 252, 254–55, 258n.
Rooms (image), 29, 39, 50–51, 52, 96–98, 108–9, 115–16, 133, 138, 145, 148, 151–52, 156, 159, 168n., 169n., 204, 205, 209, 210, 211–12, 219n., 221–22, 229, 232, 234, 237, 238, 241n., 247
Rubenstein, Roberta, 111n., 196n.
Rumi, Jalaluddin, 181
Ryf, Robert S., 197n.

Sartre, Jean-Paul, 28, 153, 256
Schlueter, Paul, 13n.
Schoeps, Hans-Joachim, 249
Scholes, Robert, 170n., 171n., 198n.
Schopenhauer, Arthur, 36
Schreiner, Olive, 253, 255
Science fiction, 154, 160, 170n., 171n., 185–86, 195, 198n., 218–19n., 225, 247, 248
Scott, Sir Walter, 253
Self, 23, 229, 231, 238. See also Jung, Carl
Seligman, Dee, 124n.
Shabistari, Mahmoud, 177, 235
Shadow, 22–23, 24, 27, 76, 80, 91, 99, 119, 133, 135, 157, 161, 176, 182, 192, 193, 232. See also Jung, Carl
Shah, Idries, 121–22, 149, 169n., 186

Shakespeare, William, 164
Showalter, Elaine, 257n.
Singleton, Mary Ann, 13n.
Spacks, Patricia Meyer P., 170n.
Spilka, Mark, 124n.
Stalin, Joseph, 49, 53–54, 66n., 78
Stendhal, 11, 253, 254
Stern, Thomas (character in *Landlocked*), 17, 116–23, 133, 134, 136, 156, 165, 176, 201, 204
Sufism, 120–23, 128, 131, 141, 142, 149, 151, 154, 162, 166, 177, 179, 181, 183, 186–87, 191, 223, 229, 230–31, 234, 238. See also Mysticism
Sukenick, Lynn, 110n., 168–69n., 196n.
The Summer before the Dark, 13, 17, 88, 200–219, 220
Swift, Jonathan, 247

Tart, Charles T., 10
Thoreau, Henry David, 253
Tolstoy, Leo, 5, 11, 253, 254
Turgenev, Ivan, 11, 210, 253
Turnbull, Colin, 242n.
Turner, Mary (character in *The Grass Is Singing*), 17, 18–29, 33, 34, 35, 37, 39, 40, 55, 57, 63, 71, 80, 87, 117, 120, 133, 147, 153, 176, 201, 204, 227, 250, 254
Tymms, Ralph, 110n.

Underhill, Evelyn, 40, 94, 95, 183

Vernon, John, 195
Vlastos, Marion, 196n.
Vonnegut, Kurt, 195, 248

Walker, Kenneth, 198n.
Wapnick, Kenneth, 158
Watkins, Charles (character in *Briefing for a Descent into Hell*), 17, 88, 175, 178–96, 200, 201, 204, 217, 222, 234, 237, 253
Wells, H. G., 247, 253, 256
White, John, 197n.
Wilson, Colin, 198n.
Wood, Jimmy (character in *The*

Four-Gated City), 135–36, 149, 154, 163
Woolf, Virginia, 103, 253, 255
Wordsworth, William, 186
Wulf, Anna (character in *The Golden Notebook*), 5, 13, 17, 26, 55, 56, 63, 65, 71–112, 113, 114, 116, 117, 120, 129, 130, 133, 142, 150, 152, 153, 156, 162, 176, 185, 186, 201, 204, 217, 230, 238, 239

Yeats, William Butler, 248

Zak, Michele Wender, 32n.
Zambesia, 33, 47n., 115, 118, 131, 140, 142